"An accessible guide that helps us understand ourselves and each other while offering opportunities to create happier, healthier, more comfortable relationships."
—JOHN GRAY, PH.D., Bestselling Author of
Men Are from Mars, Women Are from Venus

"Vicki Matthews brings a great deal of experience, expertise, and relationship clarity through her use of the Five Elements model to help people get along better."
—DONNA EDEN, Author of *Energy Medicine*

"I love this book! It has such an engaging quality; it's all my wife and I could talk about for days. I understand people better now and only wish I'd known this twenty years ago."
—JACK CANFIELD, Coauthor of the
Chicken Soup for the Soul® series

"Every now and then a book comes along that changes your life. *The Five Elements of Relationships* is just such a book for me. The information it contains makes it easier than ever to understand each other so that we can all get along better. This book should be required reading for every human being."
—PATTY AUBERY, author of the bestselling book and course, *Permission Granted*, and president of the Canfield Training Group

"Vicki Matthews offers a unique model of relationship that makes it easier than ever to understand and get along with the people in your life. Based on the ancient wisdom of the Five Elements, this approach can certainly benefit all of your relationships!"
—MARCI SHIMOFF, #1 *New York Times* bestselling author of *Happy for No Reason* and *Chicken Soup for the Woman's Soul*

THE FIVE ELEMENTS OF RELATIONSHIPS

How to Get Along with Anyone, Anytime, Anyplace

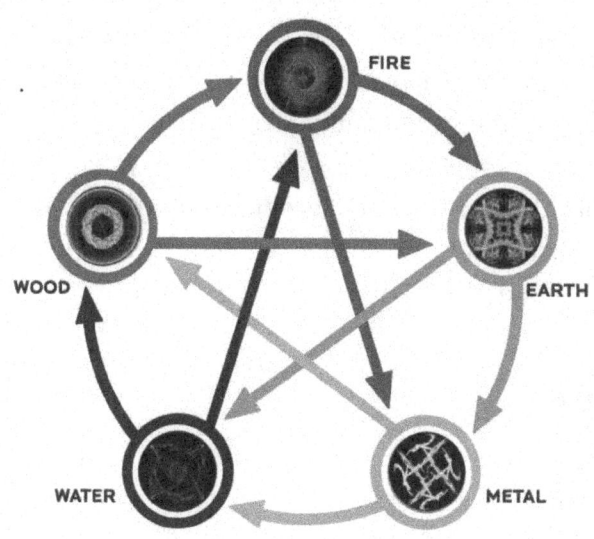

DR. VICKI MATTHEWS

A POST HILL PRESS BOOK
ISBN: 978-1-63758-451-4
ISBN (eBook): 978-1-63758-452-1

The Five Elements of Relationships:
How to Get Along with Anyone, Anytime, Anyplace
© 2022 by Dr. Vicki Matthews
All Rights Reserved

Cover design by Tiffani Shea

Although every effort has been made to ensure that the personal and professional advice present within this book is useful and appropriate, the author and publisher do not assume and hereby disclaim any liability to any person, business, or organization choosing to employ the guidance offered in this book.

No part of this book may be reproduced, stored in a retrieval system, or transmitted by any means without the written permission of the author and publisher.

Post Hill Press
New York • Nashville
posthillpress.com

Published in the United States of America
1 2 3 4 5 6 7 8 9 10

To Mark, the most wonderful husband and
partner in the world. Thank you for a lifetime of
love, comradery, fun, and understanding.

To Cindy, the best sister in the world.
Thank you for believing in me.

To my dearest friends all over the world.
Thank you for your encouragement.

To the patients who shared the highs and lows of their
journeys with me. Thank you for your trust.

And finally, to people everywhere who really do
want to get along better. This is for you.

TABLE OF CONTENTS

Introduction   How We Got Here..9

PART ONE - UNDERSTANDING OURSELVES

Chapter 1   Getting Along: Is It Rocket Science?........................ 17
Chapter 2   The Ancients Were On to Something 30
Chapter 3   The Water Club: Imagine the Possibilities 46
Chapter 4   The Wood Club: Make It Happen 57
Chapter 5   The Fire Club: Let's Celebrate! 69
Chapter 6   The Earth Club: What Do You Need?...................... 80
Chapter 7   The Metal Club: Let Me Show You the Right
             Way to Do That 92
Chapter 8   Summaries and Secondaries: Good So Far?
             Well, There's More.. 104

PART TWO - RELATIONSHIP DYNAMICS AND TENDENCIES

Chapter 9   Relationships: Highs and Lows and
             In-Betweens 121

NURTURING CYCLE RELATIONSHIPS

Chapter 10   Water with Wood: Van Gogh and Thor,
              the Artist Paints the Warrior 131
Chapter 11   Wood with Fire: Thor and the Mad Hatter,
              Celebrating the Hero... 143
Chapter 12   Fire with Earth: The Mad Hatter and Dorothy
              Gale, the Perfect Party 155
Chapter 13   Earth with Metal: Dorothy Gale and
              Mr. Spock, the Correct Way to Greet Oz............... 167
Chapter 14   Metal with Water: Mr. Spock and Van Gogh,
              Comparing Starry Skies.. 179

CONTROLLING CYCLE RELATIONSHIPS

Chapter 15	Water with Fire: Van Gogh and the Mad Hatter, A Moody, Wild Time	195
Chapter 16	Fire with Metal: The Mad Hatter and Mr. Spock, Fun and Games in Space	207
Chapter 17	Metal with Wood: Mr. Spock and Thor, Brains and Brawn Face Off	219
Chapter 18	Wood with Earth: Thor and Dorothy Gale, the Galactic Meaning of Home	232
Chapter 19	Earth with Water: Dorothy Gale and Van Gogh, Going It Alone, Together	245

SAME-ELEMENT RELATIONSHIPS

Chapter 20	Water with Water: Van Gogh and Eeyore, Maybe a Good Day	261
Chapter 21	Wood with Wood: Thor and Katniss Everdeen, Winning 101	271
Chapter 22	Fire with Fire: The Mad Hatter and the Joker, Over the Top	281
Chapter 23	Earth with Earth: Dorothy Gale and Mother Theresa, Double the Compassion	291
Chapter 24	Metal with Metal: Mr. Spock and Sherlock Holmes, It Should Be Clearly Obvious	302
Conclusion	Managing Ourselves: We Are in the Model	313

APPENDICES

Appendix I	Personality Comparisons: Response to an Invitation	323
Appendix II	Elemental Personality Quiz	327
	Scoring the Elemental Personality Quiz	331
Acknowledgments		333
About the Author		335

INTRODUCTION

HOW WE GOT HERE

*I suppose leadership at one time meant muscles;
but today it means getting along with people.*

—Mahatma Gandhi

IT HAPPENED THREE WEEKS AFTER Mark and I graduated from college, moved, and got married (yes, all on the same weekend). As realistic owners of an ancient Toyota Corolla, we'd borrowed a relative's more roadworthy car and were driving from Chicago to LA for a friend's wedding. It had been a long trip, and as we crossed into California, we hit the Mojave Desert, which, I'd just like to point out, was impossibly barren. No trees, no water, no other cars—just rocks and sand, sand and rocks.

However, there were also no highway patrol cars anywhere in sight. But despite my obvious impatience, Mark continued to drive the speed limit.

Finally, I couldn't take it any longer. "Can we speed this up?" I asked.

"Not a good idea," he replied, his eyes on the never-ending road.

"For heaven's sake," I snapped. "Why not?"

He sighed and shot a dismissive glance my way. "We are already going the speed limit."

"But there is no one else out here!" I shouted. "NO ONE!"

"The speed limit is the speed limit," he replied calmly.

And that was it.

I spent the rest of the trip wondering what I'd done. Who was this person and why had I ended up with a fellow who always drove the speed limit (I drive fast), planned budgets with a precision that would impress any one of the Big Four accounting firms (I plan, but in rather broad strokes), and had the ability to stay focused on immeasurable details seemingly forever (I'm an impatient, big-picture kind of girl)? Yes, I loved him deeply, but were we destined to fight over speed limits and spending forever?

Watching my friends and their relationships, I couldn't explain what was going on with them, either. I had a passing knowledge of astrology and even a degree in psychology, so could discuss aspects of why my friends were the way they were. Leos are usually aggressive. The baby of the family expects to be treated well. But I couldn't really explain what was happening *between* them. Why did Judy and Ross always fight while cooking, even though they both loved to cook? Why did Mary end up with the same kind of guy over and over again, even though they always broke her heart? Why couldn't they all just get along? Then quite unexpectedly, about ten years into our marriage, the answer to these questions landed smack in my lap.

After working in the business world for several years, I'd returned to school to study my first love: medicine. But ever the rebel, I went for a naturopathic degree instead of attending traditional medical school. My studies in naturopathic medicine included Chinese history, and that's what led to my relationship epiphany. Over three millennia ago, Chinese philosophers coalesced their significant understanding of the universe into a disarmingly simple model based on their observations of nature. Called the Five Elements model, not only did it serve to describe the energetic workings of the universe, I discovered it was also fantastic at predicting and explaining human relationships.

Once this clicked for me, I finally understood that Mark wasn't really anal retentive; he was wired to appreciate hierarchy, process, and protocol. I wasn't really a bossy pants; I was wired to be assertive, opinionated, and productive. And in our relationship, our individual wiring meant that we were destined to act and react in very specific ways as a couple, especially around the topic of control (more on *that* later).

Applying the Five Elements model changed how I related to everyone in my life and helped me understand how they related to me. My sister is wired to appreciate tradition, even though I'm not. Because of this, I decided it was important to include some traditions in our family events rather than always going for the new. That makes her happy. One of my good friends is a blast to be around because she's wired to be outgoing and funny, which I definitely am not. So instead of meeting in quiet restaurants over tea and wondering why she can't fit in, now we go places where being loud and boisterous is welcome and we have a much better time. I also realized that my father wasn't necessarily distant; he was wired to need time alone, which as a child I never understood. He's gone now, but in looking back, I see that it really wasn't about him not loving me. Bless the Five Elements model!

In my private practice as a naturopathic physician and relationship coach, I started sharing these ideas with my clients and light bulbs came on for them, too. A sister's marriage to a man totally unlike her suddenly made sense. A son's preference for photography over football seemed logical. Even their mothers-in-law became understandable—sort of.

And their relationships began to improve.

Using this system to understand people and their relationships has made a significant difference for me and hundreds of my clients, friends, and loved ones. I truly believe it can do the same for you. And it doesn't take a lot of work. Let me show you.

HOW TO USE THIS BOOK

In *Part One* of this book, we'll cover the basics of the Five Elements model. The five elements are Water, Wood, Fire, Earth, and Metal. All of them are present in our energetic wiring at birth, although each of us has a strong affinity for one of them. This affinity, which I call our primary elemental personality, colors everything we do, think, and feel, as well as how we relate to each other. Having this affinity is like joining a secret club when we're born. I'm a Wood person, which makes me more interested in accomplishment and willing to take risks. All members of the Wood Club will be a bit like me. Mark is a Metal person, which makes him a fan of protocol, process, and rules. All members of the Metal Club will be a bit like Mark. We'll also discuss whether we're given a lifetime club membership, how to visit other clubhouses, basic ways these clubs relate with each other, and a first quick look at how to use the Five Elements model to shift a problematic connection.

Also in *Part One*, we'll take an in-depth look at what it's like to be a member of each club. It's here that you'll start recognizing yourself, as well as your family and friends. We'll include everything you need to know about each club to help determine where you fit in: things like what makes each club happy and sad, how they react to stress, what matters most to each club, and so on. We'll also cover techniques specifically designed to de-stress the members of each clubhouse. And remember, even if you aren't a Water Club member, we all have Water moments when we're inspired, or even afraid. Certain techniques work on Water energy anytime and anyplace.

In *Part Two*, we'll look at how each club gets along with the other clubs. What's it like for me, a member of the Wood Club, to be married to Mark, a member of the Metal Club? What are the strengths

Introduction

of a Wood/Metal connection? What are the challenges? And what can be done to improve that connection? Most of this information is drawn from my years of private practice and the blog I write (*Ask Vicki*) on using the Five Elements to improve relationships. We'll also talk about relationships between two people who belong to the same club—for example, an Earth person working with another Earth person. Just like all relationships, Same-Club relationships will have strengths and challenges. You can either read *Part Two* all the way through or use it as a reference guide if, for example, you're a member of the Water Club raising a daughter who appears to be a member of the Fire Club (congratulations on that!) and want some quick help.

I can't tell you what a difference understanding the Five Elements has made in my relationships and the relationships of my clients. It's been nothing short of miraculous and has enabled us all to get along better with everyone. So read on—I know it can help you, too.

Dr. Vicki Matthews
Chicago, IL

PART ONE

Understanding Ourselves

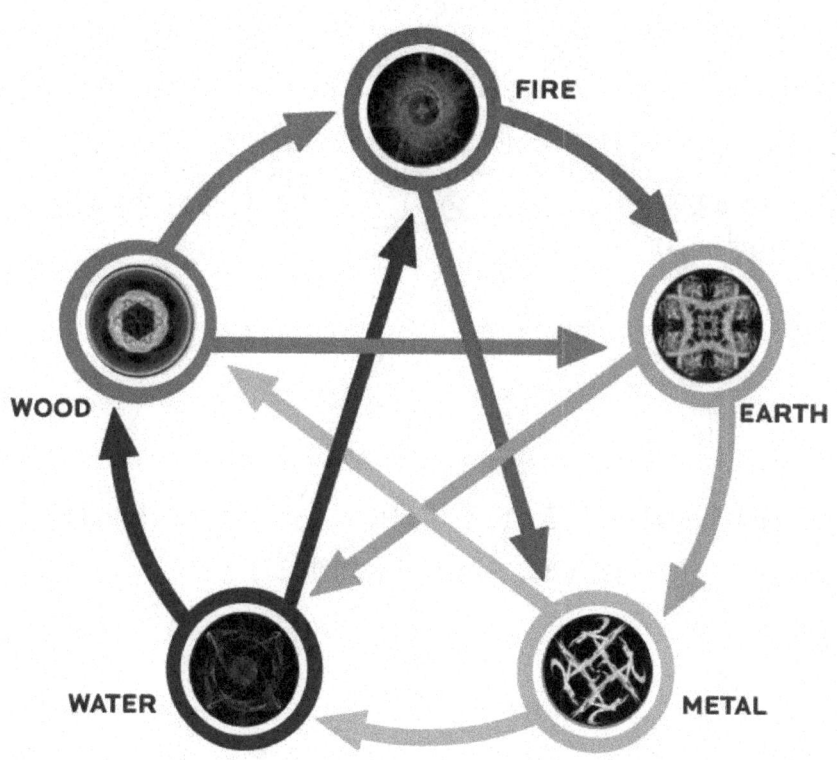

"And that, in a nutshell, is why men don't understand women."

CHAPTER 1

GETTING ALONG: IS IT ROCKET SCIENCE?

The most important single ingredient in the formula of success is knowing how to get along with people.

—Theodore Roosevelt

IT'S CLEAR THAT ONE OF the greatest challenges humans face is getting along with each other. Globally, the presence of nonstop warfare across history testifies to our failure at peaceful coexistence. On a civic level, our packed courtrooms bear witness to the fact that conflict is ever-present. More personal still, whether interacting with a mate, sibling, child, friend, or colleague, our relationships can be fraught with complications and misunderstandings. And yet, we are all human, all fundamentally the same.

Why is getting along so hard?

The answer lies in the simple truth that, at a personality level, we really *aren't* all that similar. Physically, we may carry the same genetic coding, possess the same biological functioning, and need the same environmental conditions to flourish. Yet once our physical survival is assured, how we think and act regarding a wide range of issues varies dramatically.

There are many reasons for this, not the least of which is the culture in which we're raised. Other factors include our gender, birth order, and family history. Yet even these aspects don't adequately explain every difference. Let's face it: When it comes to behavioral tendencies, we often mystify each other—and ourselves.

In truth, this shadowy arena of tendency trips us up again and again, possibly because it's very subjective. For example, I place much greater importance on accomplishment than Mark ever would. We used to argue about my workaholic ways, but he's come to accept that it's essential to my happiness, even though he still shakes his head many evenings as he passes my home office on his way to the TV room.

On the other hand, a life without order and rules would make Mark miserable. We used to fight over his need for detail, but I've come to accept it even though the tedious precision of putting together a 1,500-piece puzzle sends me screaming from the room.

It's the same with my friends. Sheila seems unwilling to take life seriously, which makes me wonder if she'll ever grow up. William spends every spare minute on his computer playing games. I want to talk some sense into them, but I'd just end up sounding bossy. Besides, they're happy, functional human beings. What's it to me?

These examples just highlight the fact that the real problem isn't what we do or think; it's how the people in our lives *react* to what we do or think. It's how we react to them, too. Most relationship issues arise when we project our own needs, desires, and priorities onto other people assuming they'll want what we want. But unless we're relating to someone with identical needs and priorities, we really don't understand why they act the way they act, and it's dangerous to assume that we do.

MAINTAINING HARMONY

Humans are set apart from other animals by our ability to love beyond instinct and our capacity for advanced cognition. When things are going well in our lives, that capacity for love will carry us a great distance down the road of "getting along." But when the going gets tough and emotions flare, the better we understand the people in our life and why they do the odd, idiosyncratic, irrational, and bizarre things they do, the easier it is to maintain harmony. That's because in these seemingly insignificant behavioral tendencies sit the seeds of relationship disaster. I know this for a fact.

At our house, we have agreed that the kitchen needs to be cleaned before we prepare the next meal. If it's Mark's turn to do the dinner dishes and he elects to wash them before breakfast the next morning rather than immediately after dinner, why should I care? Am I afraid of offending the kitchen elves by asking them to overnight in a dirty kitchen? Clearly, if he has the dishes done by 7:00 a.m. when I start breakfast, it shouldn't matter to me. But it does matter; it matters greatly. Why?

Or if my sister and I are responsible for the family Thanksgiving dinner and I make a Southern cornbread stuffing one year instead of Grandma's traditional fruit-and-nut dressing, it shouldn't matter to my sister. Both dishes taste great and are excellent gravy vehicles. But I can promise you it will matter to her very much. Why?

Other than explaining my tendency to view the kitchen as the most dangerous area of the house, what do these examples illustrate? They show how diverse our priorities can be in subtle, almost inexplicable ways. Yet it's precisely these "harmless" differences that can fuel our disagreements. The good news is that there *is* an easy way to understand each other and get along. That's what this book is all about.

I think what we cover here is unique among relationship books. The information I'm going to share is simple and straightforward; it doesn't require a PhD to understand. It's based on ancient teachings that have been used for millennia to explain relationships, and it addresses *any* kind of relationship—not just marriage or parenting issues. Plus, it can be used with big issues (*If I love him, or her, why can't I get along with him, or her?*) and small (*Who gets the remote control?*). Most importantly, it works!

MAKING SENSE OF OUR DIFFERENCES

As part of my graduate work, I studied ancient Chinese medicine, a form of healing that's been used in the East for thousands of years. It's a holistic approach that views the human as a series of interconnected energy systems working together to maintain the healthy functioning of the person. Here in the West, we're most familiar with the Chinese practice of acupuncture, using ultra-thin needles to balance channels of energy running slightly under the skin. These channels are called meridians, and too little or too much energy running through them can cause illness of the body, emotions, mind, or spirit.

But here's where it gets interesting. The energy that flows through us does so in predictable ways that manifest predictable patterns of behavior. I call this our "wiring," and it's what creates many of our personal tendencies, those pesky little issues frequently at the root of why we have trouble getting along. Why does my husband like to play it safe? Why do I like to take risks? Why does my sister appreciate traditions? Because we're each wired in that particular way. It's a wiring we're born with, a wiring we cannot change, but one we can easily comprehend once pointed out. This wiring explains our similarities and differences. It also gives us a clearer understanding of why certain relationships often seem to follow repetitive patterns. In truth, they *seem* to follow repetitive patterns because they really *do* follow repetitive patterns, all based on our wiring.

> ## WHAT IS A MODEL?
>
> *A model is an intellectual construct that takes observable phenomena and tries to give it order. A good model not only explains what's observed at the moment, it can also be used to predict what might be observed in the future. Ideally, models are based in objective reality. Because of this, as more detailed information becomes available, models are often updated, elaborated, or pitched altogether.*
>
> *The models created to explain the relationship of our Earth to the sun are good examples. Ancient astronomers observed the sun rising and setting daily in the sky and came to the brilliant, though incorrect, assumption that the sun circled Earth. By the mid-sixteenth century, astronomers had enough new information to call into question the idea of the sun orbiting Earth; the old model no longer worked within the context of the new information. Radically, an astronomer named Copernicus suggested the better model was that Earth, along with many other observable celestial bodies, actually revolved around the sun. And for centuries now, that's the model we've used to understand the relationship of our Earth to the sun.*

Does this mean that being in a relationship with someone wired differently from us guarantees ugly fights? It doesn't have to. In fact, once we understand our personal wiring and the wiring of others, we can actually *predict* how we'll act in almost every conceivable situation. This knowledge helps us build on the likely strengths between people and tiptoe gently around known challenges—or better yet, work to improve them.

To predict relationship tendencies, we're going to enlist the Five Elements model, which has been used for millennia to describe the interaction of anything with anything else. Derived from the ancient philosophies of Taoism, Buddhism, and Confucianism, this model is not only an underlying principle in Chinese medicine, it's also a brilliant tool for understanding human connections. So, without further ado, let's take a quick look at the basics of this model. We have nothing to lose except years of fighting, discord, and emotional strife.

A BRIEF HISTORICAL STROLL

To begin our study of the Five Elements model, I will greatly oversimplify millennia of Chinese history and philosophy. I offer my apologies upfront.

Two thousand years ago in China, the Han dynasty reacted to the previous dynasty—a period of strict totalitarian rule—by wisely deciding to take a synthesizing approach toward government. To do this, they incorporated diverse components of Chinese folk religion and philosophy into their guiding documents. This fusing of rival schools of thought into a single system created what is called the Han synthesis. Specifically, Confucianism (focused on personal ethics) and Taoism (focused on mystic relationship) were blended with enough Legalism (obedience to the legal system) to assure the survival of the dynasty. And it was successful; the Han dynasty's four centuries of stability and prosperity consolidated China as a unified state under a central bureaucracy that's still around today.

The philosophy that is the Han synthesis can be summarized broadly as follows: *The totality of everything can be seen as existing in two principles called yin and yang. They oppose and balance one another, always contain some of each other, and continuously create and destroy each other in their endless dance of balance. As they interact, yin and yang create energy (chi). Yin and yang are further differentiated into five elements that also dance with one another and can be used to understand and organize reality.*

In trying to create this unified philosophy encompassing the workings of the universe, the Han thinkers concluded that there is day and night, light and dark, creation and destruction in everything. This became yang and yin. They observed that the sun maps out four distinct seasons—plus transition times—per year that interact in predictable, observable ways (summer always follows spring). Finally, they noted that living organisms go through four predictable "seasons" (birth, maturity, decline, death) with accompanying transitions during the cycle of life. These four phases plus the transitions became the five phases or elements.

The Han synthesis states that anything and everything can be understood using yin, yang, and the five elements. This includes the movements of the stars, the workings of the body, the nature of foods, the qualities of music, the engagement of warfare, the progression of time, the operations of government—even history (which is the workings of yin, yang, and the five elements applied to human affairs). Understanding the relationships within these patterns gave the Chinese philosophers and physicians the knowledge necessary to maintain harmony and balance in every area of life.

This may seem pretty abstract at the moment, but by the time we're done these phases will feel like your new best friends. What's important to remember is that the entire purpose of the model is to explain relationships and how to maintain balance and harmony within them.

THE BASICS OF YIN AND YANG

Yin and yang are eternally bound polar opposites that are really two sides of the same coin. Every whole can be explained by the activities of yin and yang. They are so connected that it's impossible to describe one without the other. All the opposites we learned as children are really just yin and yang (think: dark/light, cold/hot, slow/fast, and so on).

But it's important to remember that the relationship between yin and yang isn't an either/or static state. It is a dynamic system in a constant quest for balance. If there's too much yang in the whole—let's say our bath water is too hot—we only need to add more yin (cold water) to create the perfect balance. The beauty of yin and yang is that contained within the whole is the mechanism necessary to maintain balance. So the next time you come across the yin/yang symbol, the taijitu, *don't see just a two-dimensional illustration; see a dynamic and interactive model of the universe!*

Like any useable model, the Five Elements model takes a grandiose idea and reduces it to a simple design. At its core, the Five Elements model is associated with phases and interactions found in the natural world. The phases are represented by Water, Wood, Fire, Earth, and Metal. The interactions are represented by two different cycles: one that creates and one that destroys.

Visually, this model is depicted using five colored circles, one for each element. Water is blue, Wood is green, Fire is red, Earth is yellow, and Metal is white. A color version of this model is on the back cover, but graphically, the model looks like this:

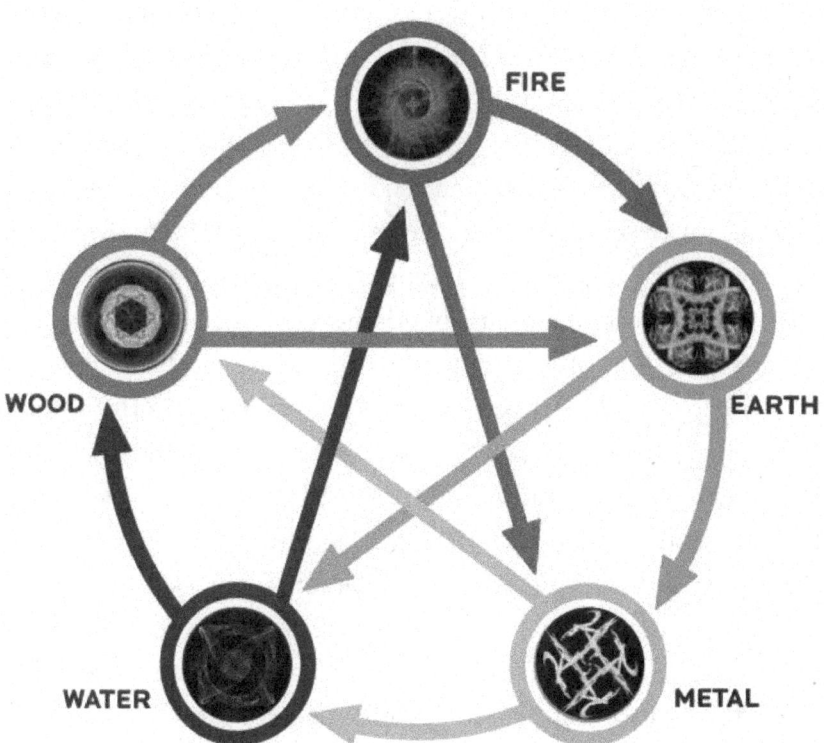

In this model, there are just two ways the elements relate to each other: the big circle and the big star. The big circle is traditionally called the Generating Cycle and connects every element to the one next to it. The big star is called the Destructive Cycle and creates a connection between every other element. Energy moves in a *clockwise* direction in both the circle and the star.

The relationship between elements on the Generating Cycle (the circle) is *creative* or *nurturing*; one element acts on another to build it. Because of this, it's also called the Nurturing Cycle and fits perfectly with how these elements relate to each other in nature. If you start at the small circle in the bottom left and follow the big circle in a clockwise pattern, you can say that Water feeds Wood (trees need water to grow), Wood feeds Fire (fire needs wood to burn), Fire feeds Earth (ash from fire adds nutrients to the ground), Earth feeds Metal (material from the earth creates metals), and Metal feeds Water (minerals from metals enrich water).

The relationship between elements on the Destructive Cycle (the star) is *depleting* or *controlling*; one element acts on another via the star to decrease it. Because of this, it's also called the Controlling Cycle and it, too, fits perfectly with how these elements relate to each other in nature. If you start at the small circle in the bottom left and follow the big star in a clockwise pattern, you can say that Water acts on Fire to put it out, Fire acts to melt Metal, Metal chops Wood, Wood anchors Earth (think of tree roots), and Earth dams Water. Clever, right? Just wait; it gets better.

Because the ancient Chinese believed that perfection rested in being able to maintain balance, this model contains everything needed to restore and sustain dynamic balance for itself. Watch: If the Fire element is out of balance because there isn't enough energy in Fire (it's under-energized), where would we look? Yes, to Wood, since Wood acts on Fire (via the big circle) in a *nurturing* way: Wood feeds Fire. If we need less energy in Fire, where would we look? If you're thinking Water, you're correct. Water acts on Fire (via the big star) in a *controlling* way: Water puts out Fire.

Every element in our model has an element that increases it and an element that decreases it, all in the quest for perfect balance. In fact, this system is so simple that there are really only two major problems that can occur in it: either too much energy in an element (excess) or too little (deficiency). And the fix for either problem is embedded in the relationship of the elements to each other. Pretty amazing, isn't it?

The way they relate to each other (via the Nurturing and Controlling Cycles) will determine the quality of the interaction between one element and its fellow elements. These inherent interaction dynamics will become very illuminating when we use the model with people. But before we do, there are just a few more quick aspects of the model we should explore.

YIN, YANG, AND THE SEASONALITY OF THE MODEL

The Han synthesis says everything can be seen as a dance between the two principles called yin and yang. And if yin and yang represent the opposing dynamics of a whole, such as expansion/contraction or nurture/control, then the elements in the model represent the predictable phases and seasons that the whole experiences during the course of one cycle. Think of the seasonality we experience on Earth during one trip around the sun.

» *Water* represents full yin: functions that have ended, are in the resting state of maximum contraction, and are about to begin again. Water corresponds to winter.

» *Wood* represents new yang: functions in a growing and expanding state. Wood corresponds to spring.

» *Fire* represents full yang: functions that have reached a maximum state of expansion and activity and are about to shift to decline. Fire corresponds to summer.

» *Earth* represents support for balance and transitions: functions that are in a state of perfect balance, total unbalance, or transition. Earth corresponds to the solstices and equinoxes.

» *Metal* represents new yin: functions in a state of contraction and decline. Metal corresponds to autumn.

Just as the ancients intended, the beauty of the Five Elements model is that we can use it to move through a whole cycle of anything, be it a twenty-four-hour day, a year, a career, a marriage, a lifetime—you name it. For example, during our lifetime we are born and spend our infancy and early childhood in the energy of Water, full of ideas and completely focused on our own needs. As adolescents, we are in a Wood stage; we are growing, and our world is expanding. Fire corresponds to the time in our lives when we are young adults, always on the go. We think we can do it all and try to prove it. Earth is a time of maturity when we (hopefully) learn to balance all life has to offer in a healthy way. And Metal is old age, the time when we ponder our life and understand its lessons. Regarding death, some teachings place it as the last act of Metal, others as the first act of Water. Personally, I place death in Metal and birth in Water, but it's really all one continuous cycle anyway, so it's kind of a moot point. The important point is that the model covers cycles that can be applied to almost everything.

THE FIVE ELEMENTS AND A SPORTS CAR

Mark has heard me wax poetic about the Five Elements for years and loves to compare the full cycle to driving a fancy sports car (in his dreams). When the car's engine is idling in neutral, it can be said that the car is in a Water phase. There's a lot of horsepower under the hood, lots of potential, but it's not manifesting yet. With one quick press of the gas pedal it's flying, but as it sits in neutral, it looks still and calm.

The Wood phase is represented by the car's rapid acceleration; the ability to go from 0 to 60 mph in five seconds. As long as the car is accelerating, that's Wood. When the car reaches its peak cruising speed and is running at full throttle zipping down the road at 120 mph (hypothetically, of course), it's in a Fire phase. The acceleration has leveled off, and the car is being held at a steady, breakneck speed.

At the point the driver takes her foot off the gas but hasn't applied the brakes, there's a moment of perfect balance before the car begins to slow. This is the Earth phase. When the driver brakes, the car begins its Metal phase of slowing down. Once it stops and is idling in neutral again, it's back to the Water phase of pure potential, maximum contraction, and no visible movement. Bravo, Mark!

CHAPTER 2

THE ANCIENTS WERE ON TO SOMETHING

The beginning of wisdom is to call things by their right names.
—Ancient Chinese Proverb

AS YOU PONDER THE MODEL we explored in Chapter 1, you may be saying to yourself, "This is a very lovely model, but how does it help me get along better with my boss?" That's a valid question, and the answer is to remind you that the Five Elements model can be used to describe anything, including people and their relationships. Modern Chinese medicine employs the Five Elements model extensively to help with the health of our physical bodies. We're also going to use it to help with the health of our relationships.

Here's the key: Just like any whole in the universe, as a whole person, we each have all five elements in our wiring. But based on that wiring, we all have a natural affinity for one of them. This means that the tendencies associated with one of these elements will feel more natural to each of us. Further, this affinity affects the colors we like, the foods we crave, the roles we take on in life, and yes, how we relate to each other. *Bottom line: You, your friends, your family, and even your boss exist in this model.* Understanding how to work with it will help you build on the strengths in your relationships and shore up the weaknesses so you get along better with everyone.

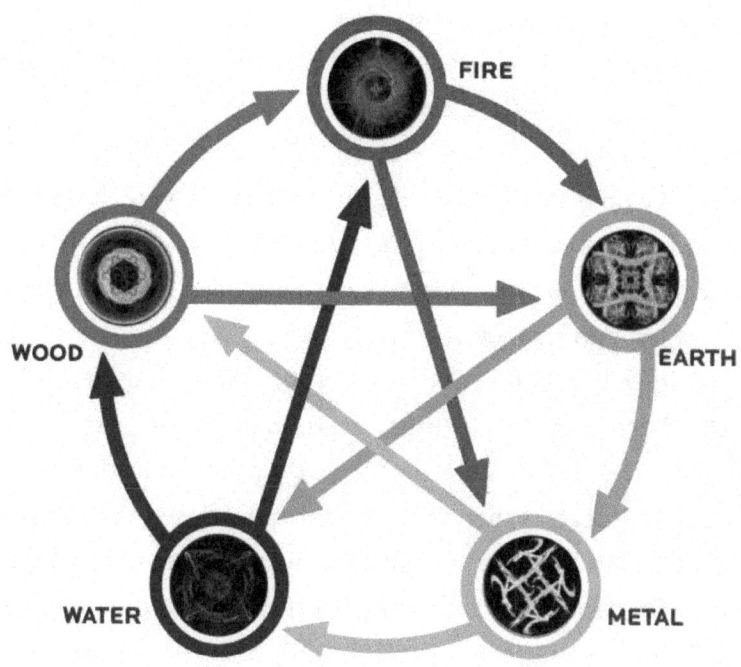

A NATURAL FIT

Think of our elemental affinity as a lens through which we view the world. It's as though at birth we're assigned to a secret club—so secret that no one tells us we belong—and we spend our life thinking, acting, and seeing the world as a member of that club. Our priorities and tendencies in life are based on our club membership, and so is the way we act when we're stressed. When we enter into a relationship with someone from a different club, which is very common, the relationship becomes a predictable dance between the two clubs.

From our model, we know that each element relates to the others in one of two ways: the big circle, called the Nurturing Cycle, or the big star, called the Controlling Cycle. Looking at the big circle, if I'm a Wood and my friend Debbie is a Water, we relate to each other via the Nurturing Cycle. This means that she and I should have a tendency to connect in a way that feels nurturing, and we do. Even though by nature she's not an overly social person (Waters rarely are), when we get together, we always have great talks about what's going on in our lives. She listens well and usually has shrewd observations. I offer (hopefully) helpful suggestions regarding ways to address situations she faces. We have a special relationship that feels nurturing to both of us.

Looking at the big star, we can say that Wood and Metal relate to each other via the Controlling Cycle. So, if I belong to the Wood Club and Mark belongs to the Metal Club, by definition he and I will relate to each other in ways that involve control. And that isn't all bad. My Wood often finds it can go further out on a limb, so to speak, because Mark's Metal is there to make sure I don't overdo it. Of course, if we're stressed, his behavior can (and does) feel downright controlling. Like the time I wanted to remodel the whole house to create more desperately needed closet space, and he prudently suggested we take it one room at a time. The process seemed unbearably slow, but I have to admit he was right (which his Metal loved).

Once we recognize our club membership and the club memberships of the people in our lives, we begin to understand why people act the way they do around us and why it affects us as it does. We can start changing the undesirable dynamics of our relationships so that we get along better, too. This seems a whole lot smarter to me than hoping the issues will magically go away on their own. They usually don't.

CLUB MEMBERS

What are Waters, Woods, Fires, Earths, and Metals like as people? Well, stereotypes come from somewhere, right? Here are some quick examples of the stereotypical people you might find in each clubhouse.

> **Water** corresponds to winter, when most of the activity is below the surface. Water people are like that; they appear almost nonchalant outside, but inside they are a flurry of thoughts, ideas, and creativity. And because everything is still conceptual, for them potential is unlimited and hope abounds. The favorite question of a Water is "Why?"

Stereotypical Waters include:

- The absentminded professor who understands the theory of a washing machine but doesn't know how to use one
- The inspired artist uninterested in eating or sleeping while painting a masterpiece.
- The laid-back, mellow friend happy just going with the flow
- The explorative toddler enthusiastically claiming the world as if it revolves around him
- The avid reader preferring time alone with a good book over almost anything else, especially a huge party

Wood corresponds to spring, a time of manifestation, growth, and expansion. "Bigger, better, more" typifies the way Woods interact with the world. And it works—Wood is where accomplishment sits. The favorite question of a Wood is "When?"

Stereotypical Woods include:

- The workaholic business executive determined to reach the top

- The daredevil adventurer ready to climb the next mountain or drive the fast car

- The decorated general willing to win at all costs because the ends justify the means

- The forceful politician loudly demanding progress and change at a packed rally

- The celebrated quarterback consistently leading the team to victory

Fire corresponds to summer, the most energetically active season of the cycle. A passion for excitement, celebration, visibility, and enthusiasm is a hallmark of Fire people. The favorite question of a Fire is "Where?"

Stereotypical Fires include:

- The talented actress comfortable doing and saying anything in front of an audience or camera

- The hysterically funny comedian improvising and spewing nonstop jokes

- The charismatic motivational speaker passionately offering ways to transcend ordinary life

- The exciting, fun-loving person at the party who everyone wants to be around

- The outgoing high school cheerleader enthusiastically rooting for the home team

Earth represents times of balance, neutrality, and transition. It's associated with late summer, the pivot point between spring/summer and autumn/winter, as well as the transition times of the solstices and equinoxes. Earth people value connections, are caring and compassionate, and love anything having to do with people and home. The favorite question of an Earth is "Who?"

Stereotypical Earths include:

- The patient teacher working hard to make sure every child learns

- The sympathetic nurse carefully tending to patients like the proverbial mother hen

- The loving parent sweetly tucking children into bed every night with a gentle goodnight kiss

- The brilliant cook happily producing memorable and satisfying dining experiences

- The talented interior designer who easily creates beautiful and comfortable homes

Metal corresponds to autumn, the time for releasing what's no longer necessary and moving forward with whatever is. Metal people are able to synthesize the wisdom from any experience and create form and protocol from it. The favorite question of a Metal is "How?"

Stereotypical Metals include:

- The detail-driven accountant diligently working to balance every line in every ledger

- The skilled attorney successfully functioning within the highly structured legal system of what is right and wrong

- The systematic engineer easily describing the detailed mechanical, chemical, or structural aspects of a given project

- The military strategist continuously studying successful historic battles to glean what worked and what didn't

- The trained physician thoroughly embracing the detailed way the physical body works

CAN WE CHANGE CLUBS?

If we belong to a specific club, are we stuck there? The short answer is yes; our club membership is it for this lifetime. However, if you're experiencing a severe case of club envy right about now, this should cheer you up: We can have temporary passes to the other clubs anytime we want. Remember, like any whole, we have *all* of the elements in us. We hang out in a specific clubhouse most of the time based on our affinity, but we can always visit the other clubhouses if we need what they have to offer. For example:

» When you simply must get something done, you can tap into the Wood clubhouse to help organize and direct you. Haven't you had days when you're amazed at how much you've accomplished? That was your Wood energy helping you out. Of course I don't have that problem—my Wood is always front and center. But lots of my friends do have trouble getting things done, and seeking out Wood energy always helps them be more productive.

- » If I have to speak in front of a large group of people and am feeling anything but dynamic that day, I will choose to visit the Fire clubhouse. By accessing my Fire energy, I find it in me to be confident, clever, and captivating onstage. Or at least interesting.
- » Whenever I work with a client or student, I tune into my Earth. They need patience and compassion, and my Earth energy brings that in spades. And speaking of spades, if you ever have trouble accessing Earth, go outside and sit in a garden. All of us are more "Earthy" when we're out in nature; it grounds us.
- » I step into the Metal clubhouse when it's time for me to follow the rules or let go of something, whether that's a person, a belief, or a habit. Hard as that might be for me, the process I find in the Metal clubhouse makes it easier.
- » The Water clubhouse probably requires the most focus for me to visit. Going with the flow seems so aimless and contrary to my Wood need to never be out of control (versus the Metal need to always be in control). But when I meditate and seek guidance, ponder a great truth, or even read a book, I'm right at home in the Water Club, which feels great.

And most importantly, for getting along with anybody you can step into any clubhouse you want whenever you want in an attempt to balance a relationship. We're going to talk a lot about that soon.

TEMPORARY AFFILIATION SHIFTS

Most of the time, I would never be mistaken for a Metal. I don't have the patience with process, nor do I value precision that much. I'm really a Nike kind of girl: Just Do It! But several years ago, I went through a period that could only be called a Metal phase. It wasn't something I tried to do. It happened because several important people and animals in my life passed away around the same time, so I experienced the grief that is one of the hallmarks of a stressed Metal. It wasn't too surprising, but what did give me pause was that during this Metal phase, I suddenly saw the value of process and precision. I even succumbed to it during that time, buying several cookbooks and following the recipes perfectly. Mark was in awe, but that's not surprising—Metals do awe great.

The point here is that each of us can, and likely will, go through phases that are different from our normal affiliation. If you're experiencing a lot of loss, you're probably going to be an honorary Metal for a while. If you agreed to babysit your three-year-old niece for a month, there's no doubt that you'll need to live in an Earth phase to survive. Life circumstances can absolutely conspire to create times when our primary affinity seems to shift. And what an excellent opportunity to walk a mile in a different club's shoes; there's nothing like personal experience to help foster tolerance and understanding. My Metal phase really did help me understand Mark better, that's for sure.

A WARNING ABOUT THAT CLUBHOUSE

Here's a serious warning: We're all so used to our secret clubhouses that it's easy for them to become our sole reality. After all, the affinity that got us there is innate; we don't have to think about it. We will automatically gravitate toward an environment that suits our club membership and act out our affinity in that environment. To paraphrase Abraham Maslow, "If all you have is a hammer, everything looks like a nail." Said another way, we all approach life through the filter of our clubs.

Let's suppose that five of us, one member from each club, are walking down the street and come upon a small riot. My Wood might view the situation as requiring organization and action, so

I would march right into the thick of things to intervene. My Fire companion might panic and run the other way. My Earth friend could be alarmed that people were being hurt and offer needed assistance. The Metal would likely be concerned about the laws being broken and call the police. Finally, the Water might seek out a few people on the periphery of the crowd and question them about the issues they are protesting.

Therein lies another reason our relationships are so difficult at times. Each club will see and react to almost everything quite differently. Remember the parable of the "Blind Men and the Elephant"? It tells of five blind men who happen upon an elephant. Each one touches a different part of the elephant and describes it based on what they feel. The one holding the trunk thinks the elephant is like a snake. The one holding the leg thinks the elephant is like a tree, etc. That parable could easily be called the parable of "The Five Different Elemental Clubs"! Each element will approach life through their own filter.

Are All Waters Created Equal?

Will every Water be like every other Water? Absolutely not! Nor will all Fires be the same, or Woods, or Earths, or Metals. All members of the same clubhouse will have key similarities and tendencies, but there will also be differences. The personality definers we discussed in the Introduction—like birth order, gender, and family history—will impact how all Waters express themselves. The same goes for the other elements. But for our purposes, there is an even more specific way that one Wood can be very different from another, and that's based on the order of influence each element has on a given individual. Here's how it works.

Again, we each have all five of the elements in our energetic wiring. Our natural affinity for a particular element is based on how the elements are wired into our circuits, so to speak. You can think of it as painting five layers of watercolor on the outside of a window. From the inside, the first layer is the main color you'll see, although you can probably get a hint of what the second color is, and possibly even a bit of the third. But by the time you get to the fourth and fifth colors, you probably can't tell what they are at all.

The way the elements stack up in your wiring is much the same. The element closest to you is what determines your natural affinity. However, the second element in the stack can also impact you. It's called your secondary affinity, or just your secondary. When we discuss personalities and relationships, secondary elements will definitely have a part to play. Just think about it: A Wood "softened" by a secondary Earth will be quite different from a Wood "strengthened" by Metal. More on this later.

Visiting Clubhouses to Shift Dynamics

The real magic of the Five Elements model is how the dynamics between the elements keep everything in balance. Need more Fire to keep the whole balanced? Wood steps up to flow energy to Fire. Need less Fire to keep the whole balanced? Water steps up to control the Fire. And not only is this true in nature, it is true in relationships as well.

If Mark and I hit a rough spot while we're paying bills (who doesn't?), I can use this concept to help us out. Let's say it appears that Mark has become rigid about what needs to be paid and what should wait, but I don't agree. Instead of arguing with him, I can try to figure out what's out of balance. It could be me; I might have too much Wood present, a situation that can make me pushy, frustrated, or snarky. Instead of going there, I can shift myself back to balance by tapping into *my* inner Metal. My Metal will prune my Wood in a way that doesn't feel threatening, and I will become more reasonable and less frustrated.

Shifting the Balance with a Boss

I'll bet you're saying, "Sure, you can use Shifting the Balance with your husband, but what about the worst boss in the world who you don't even know that well?" My answer is that it works the same way. You don't need to know him; you just need to know the priorities of each club and let his behaviors tell you where he's stuck. For example, let's say he calls you into his office to introduce himself as the new department head. As he talks, you know you're in trouble because you already want to choke him. Here's what to do:

- *Look at his behavior. What's he doing that's driving you crazy? Perhaps he's condescending and arrogant. On top of that, he hands you a folder full of the new rules and regulations he has in mind for his first phase of overhauling the department.*

- *Based on this behavior, you can guess he's probably firmly entrenched in the Metal Club and manifesting excess Metal. (Metals love rules.)*

- *Remind yourself of your club membership. Are you a Wood? A Water? A Fire? An Earth? Another Metal? If you're a Wood, you're probably upset by his obvious display of taking control, which makes things feel out of control for you, which Woods hate. If you're a Water, you might be feeling completely overwhelmed by all the rigid "stuff" he's throwing at you that signals the end of your go-with-the-flow work life. A Fire might be tempted to laugh at his belief that you would follow all the new rules. An Earth might feel overwhelmed by everything being asked of her all at once. And another Metal might feel*

> *challenged by the uncomfortable shifts in protocol and hierarchy. Each club will respond to his excess Metal display in a different way, but the cool thing is that the fix is always the same. You can always shift the energies to help bring balance back to the relationship.*
>
> - *If your new boss has too much Metal, he needs some Fire to balance it out. You can provide the Fire. Playfulness and flirting are out of the question at work, right? But you can always find an appropriate way to increase Fire. Wear Fire's color, which is bright red. Make a joke, but not at his expense because Metals are serious people. Be warm and enthusiastic to him. Smile a lot.*
>
> You may need to go back to your desk to think this through, and that's fine. Just get out of his office before you say something you'll regret, read about the Fire Club, and set to work Shifting the Balance. You'll probably never be best friends, but I promise things will change if you quietly and persistently help him regain balanced Metal.

Or maybe I determine that Mark is the one out of balance with too much Metal making him obstinate and stuck. I can bring up my Fire (Fire melts Metal) to help balance him. By nature, Fires are playful, so I can tease him, make a joke, maybe flirt a bit. Without even knowing what's happening, his adamant stance will soften and he'll become more reasonable. If he's low in Metal and starts to withdraw, I can step into an Earth place (Earth feeds Metal) and draw him back with a shoulder rub or some brownies.

And Mark can give as good as he gets. If he notices that I'm having an excess Wood moment—perhaps I'm frustrated with my computer—Mark stands firm in his Metal. He doesn't take anything personally since Metals are great at detachment, lets me rant for a bit, but then brings his Metal smarts to help solve the problem. This brings down my Wood, and all is well. Occasionally, I have deficient Wood, which usually manifests as an inability to come up with a plan. Mark will wisely step into Water (Water feeds Wood) at that point and run ideas past me until he triggers enough that my Wood springs into action. This is a simple trick we call *Shifting the Balance*, and by now we both do it pretty much automatically.

A QUICK SUMMARY OF WHERE WE ARE

Before we head off to gain a better understanding of our clubs, let's take a quick look at where we are. We've explored a pretty nifty model that summarizes relationship possibilities between five different clubs/elements. The two primary ways of relating in this model are to add energy (the Nurturing Cycle) or take it away (the Controlling Cycle). Both are important in this model because that's how the whole stays balanced.

We've explored the processes and seasonality of the elements across the whole model to get an initial understanding of what's important to each club (i.e., Wood likes expansion, Fire likes celebration, etc.). And we've suggested that while we can visit any clubhouse anytime we want, we each have a natural affinity for one of the elements, and this affinity will affect how we look at the world and interact with everything in our life. And to make things a bit more interesting, our secondary element can "flavor" how our primary element manifests.

Finally, we've determined that our club membership will affect both our relationships with others and our tendencies in times of stress. This is an important point because it's when we're stressed that our relationships usually become more challenging. Understanding our club membership and the club memberships of our friends, children, or mates gives us clues regarding why we act the way we do with them. It also helps us know how to make quick and easy shifts to the energy between us when things get a bit tense or we have to deal with someone we really don't like at all.

Claiming Your Club

It's finally time for you to claim your club membership! To do this, we're going to devote a full chapter to each of the five clubs. Here's how we'll proceed:

- » First, we'll remind ourselves of the seasonal aspects of the element. For example, why is Water considered winter and what does that mean for members of the Water Club? Do they automatically love skiing?

- » Next, we'll look at the issues that matter most to each club and their creative expression of these themes. If someone is in the Fire Club, what will they focus on in their life and how will they express that?

- » Our personalities impact how we interact with our world and each other, so we'll look there next. Where does each club stand on issues like personal expression, socialization needs, boundaries, structure, relationship focus, and those all-important personality strengths and challenges? For example, at their core, Earths are caring and compassionate people, which is a marvelous strength. But they also need to be needed, which can sometimes lead to codependency, which usually isn't so good.

- » Then, we'll look at how the members of each club react when they're stressed. Under stress, each of us actually becomes a purer expression of our primary element, but in a dysfunctional way. Sadly, that's where we often definitively claim our true club affiliation. But stressed people create stressed relationships, so I've included lots of tips and techniques for

Understanding Ourselves

getting each club out of a stressful state fast. These will be helpful for you *and* the people you relate to.

You will probably begin recognizing yourself and others from the descriptions in the next five chapters. And if you don't, the summaries in Chapter 8 should do the trick. Plus, there's also a quick quiz in the Appendix you can take, although I do believe observing ourselves (and others) is usually the best way to determine our club membership. Now, since the first element in the Nurturing Cycle is Water, we'll start with the Water Club. Are you ready? Let's dive in!

CartoonStock.com

CHAPTER 3

THE WATER CLUB: IMAGINE THE POSSIBILITIES

*In the world there is nothing more submissive and weak than water.
Yet for attacking that which is hard and strong, nothing can surpass it.*

—Lao Tzu

WATER THEMES

Water is the first element in the Five Elements cycle. It relates to winter, a time in nature when external activities are few but internal (unseen) activities abound. Water's themes are inner workings, conceptualization, and birth. The greatest strength of the Water element is the power of potential.

Water energy is the source of creativity and concepts. It is the void out of which new ideas are born, the soil in which dreams germinate, the cauldron of pure potentiality. *The inner world is the realm of Water and imagination its greatest gift.*

WATER PEOPLE

What Matters

» *Deep Issues*: People who hang out in the Water Club view life through the filter of depth. Profound issues matter to Waters, and they often seem obsessed with the pursuit of knowledge, truth, and meaning. Waters are interested in art, philosophy, and religion, but won't care about the surface aspects of these pursuits. Instead, they'll focus on the underlying meaning of it all.

» *Connecting with Something Bigger*: If not actively pursuing knowledge in isolated bliss, the more outgoing Waters will become community activists or philanthropists seeking to make the world a better place. Outgoing or not, when their connection to something greater than their selves is severed, Waters suffer deeply.

» *Quiet Time*: Water's season, winter, represents a time of solitary introspection and renewal. We all need Water time to balance our lives, but members of the Water Club need this more than most. As introspective loners, if they don't have quiet time, they lose touch with their sense of self and their place in the grand scheme of things.

Personal Expressions

» *Searchers*: Water people are wise, philosophic, and creative people. But their search for knowledge and understanding can make them penetrating and critical.

» *Loners*: Water's deep inner focus often makes them self-contained and determined to pursue their own interests regardless of what others consider important.

» *Childlike*: Paradoxically, as the first element in the cycle, Waters can also present a more innocent, childlike curiosity that's almost playful. And endearing as any child, they can be selfish and blunt, lacking tact and diplomacy, and even assume that the world revolves around them. Waters are happy playing alone.

» *Occupations*: Waters are often authors, intellectuals, philosophers, and artists who know the power of perseverance.

» *Deepest Need*: Waters need to be part of something bigger than themselves.

» *The Flip Side*: Because Water is full yin, members of the Water Club will often seem quieter or less outgoing than members of other clubs. But don't be fooled—there are still many yang members of this full-yin club, just as the seemingly still surfaces of the great oceans have pounding waves at their shores.

Structure and Boundaries

In nature, water has no boundaries of its own. It will happily flow anywhere and take any shape offered, be it drinking glass, swimming pool, or lake. This lack of boundaries is seen in Water people's tendency to be laid-back types who go with the flow. They are usually happy conforming to the structure of others as long as they can still move. And truthfully, they need structure from others. In nature, the only way water provides structure is to freeze, which markedly inhibits flow. When Water people try to create structure this way, the lack of flow always leads to problems.

In spite of what seems like aimlessness, water will end up where it wants to go. Engorged by flooding rains, a previously calm river can overspill its banks and claim any land in its path. Water people can be the same way; you may tell them no, encourage them to give up, but they won't. Instead, they'll keep at it, slowly wearing down all resistance until they get their way. Persistence and tenacity come naturally to Waters.

Strengths and Weaknesses

Strengths: Water people have a keen awareness of their inner resources and trust that they can handle whatever life brings. Exceedingly patient, Waters know that as long as they stay connected to their deep sense of self, they can ultimately triumph over any difficulty. This makes them optimistic, hopeful people.

Weaknesses: If knowing their own abilities is the greatest strength of Waters, their weaknesses are fear and lack of trust. When Waters are disconnected from the inner forces that support them, they feel vulnerable and begin doubting themselves. Fear creeps in. They usually respond to this by becoming whiny, negative, suspicious, or eventually paranoid people.

Socialization Tendencies

Water people tend to be self-sufficient loners happiest at home reading, thinking, painting, or writing. Content with a few good friends and minimal social activities, they prefer solitary projects and the ability to retreat into a quiet place where nothing distracts them.

Alone, they enjoy considering both the obscure (the meaning of life) and the relevant (the strengths and weaknesses of laptop computers). If they do gather socially, it's often with other Waters for a lively (by their standards) discussion of the nature of the Universe. Those interested in debating how many angels can dance on the head of a pin will likely be Water people. *Waters prefer the company of a few like-minded friends.*

Relationship Focus

Water people focus more on having a relationship with their inner self than on relationships with other people. Their lack of boundaries coupled with a deep inner focus makes it easy for Waters to merge with something greater than themselves, and this relationship is of utmost importance to them. In relationship with others, Waters are inclined to keep their feelings and thoughts to themselves and are very careful about what they reveal. They are self-sufficient in or out of a relationship and yearn for connections that are spiritual or mental. They can be less interested in intimate physical relationships. *Waters need to connect with their inner selves.*

Stress Behaviors: Emptiness and Hopelessness, Narcissism and Intolerance

When happy, Waters are deep, sensible, philosophic people. If stress becomes an issue, they internalize and detach. As with any of the clubs, stress takes Waters to a dysfunctional version of their normal selves. Under stress, Water's primary need to connect with their inner self will distort and manifest as either too great a sense of self (narcissism) or too little a sense of self (low self-esteem).

If Waters' response to stress takes them to a place of *deficient* Water, they become like the little donkey, Eeyore, in the *Winnie the Pooh* books. They're cheerless with a poor sense of self that makes doing anything a supreme effort. They feel disconnected and isolated from everything, including their inner world. Their emptiness inside will cause them to become absentminded, unfocused, and hopelessly gloomy or fearful. As faith in themselves and trust in others continues to dry up, they experience a loss of confidence and can become pessimistic, phobic people. When deeply stressed, they can become depressed or catatonic and lose the will to live.

If Waters' response to stress takes them to a place of *excess* Water, they become not only narcissistic, but inflexible and intolerant of other people's views. Fixated on what they want and aggravated by any who challenge them, they blame others for what goes wrong and cover their fear of inadequacy with out-of-character displays of belligerence and aggression. Their normal "go with the flow" attitude shifts to a more demanding and unforgiving posture. When really stressed, this will lead to heightened antisocial behaviors, suspicion of others, and paranoid tendencies.

> ## WATERS SHARE THEIR TRUTHS
>
> - *I'm very suspicious of other people.*
> - *I tend to avoid intimate relationships.*
> - *I am patient and persevere even when the odds are against me.*
> - *Ideas stir me and ignite my imagination.*
> - *I can become deeply depressed for no apparent reason.*
> - *It takes time for me to trust someone.*
> - *I believe the world can be dangerous and I need to be cautious.*
> - *I will stand up for myself when others disagree, but I dread when this happens.*
> - *I'm always curious about things.*
> - *I yearn for meaning in all aspects of my life.*

WATERS IN TROUBLE

When dealing with out of balance Waters, it's important to remember that their deepest need is to be part of something greater than themselves. Help them (or yourself, if this applies to you) reconnect with their inner self to rediscover a purpose to life and a way to participate in it. Perhaps they've lost touch with their ability to trust, or maybe their well of inspiration has run dry.

To help balance their Water, wisdom from Metal in the form of suggestions and new discoveries will spark their imagination (Metal feeds Water on the Nurturing Cycle of the Five Elements model). Or maybe nurturing from Earth energy in the form of guidance and love will help bring their runaway Water back into the right channels (Earth controls Water via the Controlling Cycle of the Five Elements model). And if anyone remains seriously off-balance, it's important they seek professional help.

Quick Tips to Help Balance Waters

- *Use Music*: Music touches our souls, and listening to music we love balances us. For a Water person in trouble, put on their favorite music. If you're unsure what that is, try classical music or piano music. Anything rhythmic will help balance Water. Playing an instrument keeps Water energy flowing, too.

- *Use Meditation*: Silence and solitude appeal to Waters and help them reconnect with their inner self. Almost any form of quiet meditation works with Water people.

- *Use the Energy Release Point*: The Water element is where fear sits, which means that excessive fearfulness or a tendency to frighten easily can indicate stuck Water energy. When this happens, deeply massaging Kidney 4 with your fingers will help release the energy and dispel fear. To heighten the effect, place a drop or two of an essential oil (options listed further down) on the point, then massage it in. Do this once or twice a day for at least one week, longer if needed. The point location is shown under the *Water Element Points* heading further down.

- *Use Temperature*: Water people tend to run cold, so hot baths often help them.

- *Use Color to Build Water*: The vibrations of specific colors help *build* specific elements. The color for Water is blue. If a Water person manifests behaviors that match the *deficient* Water condition described above (fearful, lethargic, hopeless, isolated, gloomy, pessimistic, depressed, etc.), surround them in blue. Blue walls, blue flowers, blue clothes (including underwear), blue anything.

- *Use Color to Decrease Water*: The vibrations of specific colors can also help *decrease* specific elements. If a Water person manifests behaviors that match the *excess* Water conditions described above (narcissistic, inflexible, intolerant, cynical, sarcastic, demanding, paranoid, etc.), surround them in yellow, the color that builds Earth, which will help bring down their excess Water. Go with yellow walls, yellow flowers, yellow clothes (including underwear), yellow anything.
- *Use Sound*: Each element has a specific sound that balances it. Use the sound several times a day. For Water, the sound is a whispered "Whooooooo." Inhale deeply, then exhale softly while making the sound as slowly as possible.
- *Use Crystals*: Colored stones can balance the energy of specific elements. For Water, use *lapis lazuli, sapphire,* or *aquamarine*. Buy jewelry made from any of these natural stones (a ring, bracelet, necklace, whatever) and wear it as often as possible, even 24/7 for a while. If the stone touches the skin, it usually does a better job of balancing.
- *Use Essential Oils*: The fragrance of selected essential oils can balance the energies of the Water element. These include frankincense and myrrh. Rubbing a few drops of the oil on the skin so that the scent is noticeable will help. Or place a few drops of the oil on a tissue and inhale. A room diffuser is also a great option.
- *Use Food*: Natural salt, in moderate amounts, will strengthen *deficient* Water. Avoid cold foods (like salads) and increase heated foods. And drink plenty of water; it balances every element.
- *Use Yoga*: Specific yoga poses work with individual elements, benefitting both the physical and energetic systems they govern. For the Water element, try the *Forward Bend* pose.

And if you've never had a yoga practice, please find a certified yoga instructor to get you started.

- *Use Personality Balancing Points*: Luo Points balance the yin and yang energies of an element. Balanced elemental energy creates balanced personality energy, which translates to happier relationships. To help balance the Water personality, on the right side of the body, place the middle finger of one hand on Kidney 4 and the middle finger of the other hand on Bladder 58. Hold these points at the same time for two minutes, then repeat on the left side of the body for two minutes. Do this once or twice a day for at least one week—longer if needed. Point locations are shown under the *Water Element Points* heading further down.

- *Use Herbs*: Parsley and peppermint can be good for Waters. A tea made from either will usually help balance Water energy. And always check with your health practitioner before using any medicinal herbs.

- *Use Nature*: Keep moving water in the environment. Buy a small tabletop fountain and run it all the time. Even better, sit by a river, lake, or ocean. Flowing water helps balance Water energies.

- *Use Emotion Stabilizing Points*: Each element has specific points on the head that balance that element's emotional state. Called Neurovascular Points (NV Points), they can be used to not only balance the energies, but also reprogram them to hold the state of balance longer. This makes NV Points both a short-term and long-term fix. To access these points for Water, place the palm of one hand across the back of the head, directly above the neck, and the other palm across the front of the forehead. Hold gently for two to five minutes, breathing normally. Do this once or twice a day for at least one week—longer if needed.

Water Element Points

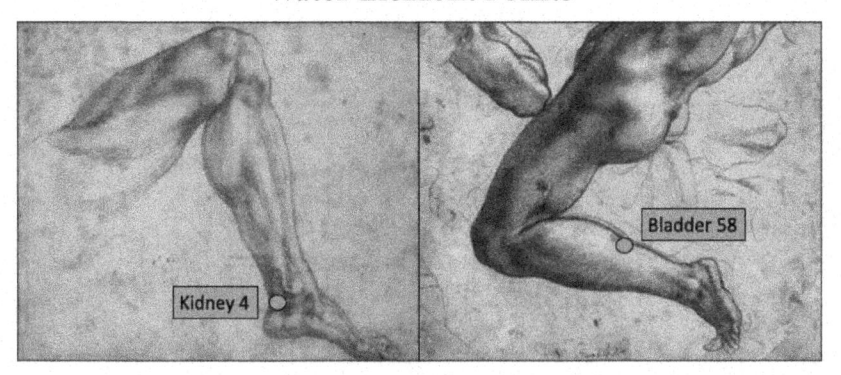

A SNAPSHOT OF WATERS

- *Introspective philosophers embracing theories and ideas*
- *Eccentric loners inspired by the depth of life*
- *Persistent, tenacious, and usually get their way*
- *Little structure, go with the flow*
- *Rarely attend parties, happiest alone*
- *When balanced: hopeful, optimistic, trusting, objective*
- *When stressed: fearful, depressed, hopeless, narcissistic*
- *When deeply stressed: intolerant, cynical, sarcastic, paranoid*
- *Color to build: Blue*
- *Color to balance: Yellow*
- *Loves: free time, deep discussions, reading*
- *Hates: tight schedules, budgets, structure*
- *Likely professions: authors, intellectuals, philosophers, artists*
- *Primary focus: INNER LIFE*
- *Favorite question: WHY?*

The Five Elements of Relationships

A Final Word About Waters

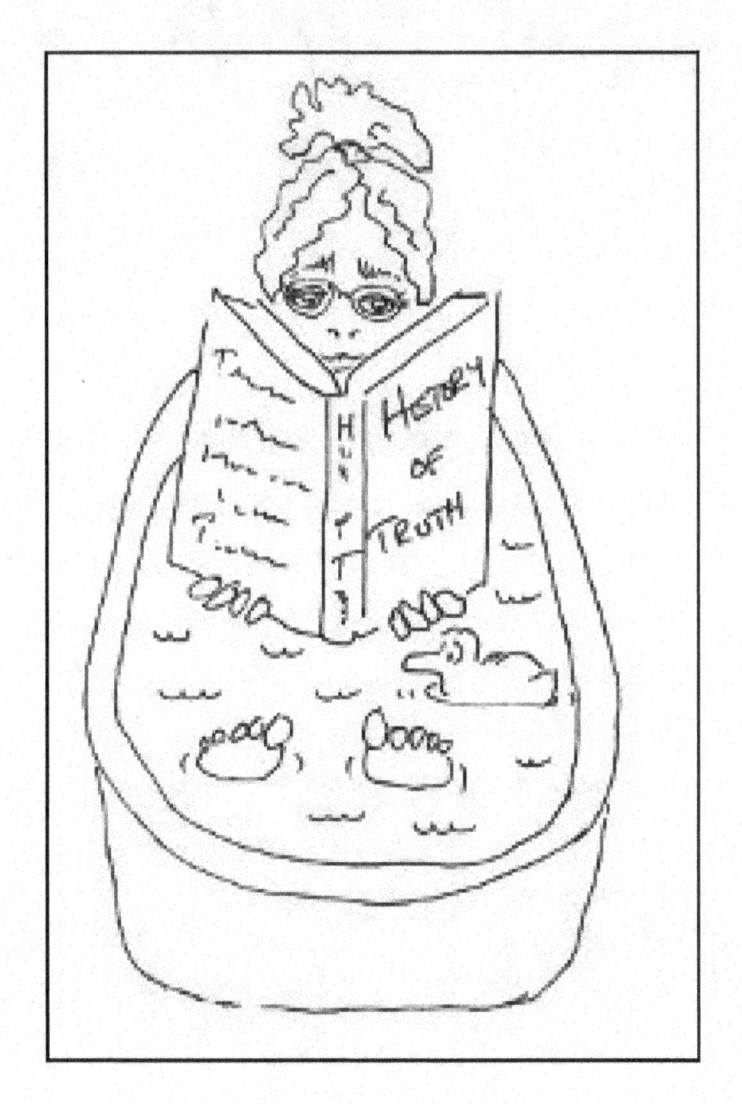

A Water Club member throws a party.
(C. Cohn)

CHAPTER 4

THE WOOD CLUB: MAKE IT HAPPEN

Trees are Earth's endless effort to speak to the listening heaven.
—Rabindranath Tagore

WOOD THEMES

Wood is the second element in the Five Elements cycle. It relates to spring, a time in nature when external activities begin to pick up and focused energy is needed for life to burst forth. Wood's themes are envisioning, acting, and producing. The greatest strength of the Wood element is the power of action and manifestation.

Wood energy is the source of actualization and growth. It is the power that thrusts crocuses up through the snow, beckons leaf buds from barren branches, and calls the whole of nature to burst forth in the spring. *The future is the realm of Wood and initiative its greatest gift.*

WOOD PEOPLE

What Matters

» *Accomplishment:* **People who hang out in the Wood Club value accomplishment and success. Good at decision-mak-**

ing and planning, Woods can see what needs to be done and rally the troops to do it (or go it alone through hard work). We all need Wood energy if we're going to accomplish anything, but members of the Wood Club need accomplishment to feel successful.

- *Fairness:* Wood people are passionate about fairness and quick to step in with their considerable power to help an underdog—be it a person, an organization, or a cause. Woods are not only ready to act; they *need* to act to right any perceived wrong.

- *Productivity*: Woods need to believe their actions are making a difference, and when they do, they will charge full speed ahead. Confusion and inactivity can create big problems for Woods, who evaluate themselves based on outcomes.

Personal Expressions

- *High Energy:* Woods are high-energy people who seek new challenges and like quick, bold results. An aspect of Wood is the wind, an energy that can be an agent of change, bringing new ideas and rearranging old ones.

- *Confident*: Blessed with drive, insight, and seemingly endless energy, Wood people move through life with confidence, ready for any situation that might present itself. Highly individualistic and willing to take charge, Woods will push themselves to the limit, enjoying both the challenge and the triumph.

- *Leadership:* Woods bring the forceful energy it takes to get things started. And with the vision that comes from long-range planning, Woods can react with steadiness when problems arise, think on their feet, then take appropriate action to stay on course. But Woods' drive to make things happen can come at a price: Sure of their goal, they may lose sensitivity and appear callous and overbearing.

» *Occupations*: Woods are often successful business executives, professional athletes, elected officials, fundraisers, or trial lawyers. They are very competitive and do well in jobs where they can play by their own rules.

» *Deepest Need*: Woods need to succeed.

» *The Flip Side*: Wood is the channel from the pure potential of winter's yin to the full actualization of summer's yang. Because of this, Wood is often called new yang or yang rising. Members of the Wood Club are frequently more yang than yin, but not every Wood will be forceful, loud, or in your face. There are quiet Woods, yet even they will stay focused on accomplishing the goal.

Structure and Boundaries

There is exquisite beauty to trees. Their branches reach for new heights driven by a sense of unlimited potential while their roots anchor deep into the ground, guided by a sense of home, the place they belong. And the organic nature of their structure allows them to bend to withstand winds of change. This same tendency toward structure is seen in members of the Wood Club. Driven to accomplish, they depend on flexibility to maintain their all-important forward movement in the face of obstacles. When Woods lose this flexibility, their stuck rigidity creates problems.

Wood people have the courage of their convictions and the capacity to hold their ground no matter what. Because of this, members of the Wood Club are often called upon to provide structure and boundaries for others. This is easy for them to do, and most Woods do this without thinking. Woods are very dependable.

Strengths and Weaknesses

Strengths: Wood people can envision their goals and firmly believe that if they try hard enough, they can manifest almost anything. Powerful and decisive, Woods count on their ability to get things done in the face of seemingly insurmountable odds. They can use their abundant energy to remove obstacles that block their way. It is their nature to be direct and assertive, hopefully in a kind way.

Weaknesses: If action and accomplishment are the greatest strengths of Woods, their greatest weakness is an explosive response to lack of movement. When things aren't happening fast enough, or at all, Woods have nowhere to focus their formidable energy. They'll push and exhaust themselves in the name of the goal and ultimately lose their ability to be flexible and adaptable. In the process they can become impatient, angry, and often quite mean.

Socialization Tendencies

Wood people tend to be workaholics who are happiest when they are making progress on an important project. They rarely have vast networks of friends because keeping up with them takes too much time. Like Waters, Woods prefer smaller gatherings where they are happy to discuss their plans and successes.

Woods are not party people and usually find large events to be a complete waste of time. However, they will attend them if it furthers their cause—personal or philanthropic—or if they have a role to play. Political fundraisers are the territory of Woods. They are happiest mixing business in with social events and can be counted on to inspire others for a cause. *Woods will socialize if they have a role to play or if it meets a goal.*

Relationship Focus

Wood people focus more on their own goals and accomplishments than on partnering. For Woods, life is usually about getting something done. To stay focused, Woods hold their boundaries and prevent outside forces from overwhelming them. In a relationship, Woods do best with people they believe are trusted allies with whom they share a common goal. Woods often resent people or situations that put limits on them; these are obstacles to growth and success. If this is the case, a Wood relationship can become one of conflict and resistance, especially when friends or partners compete for power or threaten the Wood's success. *Woods need to connect with outer accomplishment.*

Stress Behaviors: Indecision and Frustration, Impatience and Anger

When happy, Woods are confident, accomplished, and dependable people. If stress becomes an issue, Woods lose their way. As with any of the clubs, stress takes Woods to an out-of-balance, dysfunctional version of their normal selves. Under stress, Wood's primary need to succeed will distort and usually manifest as either trying to do too much too fast (impatience) or the inability to get anything done at all (indecision).

If Woods' response to stress takes them to a place of *deficient* Wood, they will become indecisive, erratic, anxious, and unable to concentrate. Their despondency over their lack of productivity will result in embarrassment and humiliation, which will cause them to withdraw from those around them. Unsure why they are failing, they'll direct the inevitable frustration at themselves, leading to internal anger and shame. As exhaustion sets in, they become more reliant on external sources of stimulation like caffeine, sugar, and alcohol, and eventually experience depression and a sense of hopelessness as they head for the inevitable collapse.

If Woods' response to stress takes them to a place of *excess* Wood, the normally thorough and competent Woods become not only impatient, but also reckless and short-tempered. They will push ahead without adequate preparation, unaware of the risks and potential damage, and respond with anger and tyrannical aggressiveness when the inevitable failure occurs. Obsessed with movement, they become driven to win at any cost and will be quick to blame others when things don't turn out well. As disaster looms, their self-destructive tendencies will increase, as will their violent and uncontrollable outbursts of rage.

> **WOODS SHARE THEIR TRUTHS**
> - *I am impulsive and need to act.*
> - *The ends often justify the means for me.*
> - *I come alive under pressure.*
> - *I am fiercely independent.*
> - *I enjoy planning and organizing everything.*
> - *Chaos brings me to my knees.*
> - *When people are treated unfairly, I stand up for them.*
> - *I am competitive and need to win, even with close friends and family.*
> - *Direct and straightforward, I sometimes come on too strong.*
> - *Taking risks is natural for me.*

WOODS IN TROUBLE

When dealing with out-of-balance Woods, it's important to remember that their deepest need is to succeed. Help them (or yourself, if this applies to you) ascertain where they feel stuck and how they might re-energize their lives and plans (Woods *always* have plans). Perhaps they've been unable to address obstacles in their path, or maybe they've lost sight of their goal.

To help balance their Wood, inspiration from Water in the form of ideas and possibilities will help ignite their vision again (Water feeds Wood in the Five Elements model). Or maybe wise advice from Metal energy in the form of reason and rationale can bring their overly assertive Wood back to pliancy (Metal controls Wood in the model). And if anyone remains seriously off-balance, it's important to seek professional help.

Quick Tips to Help Balance Woods

- *Use Music*: Music touches our souls, and listening to music we love balances us. For a Wood person in trouble, put on their favorite music. If unsure what that is, try primal melodies with wooden flutes. Anything calming will help balance Wood.

- *Use Meditation*: Woods don't do well sitting still for long, so an active meditation practice like tai chi works well for Woods. Walking meditations are good as well.

- *Use the Energy Release Point*: The Wood element is where anger sits, which means that excessive anger or a tendency to be short-tempered can indicate stuck Wood energy. When this happens, deeply massaging Liver 2 with your fingers will help release the energy and dissipate anger. To heighten the effect, place a drop or two of an essential oil (options listed further down) on the point, then massage it in. Do this once or twice a day for at least one week—longer if needed. The point location is shown under the *Wood Element Points* heading further down.

- *Use Temperature*: Wood people can chill easily, so comfortable warmth can help them. Keep a shawl, light jacket, or sweater handy.

- *Use Color to Build Wood*: The vibrations of specific colors help *build* specific elements. The color for Wood is green. If a Wood person manifests behaviors that match the *deficient* Wood condition described above (indecisive, erratic, anxious, unable to concentrate, withdrawn, etc.), surround them in green. Green walls, green plants, green clothes (including underwear), green anything.

- *Use Color to Decrease Wood*: The vibrations of specific colors can also help *decrease* specific elements. If a Wood person manifests behaviors that match the *excess* Wood conditions described above (impatient, reckless, short-tempered, unprepared, angry, etc.), surround them in white, the color that builds Metal, which will help bring down their excess Wood. Go with white walls, white flowers, white clothes (including underwear), white anything.

- *Use Sound*: Each element has a specific sound that balances it. Use the sound several times a day. For Wood, inhale sharply, then exhale quickly making the sound, "Shhhhhhhhh," pushing the last of the sound out at the end.

- *Use Crystals*: Colored stones can balance the energy of specific elements. For Wood, use either *malachite, emerald,* or *green aventurine*. Buy jewelry made from any of these natural stones (a ring, bracelet, necklace, whatever) and wear it as often as possible, even 24/7 for a while. If the stone touches the skin, it usually does a better job of balancing.

- *Use Essential Oils*: The fragrance of selected essential oils can balance the energies of the Wood element. These include peppermint and lavender, among others. Rubbing a few drops of the oil on the skin so that the scent is noticeable will help. Or place a few drops of the oil on a tissue and inhale. A room diffuser is also a great option.

- *Use Food*: Sour tastes (like lemon) will balance Wood. Sliced lemon in hot water in the morning is great for Woods. Avoid too many sour tastes if dealing with *excess* Wood. Green leafy vegetables are good to build *deficient* Wood. And drink plenty of water; it balances every element.

- *Use Yoga*: Specific yoga poses work with individual elements, benefitting both the physical and energetic systems they govern. For the Wood element, try the *Butterfly* pose. And if you've never had a yoga practice, please find a certified yoga instructor to get you started.

- *Use Personality Balancing Points*: Luo Points balance the yin and yang energies of an element. Balanced elemental energy creates balanced personality energy, which translates to happier relationships. To help balance the Wood personality, on the right side of the body, place the middle finger of one hand on Liver 5 and the middle finger of the other hand on Gallbladder 37. Hold these points at the same time for two minutes, then repeat on the left side of the body for two minutes. Do this once or twice a day for at least one week—longer if needed. The point locations are shown under the *Wood Element Points* heading further down.

- *Use Herbs*: Dandelion and milk thistle can be good for Woods. A tea made from either of these will usually help balance Wood energy. And always check with your health practitioner before using any medicinal herbs.

- *Use Nature*: Staying surrounded by green plants helps balance Wood people. Buy healthy plants and place them throughout the house, especially during winter. On nice days, go outside and walk through a forest or sit by a tree.
- *Use Emotion Stabilizing Points*: Each element has specific points on the head that balance that element's emotional state. Called Neurovascular Points (NV Points), they can be used to not only balance the energies, but also reprogram them to hold the state of balance longer. This makes NV Points both a short-term and long-term fix. To access these points for Wood, place the thumbs of each hand on the face at the outside edges of the eyes and rest the fingers of each hand across the forehead. Hold gently for two to five minutes, breathing normally. Do this once or twice a day for at least one week—longer if needed.

Wood Element Points

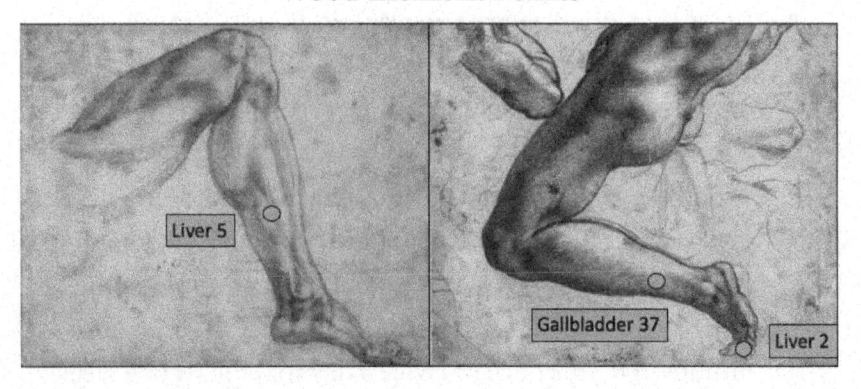

A SNAPSHOT OF WOODS

- *Goal-directed visionaries who can make things happen*
- *Assertive champions for the weak and downtrodden*
- *Productive, decisive, and usually successful*
- *Flexibly structured, likes own rules*
- *Willing to party for a purpose*
- *When balanced: fair, bold, direct, decisive*
- *When stressed: angry, frustrated, indecisive, impatient*
- *When deeply stressed: driven, explosive, insensitive, confrontational*
- *Color to build: Green*
- *Color to decrease: White*
- *Loves: challenges, accomplishment, moving forward*
- *Hates: dashed expectations, chaos, being told "No!"*
- *Likely professions: executives, sports figures, elected officials, trial lawyers*
- *Primary focus: the FUTURE*
- *Favorite question: WHEN?*

A Final Word About Woods

A Wood Club member throws a party.
(Michael Cambon, CartoonStock.com)

CHAPTER 5

THE FIRE CLUB: LET'S CELEBRATE!

Love is the Fire of Life; it either consumes or purifies.
—Swedish Proverb

FIRE THEMES

Fire is the third element in the Five Elements cycle. It relates to summer, the time in nature when external activities are at their peak and manifestation abounds. The ideas of Water and the work of Wood reach their zenith during Fire. The themes of Fire are perpetual motion, spontaneity, and passion. The greatest strength of the Fire element is the power of fully actualized potential.

Fire energy is the source of speed and maximum performance. It's the power that heats the earth, brings flowers to full bloom, and celebrates the whole of life. *The present is the realm of Fire and inspiration its greatest gift.*

FIRE PEOPLE

What Matters

» *Excitement:* People who hang out in the Fire Club have a zest for life and desire excitement. Fire's season, summer, represents a time of activity, fun, and socializing. The thrill of living life at full speed and immersing themselves completely in every experience matters to Fires. Without excitement, Fires deflate.

» *Attention:* As outgoing people, Fires love time in the limelight. They enjoy and need the attention. If ignored or left alone for too long, Fires will suffer because attention feeds them.

» *Connections:* We all need Fire energy at times because we all need relationships. The push to connect begins in Fire, and while these connections usually aren't long-term, Fires need the charge they get from spontaneous connections to feel alive. Without connections, life becomes pale and gray for a Fire.

Personal Expressions

» *Joyful:* Fire people are outgoing and fun. They laugh a lot. Their joy for living makes them popular to be around, which works well for a Fire. "The more, the merrier!" could be their creed. Their easy "Yes!" to everything makes them busy, but often finds them overcommitted or burned out.

» *Always Moving:* Fire is full yang, which means it's the time of complete actualization. Life is a banquet, and Fires want to taste it all. They celebrate life by connecting with people, places, and things, but these connections often don't last because Fires like to keep moving. They need movement so they can change direction—and their minds—rapidly.

» *Live in the Present:* Fire people are creatures of the "now" who don't like to plan. Their warmth and enthusiasm can transcend the ordinary, so the "now" is always a party with them and they are usually the stars.

» *Occupations:* Fires are often actors, comedians; motivational speakers, and public figures—people who enjoy attention.

» *Deepest Need:* Fires need movement and quick connections.

> *The Flip Side*: Fire's strong outgoing energy of expression clearly demonstrates its position as full yang, but there *are* more yin-like Fires. Yin Fires still love connecting with people, laughing, and partying, but are less inclined to do so on a public stage.

Structure and Boundaries

Just like water, in nature fire has few boundaries. It can jump a road, turn a bend, or take flight and burn a tree from the top down. Unlike water, which can be directed by offering a container, fire is very hard to focus or control. This lack of structure is seen in Fire people's tendency to act spontaneously and be easily distracted. They love the excitement of constant action so much that they will actively seek it out. Fires don't appreciate anything that tries to corral them (except Earth). Even if it's for their own good, it cramps their style. However, too much flaming yang energy will eventually burn out even the hardiest Fire.

In spite of the fact that fire can create chaos in nature, for millennia fire that is managed has warmed us all. When Fire people do what it takes to remain balanced, their genuine warmth and immediate connection is a gift to all they encounter. They easily give joy and receive it back in kind.

Strengths and Weaknesses

> *Strengths*: Fire people reach for connection and usually create paths of trust with others to accomplish this. Firm believers in the abundance and good of all creation, including people, Fires are upbeat and optimistic. Wherever they are, Fires can transform the mundane into the exceptional. They attract people, inoculate them with joy, and leave them laughing.

Weaknesses: If connection and joy are Fires' greatest strengths, their greatest weakness is not managing their energy. They thrive on drama and excitement. They can also take things too far and burn themselves out—and anyone else who is around. Fires live for opportunities to connect but can entangle themselves with others and not know clearly where they stop and someone else starts. When this happens, Fires can become anxious, irrational, and moody.

Socialization Tendencies

Fire people love to celebrate. Of all the Five Element Clubs, Fires are easily the most social. They need no excuse to throw a party or attend an event. They are charismatic hosts, and invitations to their parties are usually highly coveted. Not necessarily for the status, but because Fires are beloved, and their events are truly fun.

Fires are creative people who put effort into guaranteeing their parties are a blast. Whether a dinner for four or a banquet for forty, Fire people make sure their events are entertaining and that everyone has a good time. They are also desirable guests for the very same reason: Fires are the life of the party. Their joie de vivre draws people to them quite literally like a moth to a flame. But most will experience it as a flame of temporary transformation, not a lasting bond. *Fires are always ready to celebrate and connect.*

Relationship Focus

Fire people focus on their strong desire for intense connection. We all manifest a subtle aspect of this Fire energy because our hearts strive for union. However, there is nothing subtle about a Fire relationship. Because Fires thrive on drama, passions will flare in their relationships, as will tempers. Their intense craving for connection coupled with their poor boundaries often makes it easy for Fires to get too wrapped up with some people. They can merge with others suddenly and completely, but usually for just a short time. The intensity and chaos of the connection can burn out the Fire and everyone else. *Fires need intense connections outside themselves.*

Stress Behaviors: Scatter and Overwhelm, Anxiety and Panic

When happy, Fires are fun-loving, outgoing, and joyful people. If stress becomes an issue, Fires can destroy themselves and damage the people around them. Like all the clubs, stress takes Fires to an out-of-balance, dysfunctional version of their normal selves. Under stress, Fire's primary need to connect with someone or something will distort and manifest either as a panicked attempt to push a connection or an ineffective, scattered attempt at being with people.

If a Fire person's stress takes them to a place of *deficient* Fire, they will seem scattered, feel overwhelmed, and their trademark joy and spontaneity will desert them. They become emotionally unstable, and their desperate need to connect leads to poor judgment in love relationships, as well as an inability to change. Their intense need to be accepted will create an agitated eagerness to please and a fear of rejection. If left unbalanced, de-energized Fires find it difficult to pay attention, think logically, or speak clearly. Eventually they can become depleted, humorless, lifeless people.

If a Fire person's response to stress takes them to a place of *excess* Fire, the normally enthusiastic Fires become anxious, restless, and manic. They overload their schedules, have trouble concentrating, and can appear irrational. When they try to comfort themselves with connections, over-energized Fires scorch and drive away anyone near them. Feeling abandoned, Fires develop a deep fear of being rejected that may prompt sudden, highly out-of-character, irrational outbursts. If left unbalanced, ramped-up Fires can develop rapid, flustered speech patterns as they burn out. What will be left are frazzled, hysterical, and even delirious people.

> **FIRES SHARE THEIR TRUTHS**
>
> - *I do all I can to avoid being alone.*
> - *A yes from me doesn't always mean yes.*
> - *I am excited about life.*
> - *I laugh and giggle a lot, sometimes too loudly or at the wrong time.*
> - *Difficult situations fluster me.*
> - *Noisy, busy places make me happy.*
> - *I can easily let bygones be bygones.*
> - *Secretly, I long for support and abundant praise; I often doubt myself.*
> - *I have a thin skin; what others say about me matters.*
> - *Sensual pleasures please me.*

FIRES IN TROUBLE

When dealing with out-of-balance Fires, it's important to remember that their deepest need is for movement and quick connection. Help them (or yourself, if this applies to you) ascertain what has gone wrong and how they might re-energize their lives. Have they spent too much time alone at home? Has there been a rupture in their social circle? Investigate opportunities to socialize, whether that means coaxing them to a party or inviting people over.

To help balance their Fire, the announcement of an accomplishment from a Wood friend could offer a reason for celebration and ignite their passion again (Wood feeds Fire via the Nurturing Cycle of the model). Or maybe calm energy from a Water friend in the form of a quiet visit will help damp down their scorching flames

(Water controls Fire via the Controlling Cycle of the model). And if anyone remains seriously off-balance, it's important to seek professional help.

Quick Tips to Help Balance Fires

- » *Use Music*: Music touches our souls, and listening to music balances us. For a Fire person in trouble, put on their favorite music. If you're unsure what that is, try guitar music with a bright melody. Anything cheery will help balance Fire.

- » *Use Meditation*: Silence and solitude help calm and center Fires. Meditations that encourage intentional or focused breathing can be especially calming for Fires.

- » *Use the Energy Release Point:* The Fire element is where anxiety sits, which means that excessive anxiety and panic—and an inability to feel joy—can indicate stuck Fire energy. When this happens, deeply massaging Heart 7 with your fingers will help release the energy and calm the spirit. To heighten the effect, place a drop or two of an essential oil (options listed further down) on the point, then massage it in. Do this once or twice a day for at least one week—longer if needed. Point location is shown under the *Fire Element Points* heading further down.

- » *Use Temperature*: Fire people tend to run hot, so cool water often helps them. Splash cold water on their neck and face or have them literally jump in a lake.

- » *Use Color to Build Fire*: The vibrations of specific colors help *build* specific elements. The color for Fire is red. If a Fire manifests behaviors that match the *deficient* Fire condition described above (scattered, inflexible, humorless, emotionally unstable, illogical, overwhelmed, lifeless, etc.) surround them in red. Red walls, red flowers, red clothes (including underwear), red anything.

The Five Elements of Relationships

- *Use Color to Decrease Fire*: The vibrations of specific colors can also help *decrease* specific elements. If a Fire manifests behaviors that match the *excess* Fire conditions described above (anxious, panicked, irrational, flustered, frazzled, hysterical, delirious, etc.), surround them in blue, the color that builds Water, which will help bring down their excess Fire. Go with blue walls, blue flowers, blue clothes (including underwear), blue anything.

- *Use Sound*: Each element has a specific sound that balances it. Use the sound several times a day. For Fire, inhale slowly and exhale making the sound, "Heeeeeeeeeee," like a big sigh.

- *Use Crystals*: Colored stones can balance the energy of specific elements. For Fires, use *garnet, fluorite,* or *ruby*. Buy jewelry made from any of these natural stones (a ring, bracelet, necklace, whatever) and wear it as often as possible, even 24/7 for a while. If the stone touches the skin, it usually does a better job of balancing.

- *Use Essential Oils*: The fragrance of selected essential oils can balance the energies of the Fire element. These include rosemary and lavender, among others. Rubbing a few drops of the oil on the skin so that the scent is noticeable will help. Or place a few drops of the oil on a tissue and inhale. A room diffuser is also a great option.

- *Use Food*: If dealing with *excess* Fire, eat cooling foods like salads, raw vegetables, and fresh fruit. If dealing with *deficient* Fire, up the heat in food by using chili peppers and spices. And drink plenty of water; it balances every element.

- *Use Yoga*: Specific yoga poses work with individual elements, benefitting both the physical and energetic systems they govern. For the Fire element, try the *Star* pose. And if you've never had a yoga practice, please find a certified yoga instructor to get you started.

- » *Use Personality Balancing Points*: Luo Points balance the yin and yang energies of an element. Balanced elemental energy creates balanced personality energy, which translates into happier relationships. To help balance the Fire personality, on the right side of the body, place the middle finger of one hand on Heart 5 and the middle finger of the other hand on Small Intestine 7. Hold these points at the same time for two minutes, then repeat on the left side of the body for two minutes. Do this once or twice a day for at least one week—longer if needed. Point locations are shown under the *Fire Element Points* heading further down.

- » *Use Herbs*: Ginger and cinnamon can be good for Fires. A tea made from either of these will usually help balance Fire energy. And always check with your health practitioner before using any medicinal herbs.

- » *Use Nature*: The joy of summer makes Fire happy, so as much as possible, help Fires be outside in comfortable weather. Desert climates are usually too much heat for a Fire. Inside, fired pottery (like raku) will help balance a Fire.

- » *Use Emotion Stabilizing Points*: Each element has specific points on the head that balance that element's emotional state. Called Neurovascular Points (NV Points), they can be used to not only balance the energies, but also reprogram them to hold the state of balance longer. This makes NV Points both a short-term and long-term fix. To access these points for Fire, place the palm of one hand across the back of the head directly behind the eyes and the other palm across the front of the forehead. Hold gently for two to five minutes, breathing normally. Do this once or twice a day for at least one week—longer if needed.

The Five Elements of Relationships

Fire Element Points

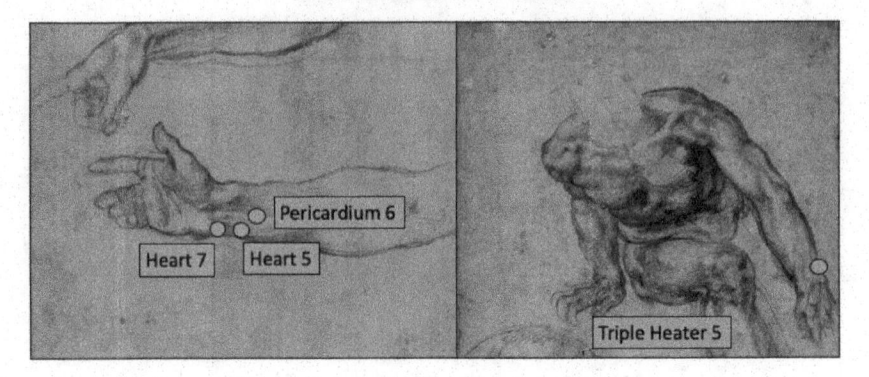

(Image: anatomical illustrations showing acupuncture points — Heart 7, Heart 5, Pericardium 6 on the wrist/forearm, and Triple Heater 5 on the arm)

A SNAPSHOT OF FIRES

- *Inspirational performers transcending the ordinary*
- *Charismatic people happy to meet and greet*
- *Enthusiastic, outgoing, and usually dramatic*
- *Little structure, poor boundaries, hard to control*
- *Willing to party and connect anytime*
- *When balanced: happy, enthusiastic, ready for fun, passionate*
- *When stressed: anxious, overwhelmed, scattered, indecisive*
- *When deeply stressed: manic, hysterical, panicked, burned out*
- *Color to build: Red*
- *Color to decrease: Blue*
- *Loves: parties, attention, and being busy*
- *Hates: boredom, ordinariness, and being ignored*
- *Likely professions: actors, comedians, motivational speakers, public figures*
- *Primary focus: the NOW*
- *Favorite question: WHERE?*

Understanding Ourselves

A Final Word About Fires

Fire Club Members throw a party.
(James Stevenson, CartoonStock.com)

CHAPTER 6

THE EARTH CLUB: WHAT DO YOU NEED?

Those who contemplate the beauty of the earth find reserves of strength that will endure as long as life lasts.

—Rachel Carson

EARTH THEMES

Earth is the fourth element in the Five Elements cycle. Its themes are balance and transitions. Earth not only governs times of balance within a seasonal phase, it also supports transitions into new phases within the larger cycle. However, unlike the first three elements, Earth does not relate to a specific season. Instead, Earth overshadows the four seasonal transition points we experience over the course of one year.

Specifically, there are two solstices where we transition either from greatest daylight toward greatest darkness (the summer solstice) or from greatest darkness toward greatest daylight (the winter solstice). There are also two equinoxes (spring and fall), points of equal day and night where we hold a state of perfect balance between light and dark. These four times, and the months in which they fall, are governed by Earth energy. *Transition is the realm of Earth and balance its greatest gift.*

EARTH PEOPLE

What Matters

» *Relationships*: People who hang out in the Earth Club value long-term relationships. The spontaneous connections forged in Fire slowly find emotional depth and reinforcement in Earth. It has been said that Earth makes order out of the Fire relationships that last. Earths also excel at making people feel safe and loved.

» *Helping Others*: Earths are compassionate people who care about others and are quick to help out in any way they can. Doing this gives meaning to their lives.

» *Inclusion:* Earths like to feel as though everyone is one big, happy family; it pains them if people (or a group of people) are left out. They will work long and hard to foster inclusion and will avoid confrontation to assure that everyone remains happily together.

Personal Expressions

» *Supporting Transitions*: Earths are comfortable with change and are ready, able, and willing to assist others. Their well-thought-out approach to transitions means they excel at making people feel safe and cared for. Earth people are happiest when they are needed, and they identify deeply with those they help. This makes them either a very effective helper or someone who suffers too much for others.

» *Mother Nature*: Earths care about the natural world and manifest this in large and small ways. They love to grow things, whether in the garden or the house, and usually have a green thumb. Earth people thrill at the expression of life and hold all life as sacred. The more yang Earths will lobby loudly, demanding better treatment for our planet, our children, and our pets. Earths are connected deeply to our planet and are a source of grounding for others.

» *Nurturer:* Earth people express their love by nurturing others, whether with food, time, advice, or the "things" they have collected along the way to share. Earths usually love to cook for others and give gifts as physical expressions of their love. The greatest joy of an Earth is to make sure that people (and animals) are comfortable, safe, and nourished.

» *Occupations*: Earths are often nurses, teachers, parents, and counselors; people who are good at helping others.

» *Deepest Need:* Earths need to be needed and help others.

» *The Flip Side*: Since Earth is neither yin nor yang, there is no "opposing force" flip side. There are, however, Earths that are more yin and Earths that are more yang. All Earths will care about nurturing and helping people, but how they do this will vary. The more yin Earths will work on a smaller scale, perhaps arranging meals for a local family having hard times. A yang Earth might create a fundraising drive to support Meals on Wheels.

Structure and Boundaries

Earth has structure, but it's the deep structure of a moveable matrix. In this way Earth is different than the other four elements. All of life, including the elements, depends on Earth for existence. Earth embraces Water to give it flow and structure. Earth is the medium that anchors and nurtures Wood. Earth is the hearth that helps contain and support Fire. And Earth feeds the minerals from her being to create Metal. Earth people are the same way—left to their own devices, they embrace, nurture, support, and feed the world.

Earth people are not quick to do anything. Their movement is slow, sometimes painfully so. But once set on a direction, they stay true to course. Earths are not good with boundaries and often find themselves caught in the middle of a situation they are trying to help. In the name of offering assistance, Earths can end up enabling someone or interfering in a situation that was not theirs to handle.

In nature, earth can be manipulated to create a stable structure; one of the oldest man-made building materials is mud brick. And just like bricks, if Earth people stay balanced, they can stand strong and do their job of holding us all for a very long time.

Strengths and Weaknesses

> *Strengths*: Earth people see the good in all beings and happily embrace them wherever they are. Loving and compassionate, Earths naturally step forward to help, giving away a piece of themselves (and anything else available) in the process. Earths use their steadying energy to stabilize people during the upheavals of transitions, allowing balance to be maintained. Earths love and honor all relationships.
>
> *Weaknesses*: If helping and supporting are the greatest strengths of Earths, helping and supporting *too much* are their greatest weaknesses. Being needed gives purpose to Earths' lives, but they can take things too far. When this happens, Earths can insert themselves into matters that aren't their business. This may cause them to smother the people they are trying to help—or alienate them altogether. Either way, Earths can worry themselves sick over the people they love.

Socialization Tendencies

Earth people love long-lasting, deep relationships, and their socialization patterns are based on this fact. Earths love to spend time with their people—those who are part of their family, tribe, or community. The focal point of most socializing that Earths do is the home. Family dinners are sacred times, as are holiday meals with extended family.

Earths will attend large social galas, but usually because someone close to them is hosting the event. If someone they care about is throwing a party, Earths will attend specifically because they care. And at the party, Earths are usually in the kitchen chatting and helping serve the abundance of food they brought to share. *Earths thrive on the chance to be with those they love.*

Relationship Focus

Earth people focus on building strong and lasting connections with others. This takes time, and Earths cannot be hurried in the process. They like to create homes, and what happens in that home is a top priority. In a relationship, a sense of deep and lasting connection is essential to the health and happiness of an Earth. Relationship discord is unbearable, and Earths will work long and hard to resolve the conflict, often accepting blame for the situation to ease the tension. Earths unconditionally love, nurture, and assist in a relationship, but their tendency to over-identify with others can make them clingy and dependent. This often makes them suffocating to be around. *Earths need deep, lasting relationships with others.*

Stress Behaviors: Needy and Clingy, Meddling and Worried

When happy, Earths are caring, nurturing, and compassionate people. If stress becomes an issue, Earths lose their all-important balance. As with any of the clubs, stress takes Earths to a dysfunctional version of their normal selves. Under stress, Earth's primary need to help will distort and usually manifest as either trying to do too much for people (meddling), or the need for others to confirm how much the Earths are needed (neediness).

If Earths' response to stress takes them to a place of *deficient* Earth, not only will they become clingy and needy, they will also manifest excessive concern for others. They become flighty, feel guilty they aren't doing enough, and suffer separation anxiety when no one needs them. Lonely and unable to muster the energy to reach out, Earths will believe they've been abandoned and develop an addictive relationship with food. As a complete lack of energy overwhelms them, Earths eventually succumb to feelings of inadequacy and a soul-deep fatigue.

If Earths' response to stress takes them to a place of *excess* Earth, not only will they become meddling and codependent, the normally grounded and stable Earths will begin obsessively worrying about everything—especially that they aren't doing enough. Their need to help causes them to insert themselves inappropriately, unaware that they are interfering instead of helping. When turned away, the hypersensitive Earths experience temper tantrums. Desperate to nurture someone, they turn to dangerous amounts of sweets to nurture themselves. Eventually they become increasingly sluggish and withdrawn, unable to satisfy their craving for love and affection.

EARTHS SHARE THEIR TRUTHS

- *I find myself in the middle a lot, but I'm only trying to help.*
- *Feeling left out hurts me deeply.*
- *I can easily mold myself to different people and situations.*
- *I am always accessible to my friends, day or night.*
- *People say it's easy to tell me their secrets.*
- *I love happy endings.*
- *I find it difficult to ask others for help.*
- *I love cooking, sewing, decorating, and everything about crafts.*
- *I tend to obsess about problems if I'm upset.*
- *Food, especially sweets, is often my best friend.*

EARTHS IN TROUBLE

When dealing with out-of-balance Earths, it's important to remember that their deepest need is to help others. Help them (or yourself, if this applies to you) discover where they have lost their own balance and how they might regain it. Has an important relationship recently ended? Have they lost their connection to their inner self?

To help balance an Earth, a party invitation from a Fire friend might offer a chance to reconnect with important relationships (Fire feeds Earth on the Nurturing Cycle of the model). Or maybe encouragement from a Wood friend in the form of a plan to get back on track could help stop their backsliding (Wood controls Earth on the Controlling Cycle). And if anyone remains seriously off-balance, it's important to seek professional help.

Quick Tips to Help Balance Earths

- » *Use Music*: Music touches our souls, and listening to music we love balances us. For an Earth person in trouble, put on their favorite music. If you aren't sure what that is, try cello music or anything with a deep, stable sound. This will help balance Earth.
- » *Use Meditation*: Guided meditations work well for Earths because the voice of someone else gives them a person-to-person connection point.
- » *Use the Energy Release Point*: The Earth element is where worry sits, which means that excessive worry and overthinking things can indicate stuck Earth energy. When this happens, deeply massaging Spleen 4 with your fingers will help release the energy and dissolve worry. To heighten the effect, place a drop or two of an essential oil (options listed further down) on the point, then massage it in. Do this once or twice a day for at least one week—longer if needed. The

Understanding Ourselves

point location is shown under the *Earth Element Points* heading further down.

- » *Use Temperature*: Cool dampness isn't good for Earths, so a cheery fire on a dreary day will help, or even a quick trip to a warm, dry desert. If travel is out, try a sauna or hot tub.

- » *Use Color to Build Earth*: The vibrations of specific colors help build specific elements. The color for Earth is yellow (or orange). If an Earth manifests behaviors that match the *deficient* Earth condition described above (needy, clingy, lonely, flighty, guilt-ridden, addiction to food, feelings of inadequacy, etc.), surround them in yellow. Yellow walls, yellow flowers, yellow clothes (including underwear), yellow anything.

- » *Use Color to Decrease Earth*: The vibrations of specific colors can also help decrease specific elements. If an Earth manifests behaviors that match the *excess* Earth conditions described above (meddling, codependent, worried, craving sweets, ungrounded, sluggish, withdrawn, etc.), surround them in green, the color that builds Wood, which will help bring down their excess Earth. Go with green walls, green plants, green clothes (including underwear), green anything.

- » *Use Sound*: Each element has a specific sound that balances it. Use the sound several times a day. For Earth, inhale deeply and exhale slowly saying the prayerful sound, "Aummmmmmm," like the OM.

- » *Use Crystals*: Colored stones can balance the energy of specific elements. For Earth, use *citrine, rose quartz,* or *tiger's eye*. Buy jewelry made from any of these natural stones (a ring, bracelet, necklace, whatever) and wear it as often as possible, even 24/7 for a while. If the stone touches the skin, it usually does a better job of balancing.

- *Use Essential Oils*: The fragrance of selected essential oils can balance the energies of the Earth element. These include peppermint and lemon balm, among others. Rubbing a few drops of the oil on the skin so that the scent is noticeable will help. Or place a few drops of the oil on a tissue and inhale. A room diffuser is also a great option.

- *Use Food*: Earths love food, and they usually love sweets the best. A *small* amount of something sweet can balance Earth energies. But just a little. And drink plenty of water; it balances every element.

- *Use Yoga*: Specific yoga poses work with individual elements, benefitting both the physical and energetic systems they govern. For the Earth element, try the *Reclining Hero* pose. And if you've never had a yoga practice, please find a certified yoga instructor to get you started.

- *Use Personality Balancing Points*: Luo Points balance the yin and yang energies of an element. Balanced elemental energy creates balanced personality energy, which translates to happier relationships. To help balance the Earth personality, on the right side of the body, place the middle finger of one hand on Spleen 4 and the middle finger of the other hand on Stomach 40. Hold these points at the same time for two minutes, then repeat on the left side of the body for two minutes. Do this once or twice a day for at least one week—longer if needed. Point locations are shown under the *Earth Element Points* heading further down.

- *Use Herbs*: Fennel and lemon balm can be good for Earths. A tea made from either of these herbs will usually help balance Earth energy. And always check with your health practitioner before using any medicinal herbs.

- » *Use Nature*: Earths love to connect with the earth. It balances and grounds them. They especially love time in a garden planting, weeding, or digging. A simple walk outside can often be enough to balance an Earth.
- » *Use Emotion Stabilizing Points*: Each element has specific points on the head that balance that element's emotional state. Called Neurovascular Points (NV Points), they can be used to not only balance the energies, but also reprogram them to hold the state of balance longer. This makes NV Points both a short-term and long-term fix. To access these points for Earth, place the thumbs of each hand on the cheekbones directly below the eyes and rest the fingers of each hand across the forehead. Hold gently for two to five minutes, breathing normally. Do this once or twice a day for at least one week—longer if needed.

Earth Element Points

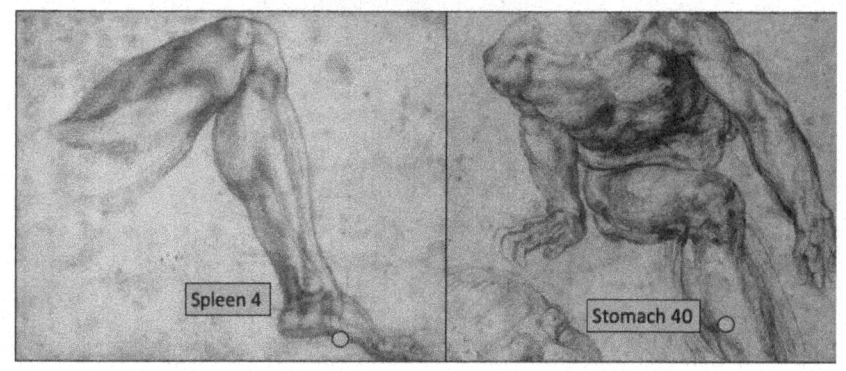

Spleen 4

Stomach 40

A SNAPSHOT OF EARTHS

- *Nurturing caregivers offering support during change*
- *Inclusive Earth Mothers embracing everyone*
- *Loving, caring, and ready to help*
- *Grounded structure, stable and steady*
- *Will help with any party*
- *When balanced: caring, compassionate, accepting, patient*
- *When stressed: meddling, worried, guilty, over-compassionate*
- *When deeply stressed: needy, obsessive, interfering, codependent*
- *Color to build: Yellow*
- *Color to decrease: Green*
- *Loves: helping people, family, and home*
- *Hates: conflict, people suffering, and not being needed*
- *Likely professions: teachers, nurses, parents, counselors*
- *Primary focus: PEOPLE*
- *Favorite question: WHO?*

A Final Word About Earths

Earth Club members throw a party.
(Courtesy of glowonconcept – stock.adobe.com)

CHAPTER 7

THE METAL CLUB: LET ME SHOW YOU THE RIGHT WAY TO DO THAT

This extraordinary metal, the soul of every manufacture, and the mainspring perhaps of a civilized society.

—Samuel Smiles

METAL THEMES

Metal is the last element in the Five Elements cycle. It relates to autumn, a time in nature when the peak activities of summer wane in preparation for winter. Metal's themes are harvest, judgment, and discarding. The greatest strength of the Metal element is the power of completion.

Metal energy is the source of separation and release. It is the power that pulls tree sap to the roots so the spent leaves will fall, calls small animals to rest safely in the bosom of the earth, and stores nature's future in tiny time capsules called seeds. *The past is the realm of Metal and discernment its greatest gift.*

METAL PEOPLE

What Matters

» *Knowledge*: People who hang out in the Metal Club value knowledge. They sit at the end of the cycle, so are better equipped than other elements to harvest what has been learned, whether over the span of a week, a year, or a lifetime. We all use Metal energy to learn and discern, but Metals thrive on synthesizing knowledge and wisdom into understanding.

» *Protocols*: Over the course of a cycle, Metals are able to glean what has worked and what hasn't. They use this information to explain reality and determine how best to interact with it. For a Metal, protocols are the distillation of experience and truth woven into ways of doing things that create success and safety. Protocols really matter to Metals.

» *Control*: If the optimal way to do anything has been determined, why would anyone want to act, respond, or engage in any way other than what's optimal? Metals are happy to share their wisdom with all and are quick to act to keep things going the way they think they should. Yes, this looks and probably is controlling, but from a Metal's perspective, there's no room for anything other than (their version of) perfection.

Personal Expressions

» *Disciplined*: Metals are disciplined people with profound inner strength and endurance. Though willful and precise, they are reasonable and wise enough to adapt to changing circumstances. Their guiding principles and character are their north star, and it's the rare Metal who strays. If something tempts, Metals' strong-willed nature allows them to turn their backs.

» *Detached*: Metals encompass the winding down of things and the need to let go of what no longer serves. To do this well, they have the remarkable ability to remain detached. When eliminating the inessential, Metals do acknowledge the grief of loss, but they are so focused on the prize being kept, their detachment keeps the experience of grief to a minimum.

» *Opinionated*: Metals value quality over quantity and have their own exacting ethical and moral standards. They are black and white people who rarely consider the gray. And because they believe they know what is best in all cases, they come off as very opinionated about a whole lot of topics. And in their Metal minds, their opinions are correct—just ask them.

» *Occupations*: Metals are successful at anything that requires detail, precision, and exactness. They also do well in hierarchical settings because they understand the need for structure. They make excellent architects, accountants, and corporate lawyers. They also do well in the military.

» *Deepest Need*: Metals are driven to pursue perfection.

» *The Flip Side*: Metal is the channel from the full actualization of summer's yang back to the pure potential of winter's yin. Because of this, Metal is often called new yin or yin rising. Members of the yin club are frequently more yin than yang, but not every Metal will be quiet, introverted, or withdrawn. There are loud Metals, yet even they will stay focused on the pursuit of knowledge.

Structure and Boundaries

Metal is often associated with the majestic mountains where many metals are mined. Reaching toward heaven, yet firmly grounded in the matrix of the earth, mountains are monuments of strength and endurance. The saying, "To move mountains," is used to express the difficulty of a task for a reason: Mountains don't move. This lack of flexibility resonates with Metal people, whether using a mountain as the metaphor or a steel building. Both are strong and practically permanent. This tendency toward strictness and lack of flexibility is seen in Metals' high regard for following the rules and doing things the "right" way. It is also seen in how deeply they value higher truths, morality, character, and everything else they deem to be of monumental importance. They have excellent boundaries and don't budge from what they believe to be true and correct.

Much like Woods, Metal people have the strength and determination to hold their boundaries. This allows them to provide structure for others willing to function within the confines of their rules/ideals/morality. This level of honorability matters to Metals.

Strengths and Weaknesses

Strengths: Metal people are kind and have the courage of their convictions. In a sense, sitting at the end of the cycle as they do, they truly have seen it all. Their keen ability to synthesize the learning, distill it into a treasure to be kept, and then let go of what doesn't serve makes them the masters of wisdom. From this knowing they derive their incredible inner resolve and willpower. But the beauty of a Metal is that if you can offer them a rational reason to change, they usually do. Precision is also a characteristic of Metals, as is the ability to compartmentalize their life and world.

Weaknesses: If incredible inner resolve and willpower are the greatest strengths of Metal people, the misuse of these abilities is their greatest weakness. These valuable traits taken too far can cause

Metals to become inflexible and dogmatic. In their all-important honoring of truth, Metals can also impose their own sense of order and discipline on others to maintain a sense of control. The end result is that people reject them, which initially might not matter to the Metal, but if it happens too frequently, will begin to erode their self-confidence.

Socialization Tendencies
If they're honest with themselves, Metals don't really need people all that much. Like Waters, they're happy to gather with like-minded friends for intellectual discussions, but beyond that, there's always work to be done. They see the approaching end of the cycle and know time is running out.

They don't like parties that much, either, because small talk bores them. Metals will attend an event if it supports an important (by their standards) cause, or if they are being honored in some way. Otherwise, Metal people are happiest left alone reflecting on life and distilling the essence of the experience to create the wisdom they hope will be carried forward into the next cycle. *Metals need separateness in any togetherness.*

Relationship Focus
Metal people focus on connecting with information and synthesizing it. Drawn to the core issues of life, Metals are passionate about acquiring knowledge and distilling it into a personal wisdom that then guides all aspects of their world. If the people around them comply, Metals are comfortable connecting. If not, they will distance themselves. Paradoxically, Metals will readily let go of something proven incorrect or unnecessary, including relationships. Metals can easily detach because they know that every ending carries within it a new beginning. *Metals need to connect with information and synthesize it.*

Stress Behaviors: Critical and Confused, Inflexible and Controlling

When happy, Metals are self-assured, rational, upstanding people. If stress becomes an issue, Metals tend to become overly judgmental and rigid. As with any of the clubs, stress takes Metals to an out-of-balance, dysfunctional version of their normal selves. Under stress, Metal's primary need to pursue perfection will distort and manifest either as excessive judgment (inflexibility) and control issues, or an inability to determine what's important (confusion), which makes them more critical of others.

If Metals' response to stress takes them to a place of *deficient* Metal, not only will they become confused, they will lose their ability to let go. This will cause them to cling more dearly to their opinions, their self-image, and the few close relationships they have. They will lose their grip on perfectionism such that all aspects of their self and surroundings sink into disarray. Deep grief will finally overtake them as they obsess about the very real fact that they could be judged as harshly as they have judged.

If Metals' response to stress takes them to a place of *excess* Metal, the normally reasonable Metals become domineering, dismissive of others, and more controlling. Unwilling to let go of anything, they insist on strict adherence to their already disciplined routines emphasizing order and protocol. Their interaction style becomes formal and even prejudiced. Once they have alienated everyone around them with their uncompromising demands, they retreat to their ivory tower where they remain self-righteous and alone.

METALS SHARE THEIR TRUTHS

- *I love puzzles, riddles, and mysteries.*
- *I put virtue and principles before having fun.*
- *I enjoy tasks that require systematic, logical, and analytical problem-solving.*
- *Life can feel sad and empty sometimes.*
- *I am a perfectionist and can be extremely critical of myself.*
- *Superficiality bores me.*
- *I set high standards for myself and expect the same of others.*
- *I often feel very inhibited.*
- *I like to do more and be better than others, and I want people to notice.*
- *Spontaneity frightens me.*

METALS IN TROUBLE

When dealing with out-of-balance Metals, it's important to remember that their deepest need is to pursue perfection. Help them (or yourself, if this applies to you) ascertain why this is difficult for them at present and how the situation can be improved. Are they overwhelmed and unable to complete something important? Have they recently lost someone or something dear to them?

To help balance their Metal, perhaps nurturing time with an Earth will make them feel special again and bring back their clarity (Earth feeds Metal in the model). Or maybe playful encouragement from a Fire friend in the form of a short visit or cheery call can bring their overly controlled Metal back to pliancy (Fire controls

Metal in the model). And if anyone remains seriously off-balance, it's important to seek professional help.

QUICK TIPS TO HELP BALANCE METALS

» *Use Music*: Music touches our souls, and listening to music we love balances us. For a Metal person in trouble, put on their favorite music. If you aren't sure what that is, try music featuring flutes or other metal instruments. Anything breathy will help balance Metal.

» *Use Meditation*: A Zen form of meditation where one sits quietly and attempts to increase self-awareness of perceptions, thoughts, and emotions will appeal to Metals and help them stay in the present.

» *Use the Energy Release Point*: The Metal element is where grief sits, which means that prolonged, unprocessed grief can indicate stuck Metal energy. When this happens, deeply massaging Lung 3 with your fingers will help release the energy and uplift the spirit. To heighten the effect, place a drop or two of an essential oil (options listed further down) on the point, then massage it in. Do this once or twice a day for at least one week—longer if needed. The point location is shown under the *Metal Element Points* heading further down.

» *Use Temperature*: Metals don't like temperature extremes. Keeping Metals warm, but not hot, and cool, but not cold, will help them stay balanced.

» *Use Color to Build Metal*: The vibrations of specific colors help *build* specific elements. The color for Metal is white. If a Metal manifests behaviors that match the *deficient* Metal condition described above (confused, clingy, sloppy, sad, disorganized, stuffy, prejudiced, etc.), surround them in white. White walls, white flowers, white clothes (including underwear), white anything.

- » *Use Color to Decrease Metal*: The vibrations of specific colors can also help *decrease* specific elements. If a Metal manifests behaviors that match the *excess* Metal conditions described above (domineering, controlling, dismissive, finicky, intolerant, obsessed with order and protocol, etc.), surround them in red, the color that builds Fire, which helps melt excess Metal. Go with red walls, red flowers, red clothes (including underwear), red anything.

- » *Use Sound*: Each element has a specific sound that balances it. Use the sound several times a day. For Metal, inhale deeply then exhale slowly making the sound, "Sssssssss," like air leaking from a tire.

- » *Use Crystals*: Colored stones can balance the energy of specific elements. For Metal, use *hematite, goldstone,* or *snowflake obsidian*. Buy jewelry made from any of these natural stones (a ring, bracelet, necklace, whatever) and wear it as often as possible, even 24/7 for a while. If the stone touches the skin, it usually does a better job of balancing.

- » *Use Essential Oils*: The fragrance of selected essential oils can balance the energies of the Metal element. These include eucalyptus and lemon, among others. Rubbing a few drops of the oil on the skin so that the scent is noticeable will help. Or place a few drops of the oil on a tissue and inhale. A room diffuser is also a great option.

- » *Use Food*: Spicy foods like vinegar, curry, or peppers in moderate amounts will keep Metal pliant. And drink plenty of water; it balances every element.

- » *Use Yoga*: Specific yoga poses work with individual elements, benefitting both the physical and energetic systems they govern. For the Metal element, try the *Standing Squat* pose. And if you've never had a yoga practice, please find a certified yoga instructor to get you started.

» *Use Personality Balancing Points*: Luo Points balance the yin and yang energies of an element. Balanced elemental energy creates balanced personality energy, which translates to happier relationships. To help balance the Metal personality, on the right side of the body place the middle finger of one hand on Lung 7 and the middle finger of the other hand on Large Intestine 6. Hold these points at the same time for two minutes, then repeat on the left side of the body for two minutes. Do this once or twice a day for at least one week—longer if needed. The point locations are shown under the *Metal Element Points* heading further down.

» *Use Herbs*: Ginger and red raspberry leaf can be good for Metals. A tea made from either of these herbs will usually help balance Metal energy. And always check with your health practitioner before using any medicinal herbs.

» *Use Nature*: Metals resonate with the energy of the mountains, so time spent in or near mountains will feed their souls. They also appreciate broad vistas.

» *Use Emotion Stabilizing Points*: Each element has specific points on the head that balance that element's emotional state. Called Neurovascular Points (NV Points), they can be used to not only balance the energies, but also reprogram them to hold the state of balance longer. This makes NV Points both a short-term and long-term fix. To access these points for Metal, place the palm of one hand on the top of the head and the other palm across the front of the forehead. Hold gently for two to five minutes, breathing normally. Do this once or twice a day for at least one week—longer if needed.

Metal Element Points

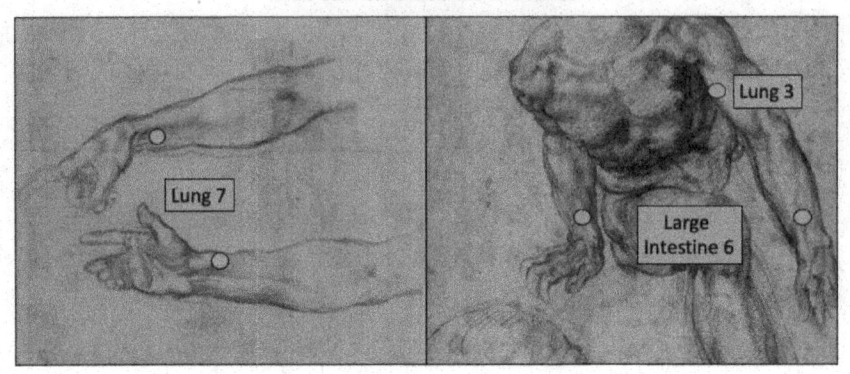

(Image: Anatomical diagrams showing Lung 7, Lung 3, and Large Intestine 6 points)

A SNAPSHOT OF METALS

- *Wise synthesizers distilling wisdom from the past*
- *Honorable people who embrace process and protocol*
- *Opinionated, forthright, and usually correct*
- *Rigidly structured*
- *Will pass on a party unless it's for them*
- *When balanced: kind, wise, honest, detached*
- *When stressed: sad, critical, empty, controlling*
- *When deeply stressed: harsh, self-righteous, inflexible, dismissive*
- *Color to build: White*
- *Color to decrease: Red*
- *Loves: understanding how things work, precision, and being right*
- *Hates: being wrong, clutter, and time running out*
- *Likely professions: architects, accountants, corporate lawyers, military*
- *Primary focus: the PAST*
- *Favorite question: HOW?*

A Final Word About Metals

Metal Club members throw a party.
(ID 66650114 © Mast3r | Dreamstime.com)

CHAPTER 8

SUMMARIES AND SECONDARIES: GOOD SO FAR? WELL, THERE'S MORE

The better you know yourself, the better your relationship with the rest of the world.

—Toni Collette

WELCOME TO THE CLUB!

Did you locate your clubhouse? Still not sure which one is your true home? No worries! Sometimes comparing key personality and behavioral aspects across all five clubs can help make things clearer. And that's what we're going to do next. As you review where each club stands on issues like priorities, personality strengths and weaknesses, and stress behaviors, your club affiliation might become obvious.

Also, the Appendix has a thorough comparison of how the members of each club might react to a party invitation, plus a short quiz. And finally, sometimes finding our club membership is a process of elimination. If you can't possibly be a member of the Water, Wood, Earth, or Fire Clubs, you're probably a Metal.

The other thing to remember is that no one is just one element. We have all five elements in our being, so there are no pure Waters, Woods, Fires, Earths, or Metals. We're all a combination. We always lead with our primary affinity, but it will be "flavored" by our secondary element. As we learned in Chapter 2, it's as though we're looking at the world through a glass window and all of the elements are layers of watercolor paint applied to that window. The layer put on first is what will be most visible to us from the inside. The second layer, our secondary element, will color the first layer and impact how our primary element expresses itself. But by the time you get to the third, fourth, and fifth layers, the effects are markedly less.

Since a Metal primary with a Water secondary will look a lot different than a Metal primary with a Fire secondary, we're also going to take a quick look here at how different secondary elements will affect the expression of a primary element. By the time we're done, I guarantee you'll have a good idea of which club is yours.

Let's start with comparisons of the primary clubhouses first.

COMPARING THE CLUBS

Superpower

- Water: The power of potential
- Wood: The power of action and manifestation
- Fire: The power of fully actualized potential
- Earth: The power of transition
- Metal: The power of completion

Focus/Gift

- Water: The inner world is the focus of Water and imagination its greatest gift.
- Wood: The future is the focus of Wood and initiative its greatest gift.
- Fire: The present is the focus of Fire and inspiration its greatest gift.

- Earth: Transition is the focus of Earth and balance its greatest gift.
- Metal: The past is the focus of Metal and discernment its greatest gift.

What Matters
- Water: Deep issues, connecting with something bigger, quiet time
- Wood: Accomplishment, fairness, productivity
- Fire: Excitement, attention, connections
- Earth: Relationships, helping others, inclusiveness
- Metal: Knowledge, protocol, control

Personality Structure
- Water: Nonlinear, go with the flow, no boundaries unless frozen
- Wood: Linear, flexibly structured, likes own rules, good boundaries
- Fire: No structure, easily scatters, hard to control, poor boundaries
- Earth: Slow structure of moveable matrix, vacillating boundaries
- Metal: Rigid structure, in control, tight boundaries

Balanced Expressions
- Water: Optimistic, hopeful, trusting, objective
- Wood: Decisive, productive, bold, direct
- Fire: Joyful, enthusiastic, passionate, spontaneous
- Earth: Caring, compassionate, accepting, patient
- Metal: Kind, wise, honest, detached

Stress Behaviors
- Water: Fearful, hopeless, narcissistic, intolerant
- Wood: Indecisive, frustrated, impatient, angry

- Fire: Scattered, overwhelmed, anxious, panicked
- Earth: Needy, clinging, meddling, worried
- Metal: Critical, confused, inflexible, controlling

Socialization Tendencies

- Water: Prefers the company of a few like-minded friends
- Wood: Will socialize if they have a role to play or it meets a goal
- Fire: Always ready to celebrate and connect
- Earth: Thrives on the chance to be with those they love
- Metal: Needs separateness in any togetherness

Relationship Focus

- Water: Connecting with the inner self
- Wood: Connecting with outer accomplishments
- Fire: Intense connections outside of the self
- Earth: Deep, lasting relationships with others
- Metal: Connecting with information to synthesize it

Deepest Need

- Water: To be part of something bigger than themselves
- Wood: To succeed
- Fire: To keep moving and make quick connections
- Earth: To be needed and help others
- Metal: To pursue perfection

Likely Occupations

- Water: Authors, intellectuals, philosophers, artists
- Wood: Business executives, sports heroes, elected officials, fundraisers, trial lawyers
- Fire: Actors, comedians, motivational speakers, public figures
- Earth: Nurses, teachers, parents, counselors
- Metal: Architects, accountants, corporate lawyers, career military

A FEW MORE QUICK COMPARISONS

They Love
- *Waters love free time, deep discussions, and reading.*
- *Woods love challenges, accomplishment, and moving forward.*
- *Fires love parties, attention, and being busy.*
- *Earths love helping people, family, and home.*
- *Metals love understanding how things work, precision, and being right.*

They Hate
- *Waters hate tight schedules, budgets, and structure.*
- *Woods hate dashed expectations, chaos, and being told "No!"*
- *Fires hate ordinariness, boredom, and being ignored.*
- *Earths hate conflict, people suffering, and not being needed.*
- *Metals hate being wrong, clutter, and time running out.*

It's Easy
- *Easy for Waters to go with the flow.*
- *Easy for Woods to get organized.*
- *Easy for Fires to speak to a crowd.*
- *Easy for Earths to create a sense of "home" anywhere.*
- *Easy for Metals to know how we got here.*

It's Hard
- *Hard for Waters to be structured.*
- *Hard for Woods to let others run things poorly.*
- *Hard for Fires to chill out.*
- *Hard for Earths to end a relationship.*
- *Hard for Metals to release control.*

OUR SECONDARY AFFILIATION

Since we have all five elements in our energetic makeup, it means that we can step into the Fire clubhouse when we want to be outgoing or visit the Wood clubhouse when we want to get something done. But our primary affiliation, the clubhouse where we naturally hang out, is what colors how we act—and react—most of the time.

Yet every now and then we might surprise ourselves. For example, my automatic reaction to Mark telling me he doesn't want to go to a movie we've planned to see for weeks is usually very Wood: I get frustrated because he's stopped something we set in motion. My expectations have been focused on seeing the movie, and Woods can get very attached to their expectations. Yet there are times this has happened, and I haven't flipped out. In fact, not too long ago, Mark said he didn't feel like a show that night, and I was actually concerned that he might be getting sick.

Other than proving I can be a nice person now and then, this illustrates that our primary affiliation isn't always front and center. Sometimes our secondary can step in and take over, or at least color how our primary acts. And this can be a good thing. In the example above of not going to the movies, my Earth colored how I responded to Mark. Earth is my secondary affiliation—a fact for which I am grateful multiple times a day. So many times, when my reaction could be that of a snarky Wood, my sweet Earth comes forward and saves the day. That means that my Wood is "flavored," as I like to call it, by my Earth.

Mark's secondary is Earth, too, which is really nice given that his primary Metal personality often feels controlling to my primary Wood personality. I know Mark subconsciously skews more toward Earth many times because he loves me. I especially remember a time I had to work late, so he'd gone to the grocery store on his way home and was making dinner for us (a very Earthy thing to do). As a Metal, he usually follows recipe directions to the letter.

The recipe in question that evening was chicken parmesan, which we both like. However, I happen to adore eggplant parmesan, but Mark dislikes eggplant, so we never have it. But that evening, as an act of kindness, he softened his Metal, upped his Earth expression, and added eggplant to the dish so that we had chicken *and* eggplant parmesan. I was floored, and very happy, but had to laugh when he picked all the eggplant out of his serving.

It's important to remember that even if we don't consciously step into our secondary, it's always there, right behind our primary, quietly whispering in its ear. This means our secondary affiliation will affect how our primary affiliation manifests, even without our knowing it. For example, I'm sure Mark wasn't thinking, "Gee, Vicki's had a bad day, so I need to be more Earthy." But nonetheless, he *was* more Earthy.

To help you further determine which clubhouse is yours, here's a list of how different secondary affiliations will slightly alter the expression of each primary elemental personality as long as they aren't stressed. Remember, when stressed, we go straight for the purest, perhaps even nastiest, manifestation of our primary affiliation. Sorry.

The Primary Elements "Flavored" by Secondaries

Water: Water people are quiet, deeply inspired loners who shy away from parties, love to discuss deep issues, and excel at going with the flow. But this will be slightly modified depending on whether their secondary is Wood, Fire, Earth, or Metal. (Remember, you only get each element once, so you can't be a Water with a Water secondary. And that's a very good thing.) One of our Water stereotypes from Chapter 2 was the inspired artist uninterested in eating or sleeping while painting a masterpiece. Let's look at how different secondaries will refine that Water stereotype. In each case, these Waters will still be quiet, deeply inspired loners who shy away from parties, love to discuss deep issues, and excel at going with the flow, but:

» *Waters with Wood secondaries* will be more inclined to do something with their ideas. Waters with Wood secondaries will also create plans for moving forward rather than just going with the flow. The stereotype for a Water with a Wood secondary could be: *The inspired artist uninterested in eating or sleeping while painting a masterpiece because he already has someone willing to pay top dollar for it when it's finished.*

» *Waters with Fire secondaries* will be more outgoing and less quiet. Waters with Fire secondaries will also attend the occasional party to connect with other Water/Fire types. The stereotype for a Water with a Fire secondary could be: *The inspired artist uninterested in eating or sleeping while painting a masterpiece because when done, she's going to throw a huge party to celebrate the fact that a Hollywood star has decided to purchase it.*

» *Waters with Earth secondaries* will have a select group of close friends with whom they relate on a regular basis. Waters with Earth secondaries will be more interested in discussing family happenings rather than just philosophic issues. The stereotype for a Water with an Earth secondary could be: *The inspired artist uninterested in eating or sleeping while painting a masterpiece because it's a birthday gift for his mother.*

» *Waters with Metal secondaries* will use lessons learned from history to spark their ideas. Waters with Metal secondaries will also embrace detailed information along with purely abstract concepts. The stereotype for a Water with a Metal secondary could be: *The inspired artist uninterested in eating or sleeping while painting a masterpiece because it's the right thing to do to finish it.*

Wood: Wood people are decisive, accomplished individuals who make things happen, fight for a cause, and enjoy leading others forward. But this will be slightly modified depending on whether their secondary is Water, Fire, Earth, or Metal. One of our Wood stereotypes from Chapter 2 was the forceful politician loudly demanding progress and change at a packed rally. Let's look at how different secondaries will refine that Wood stereotype. In each case, these Woods will still be decisive, accomplished individuals who make things happen, fight for a cause, and enjoy leading others forward, but:

» *Woods with Water secondaries* will be slightly less decisive and more willing to discuss options with others. Woods with Water secondaries will also be more interested in leading others forward for philosophic reasons instead of individual accomplishment. The stereotype for a Wood with a Water secondary could be: *The forceful politician loudly demanding progress and change at a rally because she sees the possibility for a better world.*

» *Woods with Fire secondaries* will be more interested in engaging in the social scene, whether they have a role to play or not. Woods with Fire secondaries will also be more charismatic and have more people around them than the average Wood person. The stereotype for a Wood with a Fire secondary could be: *The forceful politician loudly demanding progress and change at a packed rally because his constituents can't get enough of him.*

» *Woods with Earth secondaries* will make sure they have time for their family and friends. Woods with Earth secondaries will also champion causes that improve the lot of the less fortunate and downtrodden. The stereotype for a Wood with an Earth secondary could be: *The forceful politician loudly demanding progress and change at a rally because there are people in desperate need.*

» *Woods with Metal secondaries* will base their programs on the lessons from history. Woods with Metal secondaries will also have specific, highly detailed plans for all they do. The stereotype for a Wood with a Metal secondary could be: *The forceful politician loudly demanding progress and change at a rally because she has a detailed report showing the wisdom of her proposed changes.*

Fire: Fire people are enthusiastic, charismatic, upbeat individuals who are always on the go, focused on the present, and love connecting with others for fun. But this will be slightly modified depending on whether their secondary is Water, Wood, Earth, or Metal. One of our Fire stereotypes from Chapter 2 was the exciting, fun-loving person at the party that everyone wants to be around. Let's look at how different secondaries will refine that Fire stereotype. In each case, these Fires will still be enthusiastic, charismatic, upbeat individuals who are always on the go, focused in the present, and love connecting with others for fun, but:

» *Fires with Water secondaries* will be less inclined to run around all the time and more interested in quiet time at home. Fires with Water secondaries will also create alone time to ponder important issues rather than constantly connecting with others. The stereotype for a Fire with a Water secondary could be: *The exciting, fun-loving person at the party that everyone wants to be around because she has important philosophic points to make.*

» *Fires with Wood secondaries* will be less focused on the present all the time and more inclined to plan for the future. Fires with Wood secondaries will also be more interested in connecting with others to further personal goals and less interested in partying just for the fun of it. The stereotype for a Fire with a Wood secondary could be: *The exciting, fun-loving person at the party that everyone wants to be around because he is so successful.*

» *Fires with Earth secondaries* will want some of their quick connections to become long-term relationships. Fires with Earth secondaries will also be more likely to use their notoriety to raise awareness of the needy in the world. The stereotype for a Fire with an Earth secondary could be: *The exciting, fun-loving person at the party that everyone wants to be around because she's the one throwing the party to raise funds for the homeless.*

» *Fires with Metal secondaries* will be less scattered and more precise. Fires with Metal secondaries will also be extremely conversant regarding how the lessons of history can be applied to the present. The stereotype for a Fire with a Metal secondary could be: *The exciting, fun-loving person at the party that everyone wants to be around because he knows so much about so many things.*

Earth: Earth people are caring, compassionate, loving individuals who are always ready to offer a hand, lend an ear, and make a difference. But this will be slightly modified depending on whether their secondary is Water, Wood, Fire, or Metal. One of our Earth stereotypes from Chapter 2 was the talented interior designer easily able to create beautiful and comfortable homes. Let's look at how different secondaries will refine that Earth stereotype. In each case, these Earths will still be caring, compassionate, loving individuals who are always ready to offer a hand, lend an ear, and make a difference, but:

» *Earths with Water secondaries* will be less interested in being with people all the time and more interested in some quiet time alone. Earths with Water secondaries will also be more desirous of contemplating why things are happening and how to make a difference. The stereotype for an Earth with a Water secondary could be: *The talented interior designer easily able to create beautiful and comfortable homes because she spent time pondering the needs of the families involved.*

» *Earths with Wood secondaries* will be less inclined to collaborate and more interested in running things alone. Earths with Wood secondaries will also focus on furthering their own success as well as helping others. The stereotype for an Earth with a Wood secondary could be: *The talented interior designer easily able to create beautiful and comfortable homes because he's taken design classes to advance himself.*

» *Earths with Fire secondaries* will offer their help at the parties or large gatherings they're attending rather than one-on-one meetings. Earths with Fire secondaries will likely develop a standout style that gets them noticed. The stereotype for an Earth with a Fire secondary could be: *The talented interior designer easily able to create beautiful and comfortable homes because she's developed a flamboyant style all her own.*

» *Earths with Metal secondaries* will be less inclined to make the needs of others more important than their own *all* the time. Earths with Metal secondaries will also be a bit more neat, tidy, and organized. The stereotype for an Earth with a Metal secondary could be: *The talented interior designer easily able to create beautiful and comfortable homes because he's so organized.*

Metal: Metal people are precise, kind, and exceedingly wise individuals who focus on the past, appreciate structure and schedules, and dislike clutter. But this will be slightly modified depending on whether their secondary is Water, Wood, Fire, or Earth. One of our

The Five Elements of Relationships

Metal stereotypes from Chapter 2 was the systematic engineer easily describing how and why everything will work well. Let's look at how different secondaries will refine that Metal stereotype. In each case, these Metals will still be precise, kind, and exceedingly wise individuals who focus on the past, appreciate structure and schedules, and dislike clutter, but:

» *Metals with Water secondaries* will be slightly less stuck in their tight, rigid schedules and more willing to be flexible about time. Metals with Water secondaries will also be more interested in applying their wisdom to create new ideas. The stereotype for a Metal with a Water secondary could be: *The systematic engineer easily describing how and why everything will work well because she has new ideas to blend with the historic wisdom she values.*

» *Metals with Wood secondaries* will be less likely to focus exclusively on the past and more interested in future issues. Metals with Wood secondaries will also be more focused on expanding their businesses. The stereotype for a Metal with a Wood secondary could be: *The systematic engineer easily describing how and why everything will work well because he has additional resources at his disposal to do the job.*

» *Metals with Fire secondaries* will be less inclined to go it alone and more likely to make industry connections. Metals with Fire secondaries will also enjoy making sales pitches and presentations. The stereotype for a Metal with a Fire secondary could be: *The systematic engineer easily describing how and why everything will work well because she has the support of several important new connections.*

» *Metals with Earth secondaries* will be less likely to focus their attention solely on prestigious projects and more inclined to champion projects that help the greater good. Metals with Earth secondaries will also tolerate some clutter and include their family in their daily life. The stereotype for a Metal with an Earth secondary could be: *The systematic engineer easily describing how and why everything will work well because he has his son working with him now.*

At this point you probably have a pretty clear idea of which club you belong to, as well as the club affiliations of your family and friends. This should give you a better understanding of yourself and the people in your life. Now it's time to see what the ups and downs, highs and lows, and strengths and challenges of your relationships could be. The best way to get along with everyone is to understand the relationship dynamics and tendencies between you. And that's where we're going next!

PART TWO

RELATIONSHIP DYNAMICS AND TENDENCIES

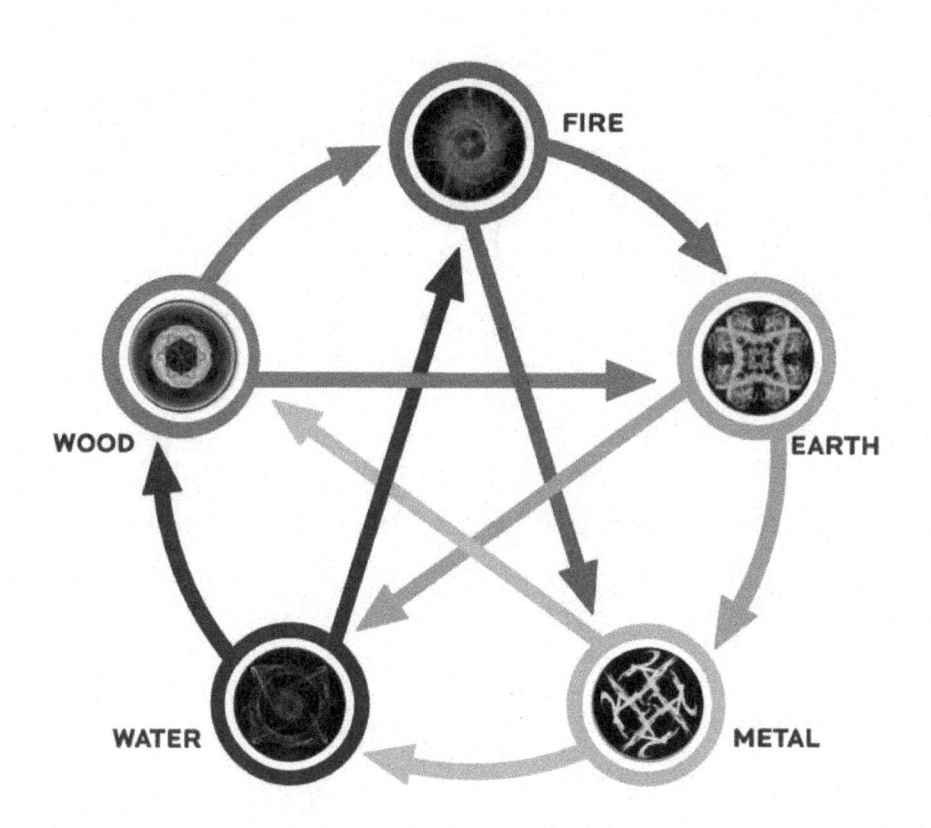

"I feel that I'm doing all the fetching in this relationship."

CHAPTER 9

RELATIONSHIPS: HIGHS AND LOWS AND IN-BETWEENS

*Remain calm, serene, always in command of yourself.
You will then find out how easy it is to get along.*

—Paramahansa Yogananda

GETTING ALONG

How do the clubs get along? At the highest level, they get along perfectly. The dynamics between the five elements are what keep any whole balanced and healthy. And that works not only in the abstract world of models, but also with people.

Each club represents an important piece of the universal puzzle. The world needs all of the clubs, and people need relationships, so it's clearly meant to work. While our relationships will all be different, we really are wired to get along. And when we aren't getting along, it's usually for one of three reasons:

- » We don't understand ourselves and each other
- » We don't understand our relationship dynamics
- » We're so stressed we create stressed relationships

I. We Don't Understand Ourselves and Each Other

This is the easiest of the three reasons to address. In the previous chapters, we covered all you need to know to understand yourself and members of other clubs. Read the behavioral tendencies for each element again so you can recognize yourself and the people in your life. For example, if your daughter is a Fire, you need to understand what matters to her as a Fire. What does she need, like, or hate?

That's what Mark and I experienced. Once we understood it, the truth of our secret clubs set us free. That's why knowing our club membership, and the memberships of family and friends, is so important. I can't help acting like a Wood because I'm a member of the Wood Club. Mark can't help acting like a Metal because he's a member of the Metal Club. The best step Mark and I can take to make sure we get along is to build on the positive aspects of our Wood/Metal relationship and avoid the pitfalls. If something around the house needs precision, it's Mark's to do; I just don't have the patience. But if something needs organizing, that's absolutely mine.

It's important to remember this in all of our relationships. Each club has strengths as well as challenges, and you can choose to emphasize the strengths. Let the Wood organize a garden, the Metal suggest the best plants for it, and the Earth plant it. We also need to adjust our expectations. As one of my clients discovered, a Water son probably won't try out for the football team; his Wood brother probably will. A Fire daughter could flirt more than her Metal sister ever did. An Earth mother will be more interested in baking cookies than a Wood mother. A Water friend will help you understand the "why" of things; a Metal will help you get your taxes done.

The good news is that you're reading this book, so you're going to be an expert on the clubs and their tendencies. But you still need to understand the dynamics of each relationship—the good, the bad, and the ugly. I'm an expert on Wood/Metal relationships, but what happens if my new brother-in-law turns out to be a Fire? I'd better become an expert on Wood/Fire relationships, too. And who knows, my new best friend might turn out to be an Earth or a Water, so it behooves me to have a grip on how my Wood relates to all of the clubs. This book will help you become an expert, too.

II. We Don't Understand Our Relationship Dynamics

The following chapters will provide detailed descriptions of the interaction dynamics between the individual clubs. The two major interactions are via the Nurturing Cycle (for example, Water feeding Wood) and via the Controlling Cycle (for example, Water putting out Fire). The third way club members can relate is to connect with someone from their own clubhouse (a Water in a relationship with another Water). There are inherent strengths and challenges in each of these relationship dynamics.

> *Nurturing Cycle Connections:* The Nurturing Cycle is the clockwise flow of energy around the big circle in the Five Elements model. It represents the truth that Water feeds Wood, Wood feeds Fire, Fire feeds Earth, Earth feeds Metal, and Metal feeds Water. If the people involved in the relationship are in balance, by definition this connection could be very nurturing. If the people aren't balanced, the relationship could feel depleting, overwhelming, or even nonexistent.
>
> *Controlling Cycle Connections:* The Controlling Cycle is represented by the straight-line flow of energy between every other element that creates a star in the center of the big circle. This relationship represents the truth that Water controls Fire, Fire controls Metal, Metal controls Wood,

Wood controls Earth, and Earth controls Water. If the people involved in the relationship are in balance, this connection will be supportive and freeing in a way that guarantees they don't get out of control. If the people aren't balanced, by definition the relationship will tend to feel overcontrolling and inhibiting.

Same-Club Connections: People from the same clubhouse do end up in relationships, and this brings its own set of opportunities and challenges. Certainly, it can feel comfortable; no one will ever understand you as well as someone from your own club. But because the energies of the Nurturing and Controlling Cycles aren't present to keep things moving and provide dynamic rhythm, Same-Club relationships can sometimes become static and feel stuck rather than familiar or safe.

As you read these chapters, hopefully light bulbs will come on for you. Perhaps you'll suddenly realize that you're a Water and your daughter is a Fire, which means you relate via the Controlling Cycle. Water controls Fire, so she may think you throw water on her flames (and at times, she'll probably be right). If you're a Wood, you relate to your Fire daughter on the Nurturing Cycle. If you're lucky, she might agree that you nurture her.

III. We're So Stressed We Create Stressed Relationships

In a perfect world, there would be no stress, we would be happy all of the time, and every relationship would be balanced. Dream on, right? Personally, I find a little bit of stress motivating, but that's a Wood Club thing. Prolonged stress is disastrous for anyone, and it's the same for our relationships. A good relationship can always manage a little personal stress now and then. In fact, a good relationship can help decrease our levels of personal stress. But prolonged stress on the part of someone in the relationship (or both people) can't help but affect the relationship.

In truth, our relationships are only as stable as we are. And while this isn't a book about individual balance, it's important to note that once you know your club affiliation, a great deal about your personal behaviors should start making sense. It was a huge aha moment for me when I realized that my tendency to be a bit bossy was because I'm a member of the Wood Club. Of course, being a Wood doesn't excuse rude behavior (which can happen when I'm stressed), but it does explain specific tendencies I see in myself again and again and again. It also helps me understand why I might be stressed to begin with, what needs to change, and how to make those changes.

EXPLORING STRESS IN RELATIONSHIPS

Normally, stress in a relationship is just a reflection of stress in the people involved. That means it's a problem with one of the clubs, and there's really only two ways individual club members can manifest stress. Using my marriage as an example, here's what can happen when either Mark or I are stressed:

» I'll have *too much* Wood energy and become an exaggerated version of my normally sweet Wood self. Maybe I interpret a given circumstance as requiring audacious action and then get angry or frustrated when things don't go the way I expect. If I have my wits about me, I can make the changes I need myself by using some of the Quick Tips in the Wood Club chapter. If I need help, Mark can help me prune my Wood by bringing more Metal (Metal controls Wood).

» I'll have *too little* Wood and become a shadow of my usual happily assertive Wood self. This is often harder for me to fix alone, but Mark will recognize what's going on by the way

I can't seem to make things happen (like using the Wood Quick Tips). When I'm like this, Mark builds my Wood by cutting back on his Metal and introducing more Water to help my Wood grow. He also hands me a copy of the Wood Quick Tips and watches while I do some of them.

» If Mark is the one stressed, that means his Metal is probably out of balance. If he brings *too much* Metal to our relationship, he might become overcontrolling. For example, he could insist on doing something the way we've always done it, even though there's a better way now (stressed Metals love rules and have trouble letting go). He doesn't see this as well as I do, of course, but I know ways to soften his Metal by introducing Fire. And then *I* hand *him* the *Metal* Quick Tips.

» If Mark ends up with *too little* Metal, he might lose his ability to stay detached about things and become clingy. Usually, he catches this and adds more Earth himself by going outside or eating some cookies. But if not, I can easily build his Metal by upping my expression of Earth (and handing him the Earth Quick Tips with his cookies).

In your own relationships, the first clue that you have a relationship problem will probably be when the stressed tendencies of your club or your relationship partner's club start showing up. You can go back to Chapter 8 and review the summaries there if you're not sure what the stress responses are for each club.

But the bottom line is still the same: If our relationships are stressed, it's most likely because we don't understand ourselves and each other, we don't understand our relationship dynamics, or we're so stressed we create stressed relationships.

THE CLUBS RELATING

In the following chapters, we're going to review the relationship dynamics between every club. That's right, fifteen possible permutations (five Nurturing Cycle options, five Controlling Cycle options, and five Same-Club options). Sir Francis Bacon said, "Knowledge itself is power," and that's what we'll discover. The more we understand the club affiliations in our relationships, the dynamics between these clubs, and where we all go when we're stressed, the quicker and easier it will be to resolve the issues that come up so we can get back to getting along.

Okay, it's time. What happens when members of different clubs, or the same club for that matter, are in a relationship? You can either read all fifteen chapters dealing with every relationship combination so you're an expert on relationships, or you can go right to the chapter that addresses a troubling relationship you have. It's up to you. Here we go! We'll start with the five Nurturing Cycle relationships.

NURTURING CYCLE RELATIONSHIPS

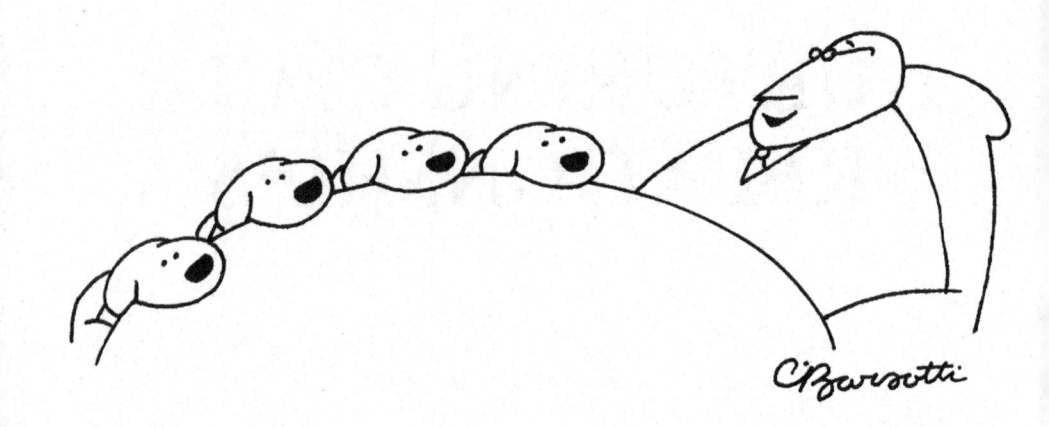

"Your love gives me strength."
(CartoonStock.com)

CHAPTER 10

WATER WITH WOOD: VAN GOGH AND THOR, THE ARTIST PAINTS THE WARRIOR

When the well's dry, we know the worth of water.
—Benjamin Franklin

Rotten wood cannot be carved.
—Ancient Chinese Proverb

WATERS AND WOODS RELATE VIA the Nurturing Cycle of the Five Elements model, which lends a flavor of interdependence to their relationship dynamics. In nature, water needs to flow or it stagnates and evaporates. And wood needs water to survive. With people, it's much the same: Water people flowing ideas to Wood people to be actualized can make them both happy. Just imagine what Van Gogh and Thor might discuss! But don't assume this means all relationships between Water and Wood people will be perfect. They won't. But many can be great.

WATER/WOOD CONNECTIONS

Friendships: Waters are usually self-sufficient loners content with a few friends and minimal social events. They're able to come up with a billion ways to conceptualize something, yet they rarely have the structure or focus to make things happen. We've all known people like that, right? Brilliant thinkers who never get organized enough to write that book? On the other hand, Woods can be workaholics who socialize only if they see a benefit in it or the event involves business. If the Water and Wood people find each other and decide to focus on creating something together, theirs will be a very viable connection.

Work: The social connections between these two will usually be based on creating together, which makes it a natural for the work environment. The Wood will provide structure and forward movement for the Water's ideas, and the Water will keep the highly structured Wood flexible, thriving, and fed with inspiration. As things progress, the Water person will be thrilled to see their ideas come to life, and the Wood person will be excited by their productivity and accomplishments. A work relationship between these two clubs is often very productive if both stay balanced.

Marriage: Waters' primary relationship focus is on connecting with both their inner selves and something greater than themselves. Woods' primary relationship focus is on individualization and personal accomplishments. For both Water and Wood people, close personal relationships aren't going to be a top priority. However, if Cupid's arrow does strike, staying home together, but involved in different activities, will usually work well.

Family: Will Water/Wood relationships create families? In a Water/Wood household, unless one (or both) has a strong secondary Earth, the couple may not want children. It just isn't their focus. If they do have a family, the Wood may be more engaged than the Water.

Over the years, I've seen dozens of excellent Water/Wood relationships:

» *Brett and Jenny, Husband and Wife:* He's an art historian (Water) and she's a paramedic (Wood). No children; neither wanted any. Jenny's politically active, and Brett uses his creative side to help her with a blog. They work on it together and love it.

» *Reba and Tina, Sisters*: Reba's a librarian (Water) who was asked to design a personal library for a wealthy patron. Her own home "library" was piles of books everywhere, so she asked her Wood sister, Tina, to help her. Their collaborated design made the local papers!

» *Stan and John, Coworkers*: Stan (Water) is a local college professor, and John (Wood) is his assistant. They coauthored a textbook on physics. Stan had most of the ideas; John helped organize them and get them down on paper.

WATER/WOOD RELATIONSHIP CHALLENGES

In the previous chapter, we mentioned that when applying the Five Elements model to people and their relationships, there are usually just three ways a relationship can get into trouble. We're going to use these three issues to explore potential challenges with Water/Wood connections.

I. We Don't Understand Ourselves or Each Other

When we understand someone's club, we understand *them*. When we look at them through the lens of their club, their apparent bizarre or disturbing behavior makes total sense. Of course a Water is going to leap up from bed to write down the brilliant thought they just had. Of course a Wood is going to discuss their exciting business project over a candlelit dinner for two. And when any of these behaviors aren't exactly appropriate, understanding that club will make it easier to talk to the Water or Wood in a language they will hear. The good news with a Water/Wood relationship is that they're both fairly rational people. But as my friend's Water daughter found out, that won't matter if you just don't understand your Wood sister.

CASE CORNER
Karen and Leslie, Sisters

Karen was a very creative Water teen. She loved to design clothing, pottery, and even scenery for her local theater. With no shortage of ideas, Karen frequently started one project but then jumped to another. Her early teen years were spent in a happy haze of creativity and going where the muses led.

Things took a decided turn for Karen when her older sister, Leslie (a Wood), moved back home after working out of state for five years. Leslie helped around the house but spent most days looking for a new job. Initially, Karen was thrilled to have her big sister home, but as the newness wore off, so did the good behavior between the sisters, especially Leslie. She teased Karen frequently about all of the partially started projects in her art room and questioned when she was going to finish them.

But the final straw was when Leslie asked if Karen's "junk" could be moved to the basement so she could use the art room as an office for a work-from-home job she was pursuing. Karen's mom asked Karen what she thought of the idea, and Karen was crushed. Her Water didn't know what to do with the idea of structure around art. Things were pretty icy in the house for almost a week. Finally, Karen's mom asked if I could help Karen understand Leslie.

When Karen came to my office, she was quiet and withdrawn. I asked her what was wrong, and she said she couldn't understand how her sister could be so cruel. I pulled out the Five Elements model and explained that while Karen was a Water, Leslie was a Wood. As a Wood person, Leslie would think it natural for Karen to give her what she wanted (Water feeds Wood). I also explained that Woods value fully manifested projects, and in fact, believe anything that doesn't manifest fully isn't a success.

We talked further about Wood, and Karen asked if Leslie understood what it meant to be a Wood person. I wasn't sure, but lent Karen a book that Leslie did read. She totally recognized the highs and lows of being a Wood, too. The happy ending is that Leslie used her organizing skills to help Karen rearrange the room and prioritize what she wanted to finish. There was even enough space left to fit a desk for Leslie. The girls had great fun for two years sharing their "art office." About the time Karen went off to college, Leslie took a job out of state. When they left, Karen's mom already had plans for the empty room.

II. We Don't Understand Our Relationship Dynamics

Water and Wood relate on the Nurturing Cycle, which as we've said, has pluses and minuses. Nurturing is good; too much nurturing is bad. Expecting nurturing and not getting it is bad, too. For Water and Wood people, the energy flows from Water to Wood, so Woods will probably feel more nurtured than the Waters. And that's okay; Waters are loners, but Woods usually like the attention.

Example: Beth discovered how important it is to understand the relationship dynamic between people when she hired David, her new assistant. Beth (Wood) needed someone to manage a research facility, and David came highly recommended. She asked him to keep her informed regarding developments but was ill-prepared for the fact that David sent her two to five emails daily on what he was finding. Beth and I talked about it and pieced together the fact that David was a Water person. Waters need to flow, and their primary target is Wood. Once Beth gave David guidelines around communication frequency, it worked out perfectly. Plus, Water people usually appreciate reasonable structure and boundaries; they have so little of their own.

III. We're So Stressed We Create Stressed Relationships

Even if we understand our clubs and relationship dynamics, it's not always easy to get along. The problems usually start when life intervenes and opens the door to stress. Knowing what a stressed Water/Wood relationship looks like not only helps you recognize problematic aspects in your own Water/Wood relationships, it also helps you fix them. As we discussed in the last chapter, when stress is a factor, Water and Wood can each only go to one of two places: an excess state or a deficient state. Let's see what that can look like, Water first.

> **REMINDERS FOR WATER/ WOOD CONNECTIONS**
>
> *If you find yourself in a Water/Wood relationship that isn't going the way you'd like, take a moment to remind yourself what's important to the other person. If you're the Water, remember that Woods need to be productive to feel good about themselves. If they elect to work instead of staring at the stars with you or attending a scintillating lecture on fractals, that's normal for a Wood. If you're the Wood, remember that Waters need alone time to read and ponder; don't take it personally when they refuse to help you paint your office or wash the car. And if things get stressed, reach for the Water and Wood Quick Tips covered earlier.*

Water Out of Balance

» *Deficient*: A Water person with too *little* Water energy will lack confidence in their ideas, so will retreat and have nothing to offer the Wood. When questioned, the Water will lose focus and begin to distrust the intentions of the Wood. This lack of connection with the Water will make the Wood feel "dead in the water." They will grow irritated by the absence of progress or nurturing. Wood becomes rigid and dies without Water.

Example: Tom, a Wood client of mine, hired Simon (Water) to illustrate a book. But in spite of Simon's excellent portfolio, when it came time to provide Tom with drawings, Simon sent only weak sketches that were two months late. Impatient, Tom finally pressed him and discovered that Simon's father had died three months earlier and Simon was immersed in the Metal place of grieving and settling his father's estate. Simon was so stuck there that little energy was flowing from his Metal to his Water, which meant he just didn't have enough creative Water energy to give to Tom's project. Tom hired a different artist.

» *Excess*: A Water person with too *much* Water energy can throw too many unprocessed, disorganized ideas or theories at the Wood. When Wood expresses concern, the Water can seem intolerant of the Wood and blame them for whatever goes wrong, even suggesting that the Wood is creating problems on purpose. When this happens, the Wood will feel overwhelmed, frustrated, and angry.

Example: My friend Joelle (Wood) chaired a city beautification committee where one woman, Fiona, drove her nuts. Fiona (Water) donated great sums to the beautification projects so assumed that her ideas were the most valuable. Time and again she brought suggestions to the committee that were irrational, unrealistic, and not well thought out. But when Joelle and others tried to explain the problems to Fiona, she grew hostile and accused them of sabotaging her. There were many times I talked Joelle down after one of these meetings, her Wood drowned by Fiona's Water. Finally, Joelle decided to offer her volunteer service in other areas.

» *Result*: Whether the relationship is suffering from too much or too little Water, the Wood person is going to question the value of the Water's contributions. Too little Water will starve the Wood of ideas. Too much Water will overwhelm and rot the Wood. If either occurs, Wood's need for accomplishment will trump a stalled relationship, and Wood will move on. To save relationships where this is happening, the Water person needs to be brought back into balance.

Wood Out of Balance

» *Deficient*: A Wood person with too *little* Wood energy will be unable to concentrate and make use of what Water gives them. Erratic and humiliated by the lack of progress, the Wood will withdraw from the Water. The Water will feel confused and possibly even fearful that the lack of accomplishment is their fault. Water without structure goes every which way; we've all seen what happens when a river breaches its banks.

Example: Pamela, a marketing executive, lost her job. Deflated, she couldn't bring her normal Wood skills to help her younger sister (Water) with her science fair project as she had promised. Her sister was devastated, but we were able to rebuild Pamela's Wood energy in time to help her sister. Their project won third place!

» *Excess*: A Wood person with too *much* Wood energy might demand too much from their Water partner or become reckless with what they are given, pushing ahead without adequate preparation. If things fail, they will be quick to anger and blame the Water, who will feel hurried by the Wood, overcontrolled, and pressured. Too much Wood energy also creates an excess of structure that the Water will find stifling and likely depleting. This became especially apparent to my clients Tami and Pete who are featured in the next CASE CORNER.

» *Result:* Whether the relationship is suffering from too much or too little Wood energy, the Water is going to feel betrayed by the Wood's inability to provide appropriate structure and accomplishment. Too little Wood will allow the unstructured Water to spread too thin. Too much Wood can cause the Water to feel confined, used up, and depleted.

Unless things change, Water's need to connect with something greater will end up trumping a stalled relationship, and Water will flow toward the next opportunity. To save relationships where this is happening, the Wood person needs to be brought back into balance.

CASE CORNER
Excess Wood: Tami and Pete, Husband and Wife

Pete's a powerful Wood trial attorney and Tami's a talented Water painter. Several years ago, they went through a tough spot while Pete was defending a man accused of murder. Pete was obsessed with this case, his Wood sense of justice inflamed because he firmly believed his client was innocent.

Pete spent long hours at his office poring over depositions, desperate to find something that would help clear his client. This left Tami to pick up much of what Pete did at home. She walked the dogs, made the meals, did the laundry, and helped their son with his homework. Bothered by Pete's lack of support, Tami found herself drawn more and more to her studio on the back of their property. She often returned there after their son was in bed, which meant she wasn't waiting for Pete when he finally arrived home.

This irritated Pete, as did Tami's performance of the chores since her Water approach was much more "go with the flow" than his Wood approach. But without Pete, Tami really didn't have the structure she needed. Plus, Pete's excessive Wood was sucking her dry, so she wasn't as nurturing with him as he thought she should be. Since Wood looks to Water for nurturing and Water looks to Wood for structure, they were both upset.

We'd worked together in the past, so they knew their club affiliations. When they came to see me, it didn't take long to sort things out: Pete was in a state of excess Wood energy as he focused single-mindedly on successfully defending his client. With Pete's structure gone, Tami's Water flowed all over the place, giving her deficient Water energy.

In our session, we created a plan for Pete: He'd chill out more, make it home for dinner at least two nights a week, and be home every night in time to walk the dogs. Tami stepped into her secondary Earth and agreed to cut Pete some slack. And they both promised to do at least three things daily from the Quick Tips lists for their Water and Wood Clubs.

This process worked, and harmony returned. Pete started talking more about the case with Tami who, as a Water, had no shortage of ideas. And the case? Pete won it. While walking the dogs one night, something Tami said at dinner reminded Pete of a comment in a deposition, and several important pieces fell into place. It turned out the gardener did it.

WATER/WOOD RELATIONSHIPS: THE BOTTOM LINE

Close personal relationships aren't usually a high priority for either the Water or the Wood Club. Waters value connecting with something greater than themselves. Woods value accomplishment and success. If something develops between these two clubs that takes ideas and makes them happen, it will be glorious at the start. Going forward, if they can address their individual issues around structure, a relationship between a Water and a Wood could be stable.

But if stress is part of the picture, without intervention a troubled Water/Wood relationship will likely see the Water drifting off for the freedom of flow and the Wood getting down to business.

If you find yourself in a Water/Wood relationship that's having trouble, ask yourself the following questions:

» Do you understand the priorities and needs of your club and your partner's club? Are your expectations for the relationship realistic?

» Do you understand the tendencies of relating on the Nurturing Cycle? Is this helping or hurting what you want from the relationship?

» Are either or both of you stressed? If so, start using the Quick Tips for Waters and Woods at the ends of Chapters 3 and 4.

A QUICK WAY TO DEFUSE WATER/WOOD PROBLEMS

In the middle of a fight, we all know it's difficult to pull back (Metal people are usually the only ones who can do it). For Waters and Woods in combat, here's a quick way to take down some of the intensity.

Water: Put one hand across the back of your head at the base of your skull and the other across your forehead. Look the troublesome Wood in the eye, take a deep breath, and exhale a soft "Whoooooooo." If there's energy behind it, so much the better.

Wood: Put your thumbs at the outside edges of your eyes and rest your fingers across your forehead. Look the weary Water in the eye, take a deep breath, and exhale a sharp "Shhhhhhhhh." Push that sound out vigorously at the end.

Repeat the process until you both feel a shift in the dynamics and begin to smile.

CHAPTER 11

WOOD WITH FIRE: THOR AND THE MAD HATTER, CELEBRATING THE HERO

Wood burns because it has the proper stuff in it.
—Johann Wolfgang von Goethe

It is your business when the wall next door catches fire.
—Horace

WOODS AND FIRES RELATE VIA the Nurturing Cycle of the model which, as we said, can lend a flavor of interdependence to their relationship. In nature, trees need to drop dead wood to stay healthy. Fire needs wood for fuel. With people, it can be the same: Woods flow success and accomplishments to Fires to fuel their passions. Just imagine the crazy party the Mad Hatter could throw for Thor! And like any Nurturing Cycle relationship, things won't automatically be perfect, but several types of relationships between Wood and Fire will work very well.

WOOD/FIRE CONNECTIONS

Friendships: Wood people are serious individuals who rarely make time for social events unless they have a role to play or it furthers a goal. We all know a few workaholics, right? Most of them are Woods. Fire people love exciting gatherings; the festive energy feeds them and provides the perfect opportunity for the spontaneous connections they crave. If a Wood and Fire want to focus on socializing together, their relationship can be very successful. The Wood will provide the reason for the gathering and some degree of structure for the event. The Fire will be thrilled to share the excitement and celebration. This means a Wood and Fire could be happy together at the same party but for different reasons.

Work: We know social connections between these two can be compatible, but work relationships might be less comfortable. Woods will be deathly serious about business, and Fires can bring a flighty energy that the structured Wood usually finds frivolous. But if the Fire has a strong secondary Wood or Metal, the business connection can work, especially since the Fire will tend to laud the Wood's accomplishments and the Wood will be attracted to the Fire's passion.

Marriage: Woods' primary relationship focus is on individualization and personal accomplishments, not personal relationships. Fires' primary relationship focus is on intense short-term connections outside of themselves, not lasting relationships. For both Wood and Fire people, then, lasting personal relationships aren't a top priority. Neither club is deeply into house and home, either. Although a Wood will value home as the place of its roots and a symbol of accomplishment, a Fire will value home as a place to invite people. A personal relationship between the two can be stable if it's centered on social activities. And that's okay. Great relationships have been built on less.

Family: Will Wood/Fire relationships create families? In a Wood/Fire household, unless one of them has a secondary Earth, the couple will likely choose not to have children. If they do have a family, the Wood will consider it their legacy; the Fire will find it an adventure.

Over the years, I've seen dozens of great Wood/Fire relationships:

- » *Ken and Terry, Brothers:* Ken and Terry own a construction business. Ken (Wood) does most of the planning and purchasing, Terry (Fire) does most of the client selling, and they both build great houses!
- » *Frederic and Anna, Husband and Wife*: Frederic (Wood) is a high-profile attorney married to Anna (Fire). In this very stereotypical Wood/Fire connection, she plans the social events, he pays for them, and they are both very happy.
- » *Sally and Paul, Associates:* Paul (Fire) is a local actor whose star is rising. He's getting busier and busier, so he hired Sally (Wood) to manage his bookings. It's working perfectly for both of them.

WOOD/FIRE RELATIONSHIP CHALLENGES

As we've discussed, when using the Five Elements model with people and their relationships, there are only three ways any kind of relationship can get into trouble. We're going to use those three issues to explore potential challenges with Wood/Fire connections.

I. We Don't Understand Ourselves or Each Other

Once we understand the tendencies of another person's club affiliation, we understand *them*. Yes, Wood people will take a business call during a movie. Yes, Fire people will lobby for attention if no one is noticing them. And when these behaviors aren't exactly appropriate, understanding their club will make it easier to talk to the Wood or Fire, if necessary, in a language they will hear. Fortunately, Wood/Fire relationships can be fun, which should keep things upbeat. But as my Wood client Marta found out in the next CASE CORNER, that won't matter if you just don't understand your Fire cousin.

CASE CORNER
Marta and JoJo, Cousins

Marta is a lovely member of the Wood Club, and her cousin JoJo is a Fire. Marta has worked in Chicago as a marketing executive since receiving her MBA four years ago. JoJo, who is three years older than Marta, works as a model in Manhattan. While growing up, the girls usually saw each other over the summers and on most major holidays. Marta always looked up to JoJo, wanting to be "fun" like her when she grew up.

Two years ago, Marta became engaged to Frank, an accountant at a large firm in Chicago. They got on well, and everyone was pleased as the large formal wedding drew near. JoJo was one of the seven bridesmaids and flew out to Chicago for the bridal shower. It was a beautiful event, and JoJo was the life of the party. She laughed all the time, told hysterical jokes, and shared photos of her boyfriend, a male model she'd known for years. Several of Marta's closest friends told her how lucky she was to have JoJo as a cousin, and Marta agreed. But that changed at the wedding.

According to Marta, the ceremony was beautiful, and everything went well until the reception. Even though it was Marta's day, JoJo was once again the life of the party. She'd broken up with her boyfriend and was clearly "shopping around," as Marta put it. JoJo laughed the loudest, danced the wildest, and was everywhere photos were being taken. At least that was Marta's perception.

The month after her honeymoon, Marta made her way to my office, unable to forgive her cousin for ruining her wedding. I'd asked Marta to bring the wedding photos, and as we looked through them together, it became apparent that JoJo really wasn't in *all* of them, or even most of them. There were photos of JoJo laughing and having a great time, but the people around her were laughing and having a great time, too. Even Marta had to admit that the JoJo in the photos seemed to fit in rather than stand out.

I explained to Marta about the Fire Club and pointed out that JoJo was clearly a member. As we talked, Marta came to see that JoJo wasn't trying to hog the spotlight on Marta's special day; she was just having a great time connecting with people, as is the Fire way. Once Marta understood that, she was able to reframe how she looked at JoJo's behavior at the wedding. She realized that it really wasn't much different from JoJo's behavior at Christmas parties or summer barbecues—good times that Marta remembered with JoJo. The problem was that Marta's Wood wanted to be the star of her own wedding. And a quick examination of all the photos showed that, indeed, she had been.

II. We Don't Understand Our Relationship Dynamics

Wood and Fire relate on the Nurturing Cycle, which we know has pluses and minuses. Nurturing is good; too much of a good thing is bad. For Woods and Fires, the energy flows from Wood to Fire, meaning that Fires will probably feel more nurtured than the Woods. But both need attention, so if Fires remember to shine their light back on their partner Woods, everything will be fine.

Example: My sister's friend Tricia (Fire) illustrated this well when she started dating a Wood. Tricia fell hard for Hans. According to my sister, Tricia couldn't get enough of him. She wanted to be with Hans all the time because he made her happy. Ignoring the fact that we should all be able to make ourselves happy, I knew what was happening: Hans's Wood was feeding Tricia's Fire. But apparently she wasn't showering enough attention back at him. Hans broke it off after six months because he found Tricia "exhausting." If Tricia had understood her dynamic with Hans, the relationship might have lasted.

REMINDERS FOR WOOD/FIRE CONNECTIONS

If you find yourself in a Wood/Fire relationship that isn't going the way you'd like, take a moment to remind yourself what's important to the other person. If you're the Wood, remember that Fires need excitement, connection, and attention in their lives. Don't be surprised if they don't like staying home alone while you work late hours. If you're the Fire, remember that Woods need accomplishment and success. Don't take it personally when they want to be productive instead of party. And if things get stressed, reach for the Wood and Fire Quick Tips covered earlier.

III. We're So Stressed We Create Stressed Relationships

Understanding our clubs and relationship dynamics will always help us get along with others, but there's another factor to consider: stress. Knowing what a stressed Wood/Fire relationship looks like not only helps you recognize problematic aspects in your own Wood/Fire relationships, it also helps you fix them. And it's not hard. As we've already discussed, when stress is a factor in a Wood/Fire relationship, Wood and Fire can each only go one of two places: an excess state or a deficient state. Let's see what that looks like, Wood first.

Wood Out of Balance

» *Deficient*: A Wood with too *little* Wood energy will be low on motive power, which means they'll most likely be unsuccessful at manifesting anything. This will result in feelings of humiliation that will cause the Wood to lose their structure and withdraw from the Fire. The Fire will wonder why they aren't being given the attention they're used to, because it fuels them. Fire without fuel (or structure) scatters quickly.

Example: Warren, a gentle Wood, lost his business during the recession, and it really took him down. Peggy, his Fire girlfriend, stuck by him for several months, staying upbeat and optimistic. But it took Warren longer to get back on his feet than she was willing to wait, so their relationship ended.

» *Excess*: A Wood with too *much* Wood energy will demand more and more of their Fire partner: more fun, partying, or accolades. The excessive Wood will put more structure in place, too, which will be a downer to the spontaneous Fire. The excess fuel the Wood creates for the Fire will cause them to burn brighter and brighter, and possibly burn out. This will frustrate the Wood, who might even push harder.

Example: Sandy (Fire) was an event planner who was so good at her job that she made it look easy. Thinking she could handle it, her boss (Wood) bought another company to grow his business faster. Suddenly, Sandy had too many events to plan. She gave it her best and even asked for assistance, but it wasn't until she literally burned out that her boss finally hired extra help.

» *Result:* Whether the relationship is suffering from too much or too little Wood, the Fire is going to be confused by the Wood's inability to provide a steady flow of accomplishments, which is Fire's fuel. Too little Wood means the Fire will lose structure and scatter. Too much Wood will cause the Fire to burn too hot and burn out. And when things do end, the Wood will still think it was their idea to split. To save relationships where this is happening, the Wood person needs to be brought back into balance.

Fire Out of Balance

» *Deficient*: A Fire with too *little* Fire energy will be unable to use what the Wood sends them. They will appear scattered, overwhelmed, and unstable. The Wood will become frustrated by Fire's inability to hold up their end of the relationship. Wood needs to stay on track. Depleted of joy, the Fire will fail at the one thing they value most: connecting. The downward spiral of this kind of relationship became apparent to my client Linda and her business partner, Abby, who are featured in the next CASE CORNER.

» *Excess*: A Fire with too *much* Fire energy will fill their life with too much of everything. They'll overbook themselves and accept random invitations, then become restless and overly dramatic. Everything will become an issue. The Wood will feel used up by the burning Fire and tired of the sensational dramas that distract them from their important work. Eventually, the depleted Wood will leave and the Fire will collapse, overwhelmed.

Example: Mason (Wood) was the principal of a nearby school. He had a teacher on his staff named Jane (Fire) who, as he put it, "drove him nuts." She was flighty and what he called "terminally perky." She agreed to attend faculty meetings and then didn't show. And whenever she *was* there, she joked around so much he couldn't get down to business. He tried talking to her, asking her to tone it down, but it didn't work. He ended up having to fire the Fire.

» *Result:* Whether the relationship is suffering from too much or too little Fire, the Wood will feel frustrated by the Fire's inability to uphold their end of things and their apparent out-of-control, scattered behaviors. Too little Fire will eventually cause Wood to warm itself elsewhere. Too much Fire will scorch and burn the Wood, driving it away. To save relationships where this is happening, the Fire needs to be brought back into balance, as we will see in the next CASE CORNER.

CASE CORNER
Deficient Fire: Abby and Linda, Business Partners

My client Linda (Wood) runs a small public relations business with Abby (Fire). As one might imagine, Linda is the organizational force behind the firm; Abby is the enthusiasm and presentation side. Over the years, they've built up a respectable company, one that Linda depends on for income—and prestige.

Several years ago, they hit a rough spot because the normally upbeat and enthusiastic Abby had changed. According to Linda, she was distracted and scattered, and talking a lot about the past. They had numerous people interested in PR proposals, and Linda had started many of them, but Abby just didn't have the enthusiasm needed to help finish and pitch them. And whenever Linda asked her, Abby just said that she was processing something and would be fine. But months later, she still wasn't fine.

Linda finally came to me with the issue. As we talked about it, she mentioned that six months ago, Abby's adult daughter had moved out of state to take an important job. When I asked if that could be bothering Abby, Linda didn't think so. Years earlier, Abby and her husband had divorced, and Abby barely skipped a beat over that. But the more we discussed Abby's daughter moving, the more Linda realized that the timing matched rather perfectly. She also acknowledged that Abby and her daughter were very close and had lunched together several times a week before the move. Currently, Abby didn't want to connect with anyone.

It became clear that Abby's Fire was suppressed by the grief she felt around the loss of her daughter on a daily basis. In truth, Abby wasn't a member of the Fire Club those days; she'd taken a temporary membership in the Metal Club. This helped Linda understand what was happening, but she (and the business) needed Abby and her Fire back in place soon. Their bottom line was suffering.

Based on my suggestions, Linda insisted she and Abby have lunch together. At a quiet table, Linda asked her if she was missing her daughter. The tears Abby shed confirmed it: Her Fire was deficient because of grief. Once Linda knew what she was dealing with, she stepped up in good Wood fashion and insisted Abby take a week to go visit her daughter. Linda also gave Abby a copy of the Fire Quick Tips and extracted a promise from her that she would do at least three things on the list every day. And it worked. As Abby's Fire built, it banished the excess Metal she was experiencing (Fire melts Metal). Soon the business was back on track. Linda was thrilled, and very relieved.

WOOD/FIRE RELATIONSHIPS: THE BOTTOM LINE

Long-term personal relationships aren't a high priority for either the Wood or the Fire Club. Woods care about accomplishment and success. Fires care about short-term connections with something or someone exciting. If these two clubs connect over partying with a purpose, it will be compelling for both. Going forward, if they can address their issues around the work-versus-play dilemma, a relationship between a Wood and a Fire could be stable. But if stress is part of the picture, without intervention, a troubled Wood/Fire relationship will likely see the Wood alone focused on work and the Fire out seeking new connections.

If you find yourself in a Wood/Fire relationship that's having trouble, ask yourself the following questions:

- » Do you understand the priorities and needs of your club and your partner's? Are your expectations for the relationship realistic?
- » Do you understand the tendencies of relating on the Nurturing Cycle? Is this helping or hurting what you want from the relationship?
- » Are either or both of you stressed? If so, start using the Quick Tips for Woods and Fires at the ends of Chapters 4 and 5.

> ## A QUICK WAY TO DEFUSE WOOD/ FIRE PROBLEMS
>
> *Unless we're Metals, we all know it's difficult to pull back in the middle of an argument. For Woods and Fires in battle, it could be a shouting match. Here's a quick way to take down some of the intensity.*
>
> *Wood: Put your thumbs at the outside edges of your eyes and rest your fingers across your forehead. Look the hysterical Fire in the eye, take a deep breath, and exhale a sharp "Shhhhhhhh." Push that sound out vigorously at the end.*
>
> *Fire: Put one hand across the back of your head directly behind your eyes and the other across your forehead. Look the stuffy Wood in the eye, take a deep breath, and exhale a soft "Heeeeeeee." Emphasize the sighing aspect of this sound.*
>
> *Repeat the process until you both feel a shift in the dynamics. At that point you'll probably be laughing instead of fighting.*

CHAPTER 12

FIRE WITH EARTH: THE MAD HATTER AND DOROTHY GALE, THE PERFECT PARTY

Love is a fire. But whether it is going to warm your hearth or burn down your house, you can never tell.

—Joan Crawford

That is your legacy on this Earth when you leave this Earth: how many hearts you touched.

—Patti Davis

AS WITH EVERY NURTURING CYCLE relationship, the connection between Fire and Earth will carry a flavor of interdependence. In nature, fire needs to burn but can scatter and easily burn out. Earth has been used for millennia to create ovens and hearths for fire. It works the same way with people: Fires need to be contained to burn steadily, and Earths, who need to be needed, are happy to hold the Fire. Dorothy could definitely rein in the Mad Hatter, and in a kind way! That doesn't mean all relationships between them will be perfect. But there's a lot to work with between Fire and Earth at a relationship level.

FIRE/EARTH CONNECTIONS

Friendships: Members of the Fire Club are high-energy people who enjoy being busy and thrive on attention. We all know people who love the limelight, right? Most of them are Fires. Earths, on the other hand, want to be with people they love and can help; it makes them feel needed. If Fire and Earth meet, the emphasis they both have on connecting will guarantee they bond, perhaps just for a short time. If a friendship lasts, they would be the perfect pair for hosting gatherings: the Fire will keep guests entertained, and the Earth will guarantee that everyone's needs are met.

Work: Social connections between these two clubs can be very compatible, but depending on the occupation, work relationships will be less straightforward. Earth people will be invested in making sure everything goes well so others are happy. And unless the work builds on a Fire's strengths, the Fire's tendency to scatter under pressure could require the Earth to run interference for them. Most Earths won't care, though, because they like to help so much.

Marriage: The primary relationship focus of a Fire person is on intense, short-term connections. Earth people, however, need deep lasting relationships. So, unless the Fire has a secondary Earth or some other compelling reason to stay in a long-term relationship, a marriage between these two clubs will probably not last, even though the Earth will want it to. While together, the Fire will value home as a place to entertain people, which will appeal to the Earth. But the Earth will view quiet time together at home as crucial, which might cramp the Fire's style. But Fire's natural flow toward Earth in the Five Elements model, and Earth's ability to safely embrace their passion and flames, may be a compelling enough reason for some Fires to stay.

Family: Will Fire/Earth relationships have children? If they've worked out the dynamic of long-term versus short-term connections, a Fire/Earth relationship will absolutely want children because this is of paramount importance to an Earth. In parenting, the Fire will bring the fun; the Earth will bring everything else.

Over the years, I've seen dozens of wonderful Fire/Earth relationships:

» *Noland and Wanda, Brother and Sister*: Noland (Fire) and Wanda (Earth) own a catering business. Noland runs the business end, and the variety of events keeps him happy. Wanda loves the cooking. And they both keep the parties fun and fantastic in their own way.

» *Janice and Marie, Actress and Agent*: Janice (Fire) is an actress, and Marie (Earth) is her agent. They've been together for a decade now, each doing what they do best.

» *Frank and Candy, Husband and Wife*: Frank (Fire) is an excellent salesman, and Candy (Earth) stays home with their children. Frank is on the road a lot, but the relationship works well. They have a great time when he's home, and the rest of the time Candy has her deep connection with her young children to keep her happy.

FIRE/EARTH RELATIONSHIP CHALLENGES

As we know, there are three basic ways a Five Elements relationship can get into trouble. We're going to use those to explore potential challenges with Fire/Earth connections.

I. We Don't Understand Ourselves or Each Other

We understand another person when we understand the tendencies of their club. Yes, Fire people will be gone from home more than almost any other club. Yes, Earth people will bake high-calorie goodies because they love you. And when these behaviors aren't exactly desirable, understanding their club will make it easier to talk to the Fire or Earth in a language they will hear. In truth, Fire/Earth relationships can be strong. But as my Fire client Chelsea found out in the next CASE CORNER, that won't matter if you just don't understand your Earth mother.

CASE CORNER
Reva and Chelsea, Mother and Daughter

Chelsea was a sixteen-year-old member of the Fire Club. She became a client of mine when her mother, Reva, caught her sneaking out at night to meet with her friends—a very Fire thing to do. We had long talks about boundaries and rules, which Fires don't embrace anyway, but during one of these conversations, Chelsea mentioned that she just didn't understand her mother.

When I asked her what she didn't understand, she gave me a list of what bothered her (besides having rules). One was that her mother insisted on meeting her friends before she could go out with them alone. None of her friends' parents required that. Her mom also insisted that Chelsea get good grades so she could attend a good college (Chelsea wasn't even thinking of college yet—Fires are creatures of the now). Her mom also insisted she eat healthy food; her friends got to eat anything they wanted.

I spent some time explaining the five clubs to Chelsea that afternoon, placing special attention on the Fire and Earth Clubs. She had to admit that it was uncanny how much like a Fire she sounded, and agreed completely that Reva was a "total Earth." I also explained how a relationship between a Fire and Earth could be supportive, fun, and upbeat if the Fire would accept the Earth as the perfect container.

Chelsea thought about it for a week, and the next time I saw her she acknowledged that her mother was pretty gentle with rules compared to some of her friends. She also admitted that some of her friends thought Reva "rocked." When Chelsea looked at her mom through the lens of the Earth Club, she understood better why she did what she did. Chelsea agreed to try to work with her mom instead of fighting her on all the boundaries. She also agreed to thank Reva once a day for something she did that Chelsea appreciated.

I wish I could say that Chelsea magically changed, but she didn't. Once a Fire, always a Fire. But Reva reported that Chelsea was less quarrelsome at home and more willing to try to work with her on issues she felt were restricting her. And I think that's about all you can ask from a teenage Fire.

II. *We Don't Understand Our Relationship Dynamics*

Fires and Earths relate on the Nurturing Cycle, which we know has its ups and downs. Nurturing can be good or bad, depending on the details. For Fires and Earths, the energy in the model flows from Fire to Earth. This would usually mean that the Earth would feel more nurtured than the Fire. But in this case, everyone will feel nurtured—the Earth because of the energy flowing to it from the Fire, and the Fire because Earth's greatest desire is to nurture everyone, so they will send the energy right back to the Fire. In fact, the saving grace of a Fire/Earth connection is the reality that the nurturing goes both ways. That can often make up for the difference in their relationship needs.

Example: Chester is an Earth, and his relationship with Sela (Fire), his girlfriend, perfectly illustrates the dual nurturing aspect of a Fire/Earth connection. Even though Sela doesn't spend as much time with Chester as he'd like, he feels so good with her that it doesn't seem to matter. Sela even appreciates his caring, Earthy ways, which makes him very happy. The fact that she feels so comfortable and safe with him makes sense—his Earth is the perfect container for Sela's Fire. For the time being, they are both very happy. And as long as Chester gives Sela the freedom her Fire needs, it might well last.

> ### REMINDERS FOR FIRE/EARTH CONNECTIONS
>
> *If you find yourself in a Fire/Earth relationship that isn't going the way you'd like, take a moment to remind yourself what's important to the other person. If you're the Fire, remember that Earths need deep, lasting connections. Of course they'll want you to stay home with them instead of going out all the time. If you're the Earth, remember that Fires need excitement and connections. Of course they will want to go out more than you might like. And if things get stressed, reach for the Fire and Earth Quick Tips covered earlier.*

III. We're So Stressed We Create Stressed Relationships

We will always get along better with others if we understand our clubs and their inherent relationship dynamics. But much of that can go out the window when stress is a factor. Knowing what a stressed Fire/Earth relationship looks like not only helps you recognize problematic aspects in your own Fire/Earth relationships, it also helps you fix them. And it's pretty straightforward. When stress is a factor in their relationship, Fire and Earth can each only go one of two places: an excess state or a deficient state. Let's see what that looks like, Fire first.

Fire Out of Balance

» *Deficient*: A Fire with too *little* Fire energy will leave the Earth feeling chilled and empty without the heat of the Fire. When the Fire scatters and is unstable, the Earth will try harder to help. But when joy leaves the Fire altogether, they will fail at the one thing they value most: connecting. When this happens, the Earth will worry and feel guilty that they're the reason the relationship is failing.

Example: Becky (Earth) fell in love with a Fire; she thought the sun, the moon, and the stars all rose over Jason (Fire). The beauty of a developing relationship thrilled Becky, and Jason reveled in the fun and intensity of the initial contact. But as the connection progressed, Jason's Fire decreased because the rush of newness that had been energizing him was gone. With no Fire to feed Becky's Earth, she worried for a while, but then even she had to admit the party was over.

» *Excess*: A Fire with too *much* Fire energy will scorch the Earth with their presence. When the Fire jokes inappropriately, says yes to every invitation, and succumbs to the drama in everything, the Earth will worry that the problems are somehow their fault.

Example: My client Dory (Earth) got a good dose of what too much Fire feels like when her good friend Kate (Fire) spontaneously invited her sister (also a Fire) to join Kate and Dory for lunch one day. Initially, Dory enjoyed the connection, but as the energy between the sisters ramped up, Dory tried to balance them. By the end of the lunch, she was completely spent and worried that the whole thing was somehow her fault. I helped her see otherwise.

» *Result:* Whether the relationship is suffering from too much or too little Fire, the Earth is going to overcompensate and try harder; few Earths voluntarily end a relationship. Sadly, too little Fire will leave the Earth undernourished and feeling needy; too much Fire will scorch the Earth and make them weary. To save relationships where this is happening, the Fire needs to be brought back into balance.

Earth Out of Balance

» *Deficient*: An Earth with too *little* Earth energy will need connection and reach out with excessive concern for the Fire. When the Fire pulls back, the Earth will feel guilty that they aren't doing enough. As the presence of the Earth diminishes, the Fire will discover that no one is containing them and burn hotter, which will make the Earth feel even worse.

Example: Even though Joan's mother was an Earth, she wasn't "warm and fuzzy" like other moms. She never baked cookies, never took them shopping, never cuddled them. Hungry for attention, twenty-something Joan (Fire) started running around with a fast crowd that fed her need to connect. Fortunately, she pulled her life together and eventually married a nice Earth guy who could give her Fire the container it needed. These days, she's happy and settled.

» *Excess Earth:* An Earth with too *much* Earth energy will start meddling in the Fire's life. They'll insert themselves where they really aren't needed and try to create a codependent relationship. When the Fire feels smothered and pulls back, the Earth will worry obsessively that they aren't doing enough and try even harder, but too much Earth puts out Fire. The dynamic became apparent to my client Leila when she moved in with her cousin Susan. Their story is featured in the next CASE CORNER.

» *Result:* Whether the relationship is suffering from too much or too little Earth, the Fire is going to be confused by the Earth's inability to help it hold its boundaries. Earth is supposed to contain Fire. Too little Earth will allow it to burn out of control; too much Earth will suffocate it. Either way, the Fire will probably leave. To save relationships where this is happening, the Earth person needs to be brought back into balance.

CASE CORNER

Excess Earth: Leila and Susan, Cousins

Leila (Fire), a recent college graduate, moved to Chicago to look for a job in broadcasting. Her cousin Susan (Earth) lived in a suburb with her husband and three children and offered Leila a room over their garage rent-free for six months. Knowing it might take her that long to find a full-time job, Leila jumped at the chance.

It was a great setup at first. Leila didn't feel alone and could drop in to connect with the family whenever she wanted. She especially loved playing with Susan's twin girls who, at eight years old, were rambunctious and fun. Susan made sure that Leila had meals with them when she was home, which also made Leila happy.

About two months into this arrangement, Susan's husband took a new position with his firm that required him to live in LA. He made it home a few weekends a month, but the rest of the time Susan was left with a house to run on her own. It wasn't long before the stress of being mother and father to her children took its toll and Susan's Earth ramped up. Soon, Susan was checking in with Leila daily, and then multiple times a day. She asked Leila about her interviews, offered to lend her clothes for the interviews, and called her after the interviews to see how they'd gone.

Leila appreciated the caring but was beginning to feel smothered. She had started a temp job, so was able to stay away from her garage apartment most of the day and only returned home to sleep. And when she did, Susan would call or knock on the door to see if she was okay. Did she need something? Could she help her in any way? Was anything wrong? When Leila said everything was fine, Susan seemed irritated.

Concerned by Susan's changed behavior, Leila arranged to share an apartment with a new friend. She thanked Susan, said she was grateful for the help, but was ready to fly on her own. When she did, Susan threw a tantrum over Leila leaving. At her new roommate's insistence, Leila called me to talk about what was happening with Susan. She also called Susan's husband and expressed concern.

I helped Leila understand that Susan was undoubtedly in an excess Earth place as she tried to be mother and father to her children, run a house, and be available to her husband the weekends he was able to get home. Leila understood and felt bad, but went on with her life.

The next time Leila saw Susan at a family gathering, she was back to normal. It turns out Leila's spontaneous call to Susan's husband made all the difference. He told Leila that he'd noticed the change in Susan and was equally worried. The new position wasn't all he thought it would be, so he returned to his old position in Chicago. Once he was home, Susan relaxed, lost some of the weight she'd gained from the extra sweets she'd craved, and returned to her balanced, caring self.

FIRE/EARTH RELATIONSHIPS: THE BOTTOM LINE

The Fire and the Earth Club both value connections. Earths want connections that turn into deep relationships. Fires want connections that are spontaneous and exciting, yet they usually don't last. Anything that develops between these two clubs will feel wonderful at the start. Going forward, if they can address their issues around going out versus staying home, a relationship between these two clubs could be stable. But if stress is part of the picture, without intervention, a troubled Fire/Earth relationship will find the Fire seeking fun and new connections while the Earth is left wondering what they did wrong.

If you find yourself in a Fire/Earth relationship that's having trouble, ask yourself the following questions:

» Do you understand the priorities and needs of your club and your partner's? Are your expectations for the relationship realistic?

» Do you understand the tendencies of relating on the Nurturing Cycle? Is this helping or hurting what you want from the relationship?
» Are either or both of you stressed? If so, start using the Quick Tips for Fires and Earths at the ends of Chapters 5 and 6.

A QUICK WAY TO DEFUSE FIRE/ EARTH PROBLEMS

Most people find it difficult to pull back in the middle of an argument. Although Fires and Earths probably won't have huge fights (the Earth couldn't bear it), here's a quick way to balance the energy between you if times get tense.

Fire: Put one hand across the back of your head directly behind your eyes and the other across your forehead. Look the smothering Earth in the eye, take a deep breath, and exhale a soft "Heeeeeeee." Emphasize the sighing aspect of this sound.

Earth: Place the thumbs of each hand on your cheekbones directly below your eyes and rest the fingers of each hand across your forehead. Look the scattered Fire in the eye, take a deep breath, and exhale softly making an "Aummmmm" sound, like the OM. Make the sound prayerful.

Repeat the process until you both feel a shift in the dynamics. The good news is you'll probably feel reconnected, which will make you both happy.

CHAPTER 13

EARTH WITH METAL: DOROTHY GALE AND MR. SPOCK, THE CORRECT WAY TO GREET OZ

Life comes from the earth and life returns to the earth.
—Zhuangzi

It is by presence of mind in untried emergencies that the native metal of man is tested.
—James Russell Lowell

AS IS COMMON WITH NURTURING Cycle relationships, the connection between Earths and Metals will embody an aspect of interdependence. In nature, earth is the stable matrix in which metals develop and grow. It's the same with people. Earths naturally want to take care of Metals, and Metals feel they deserve it. Just imagine how Dorothy would take care of Mr. Spock if he joined her in Oz! This doesn't mean all Earth/Metal relationships will be perfect, but they will usually start out on good footing.

EARTH/METAL CONNECTIONS

Friendships: Members of the Earth Club want to help people and make a difference. We all know people who are Earth Mother types, right? Most of them *are* Earths. Metals, however, are highly structured people who have distilled their version of excellence and want to spread it across the globe. If an Earth and Metal meet, the naturalness of their connection will feel comfortable. Yet even though the Earth person will feel like they have found a long-lost child, the Metal person will likely remain somewhat distant. However, if the Earth wants to include the Metal in their life, the Metal won't fight it, to a point.

Work: The likelihood of an Earth and Metal working well together is small, unless the Earth has a secondary Metal or Wood to provide needed structure. Without that, the Metal will insist on a level of exacting perfection that will be difficult for the Earth to accomplish. And when the Earth offers suggestions to ensure that everyone gets along well, the Metal will turn a deaf ear. Precision and perfection are the Metal's goal, no matter whose feelings are hurt.

Marriage: The primary relationship focus for Earths is on deep, lasting connections with others. Metals need to connect with information they can synthesize. But the strong feeling an Earth has to nurture a Metal, combined with the Metal's belief that the attention is right and natural, could make for a stable marriage as long as it conforms to the Metal's rules. At home, the Earths will love decorating and making a home, but will also want quiet time together. The Metals will want a minimum of clutter and quiet time alone. If they can find a meeting place on these issues, they have a good chance of a stable connection.

Family: Will Earth/Metal relationships have children? Probably. The Earths will want a family, and the Metals will be happy to oblige as long as they don't have to be too involved. In parenting, the Metals will provide the structure and rules; the Earths will provide the rest.

Over the years, I've seen dozens of successful Earth/Metal relationships:

» *Sharon and Sami, Sisters:* Sharon (Metal) is an architect, and Sami (Earth) is an interior decorator. They run a design business together that's very popular.

» *Charles and Liz, Business Associates:* Charles (Metal) is an accountant, and Liz (Earth) runs his office. They both agree they couldn't do what they do without each other.

» *Jack and Jill (seriously!), Husband and Wife:* Jack (Earth) is a school principal, and Jill (Metal) is an accountant. They have a happy life with two children. Jack does most of the cooking.

EARTH/METAL RELATIONSHIP CHALLENGES

As we know, there are only three ways a Five Elements relationship can get into trouble. We're going to use those to explore potential challenges with Earth/Metal connections.

I. We Don't Understand Ourselves or Each Other

Knowing the tendencies of their club helps us to understand another person. Of course Earths will love displaying treasured objects all over the house. Of course Metals will correct what you say in front of people. And when these behaviors aren't exactly desirable, understanding their club will make it easier to talk to the

Earth or Metal in a language they will hear. Usually, Earth/Metal relationships are pretty stable. But as my Earth client Becca found out, that won't matter if you just don't understand your Metal boss.

CASE CORNER
Becca and Marilyn, Assistant and Engineer

Becca began working for Marilyn straight out of college. Becca's a clever girl, but still has the Earth tendency of wanting everyone to be happy. Eager to please from the day she started, Becca was disheartened that nothing she did for Marilyn seemed good enough. Whether it was margins on memos, the way she answered the phone, or copying documents, Marilyn always had suggestions. After six months of hearing, "This is fine, but..." every day, Becca was miserable. No matter how hard she tried, she just couldn't please Marilyn. Becca's mother suggested Becca and I chat, so she ended up in my office.

The more Becca described Marilyn's behaviors and priorities to me, the more I was sure that Marilyn was a Metal. It was apparent in how organized Marilyn's office was in spite of the tremendous number of drawings and files to be stored. Or the fact that Marilyn's desk was never cluttered, a problem with Becca's desk that had been pointed out to her several times. Even Marilyn's clothing was streamlined and sharp, unlike Becca's more "comfortable" attire. The biggest problem was that Marilyn rarely thanked Becca, which meant Becca didn't feel appreciated. That's really hard on an Earth.

Grabbing my Five Elements chart, I showed the model to Becca and explained that she was an Earth and Marilyn was a Metal. As we talked about what matters to Metals, Becca began to understand that, while any engineer will expect precision, Metals need it to feel right about their world. I also helped Becca see that the reason Metals want process and protocol is because it's their way of honoring the excellence of all that's come before. Metals distill experience into wisdom, then expect the rest of us to take that wisdom forward. And we usually do.

Becca left with a better understanding of her Metal boss. She also left with a few tips for making sure Marilyn didn't get too rigidly stuck in a "control everything" mode. I suggested that Becca bring more Fire energy into the office to help control Marilyn's excess Metal. To do this, I encouraged Becca to start wearing red at work (red builds Fire) and also bring out her own natural Fire by smiling a lot and even telling a few jokes. Becca wasn't sure she knew any jokes but was definitely up for buying a red sweater.

I ran into Becca's mother a few weeks later, and she confirmed that Becca was still working for Marilyn. Becca's mother wasn't sure how long it would last, but for the time being, Becca had a new appreciation of Marilyn's wisdom and was sticking around. That didn't surprise me, either. Earths are usually the last ones to leave any relationship because they never give up on people.

II. We Don't Understand Our Relationship Dynamics

Earths and Metals relate on the Nurturing Cycle, which is a mixed bag. Earths love to nurture, but too much nurturing is usually bad for a Metal. The energy flows from Earth to Metal, which works well for both: The Metal will be the one who accepts the nurturing, and the Earth will feel great taking care of someone. The level of stability this provides an Earth/Metal relationship can often counter the extreme differences in their relationship needs. But not always.

> *Example*: After graduate school, Margo's son Gilbert (Metal) moved five hours away from home. A research specialist who was the last child to leave the nest, Gilbert worked long hours and rarely got home to see his parents. Deeply missing her role as an active mom, Margo (Earth) started casually "dropping in" to visit Gilbert on weekends. At first, he welcomed her, but eventually she impinged on his time alone and he told her (kindly) that she needed to stop coming. This broke her heart, but if she'd understood Gilbert's "Metalness" she would have known he needed his space.

REMINDERS FOR EARTH/ METAL CONNECTIONS

If you find yourself in an Earth/Metal relationship that isn't going the way you'd like, take a moment to remind yourself what's important to the other person. If you're the Earth, remember that Metals thrive on order and discipline. Of course they'll expect everything to be shipshape all of the time! If you're the Metal, remember that Earths use mementos to remind themselves of their lasting connections with the people who gave them the mementos. Of course they'll want them scattered all over the house so they can see them! And if things get stressed, reach for the Earth and Metal Quick Tips covered earlier.

III. We're So Stressed We Create Stressed Relationships

When we understand our club tendencies and relationship dynamics, it makes it much easier to get along with others. But relating is always made harder when stress is a factor. Knowing what a stressed Earth/Metal relationship looks like not only helps you recognize problematic aspects in your own Earth/Metal relationships, it also helps you fix them. And it's pretty straightforward. When stressed, Earth and Metal can each only go one of two places: an excess state or a deficient state. Let's take a look, Earth first.

Earth Out of Balance

» *Deficient*: An Earth with too *little* Earth energy will become fearful that they aren't needed. This will make them flighty, ungrounded, and frequently unable to reach out. The Metal will read this as unavailable and look elsewhere for the nurturing they expect, which will make things even worse for the Earth.

Example: Ginny (Earth) worked in the office of Dr. Lentz (Metal). When her mother died, Ginny took it hard but was back at work one week after the funeral. Losing her mother really depressed Ginny's Earth, so she had a hard time getting back into her groove at work. She was frequently spacey and unfocused at the office and even left early a few times a week. Dr. Lentz perceived this as Ginny pulling back and talked to his office manager about firing her. Fortunately, the office manager knew that Ginny's mother had recently passed and suggested they ask her to take a few more weeks off. They did, and it really helped. When Ginny came back, her Earth was much more balanced and ready to work.

» *Excess Earth*: An Earth person with too *much* Earth energy will over-focus on the Metal and become a constant presence in their life. Metal people cannot stand to be smothered so will separate even further from the Earth. This will create feelings of guilt in the Earth that somehow they aren't doing enough, and they will try harder. At this point, the Metal will pull back even more to protect their space, or simply leave.

Example: Patty (Metal) and Bill (Earth) had been married for years and weren't able to have children. He was a teacher, and she was a recently promoted attorney who hadn't been home much lately. Lonely and unable to share as much with Patty as he used to, Bill ended up with too much Earth. This became apparent to Patty at a rare dinner out with friends when Bill's need to connect in a meaningful way caused him to share details from their life that she, as a Metal, felt were better kept private. They talked about it once home and agreed to try harder to connect more often going forward.

» *Result:* Whether the relationship is suffering from too much or too little Earth, the Metal is going to be displeased by the change in dynamics in their well-ordered world. Too little Earth will cause the Metal to feel under-supported, and too much Earth will overwhelm them. If the situation doesn't improve, the Metal will leave. To save relationships where this is happening, the Earth needs to be brought back into balance.

Metal Out of Balance

» *Deficient*: A Metal with too *little* Metal energy will lose their ability to discern right from wrong and good from bad. Their orderly ways will desert them as they hold tightly to their precious opinions in the face of mounting confusion. The Earth will suffer from the lack of structure and, of course, assume they've done something wrong. But the worried and forlorn Earth will stay and try harder.

Example: Howard (Metal, early sixties) lost his job as an accountant when his firm merged with a larger one. Howard's whole life had been structured around the rhythm of going to work; coming home; eating the dinner his wife, Lucy (Earth); and going to bed. Without this structure, his Metal depleted, and he became confused and lost. Without the structure Howard provided, Lucy also floundered and assumed everything was somehow her fault. Fortunately, they had grown children who helped them get things back on track. The couple eventually embraced their early retirement and have been busy ever since.

» A Metal with too *much* Metal energy will find their normally reasonable style become harsh and unforgiving. Their desire for order and control will escalate, creating behavior that can only be called domineering. The Earth will compassionately try to work with the Metal's unreasonable demands, but the Metal will retreat completely to be alone with their perceived perfection. Sadly, the beginnings of this dynamic became apparent to my client Corrine when her mother put propriety over heart. Their story is featured in the next CASE CORNER.

» *Result:* Whether the relationship is suffering from too much or too little Metal, the Earth is going to worry that it's their fault. Too little Metal will cause the Earth to feel abandoned and adrift. Too much Metal will make the Earth feel pressured to adapt to circumstances that feel harsh or unrealistic to them. Either way, the Earth will probably stay and try harder. To save relationships where this is happening, the Metal needs to be brought back into balance.

CASE CORNER

Excess Metal: Jody and Corrine, Mother and Daughter

Several months after her father passed away, twenty-four-year-old Corrine (Earth) received an upsetting email from her mother, Jody (Metal). It dealt with the details of an upcoming memorial service for her father. At the time of his death, the immediate family held a simple, private funeral for him, which Tracy, Corrine's partner of several years, attended with her.

The email from Jody announced that Corrine's father's family was planning a service in his hometown several states away. Jody went on to remind Corrine how conservative her father's family was, and because of that, she thought it best that Tracy not attend the service with the rest of the family. Jody was concerned about appearances and possible flak from his family.

When Corrine came to see me, she was understandably upset that Tracy was being left out (inclusion is very important to Earths). Corrine was also worried that she had somehow angered her mother. Jody had always been a "by the book" mom, very neat and tidy and tied to rules, but for the three years Corrine and Tracy had been together, Jody had been very accepting of Tracy. Corrine couldn't understand why her mother had taken this new position against Tracy.

I explained to Corrine that Jody was a Metal person, someone who lived life embracing protocol, rules, and "the way things should be." But as Jody dealt with the grief of losing her husband, she was clearly in an excess Metal place (grief and loss sit in Metal). People with excess Metal energy become domineering, controlling, and even more determined than ever to stick to rules. And in this case, it appeared Jody was trying to stick to her husband's family "rules," which seemed unwilling to embrace Corrine's relationship with Tracy.

But the good news with Metals, even Metals in an excess state, is that along with rules, they value priority and hierarchy. Almost any mother, even a grieving Metal one, would agree that the feelings of her daughter should matter more than the feelings of distant relatives. Corrine went home and shared with Jody that it felt as though when she needed her most, Jody was alienating her. To Jody's credit, she thought about it and then agreed that Corrine's feelings were most important; Tracy would go to the service.

EARTH/METAL RELATIONSHIPS: THE BOTTOM LINE

Personal relationships are everything for members of the Earth Club, but they aren't a high priority for the Metal Club. Earths love to nurture, and Metals feel it's their right to be nurtured, so a relationship between these two clubs could start out well. Going forward, if they can address their issues around togetherness versus separateness, a relationship between these two clubs could be stable. But if ongoing stress is part of the picture, without intervention a troubled Earth/Metal relationship will likely see the Metal retreating for time alone and the Earth trying harder to connect.

If you find yourself in an Earth/Metal relationship that's having trouble, ask yourself the following questions:

» Do you understand the priorities and needs of your club and your partner's? Are your expectations for the relationship realistic?

» Do you understand the tendencies of relating on the Nurturing Cycle? Is this helping or hurting what you want from the relationship?

» Are either or both of you stressed? If so, start using the Quick Tips for Earths and Metals at the ends of Chapters 6 and 7.

A QUICK WAY TO DEFUSE EARTH/METAL PROBLEMS

While Earths will find it almost impossible to pull back in the middle of an argument, the Metal will be able to detach and leave. For this reason, Earths and Metals probably won't have huge fights. But here's a quick way to balance the energy between you if times get tense.

Earth: Place the thumbs of each hand on your cheekbones directly below your eyes and rest the fingers of each hand across your forehead. Look the minimizing Metal in the eye, take a deep breath, and exhale softly making an "Aummmmm" sound, like the OM. Make the sound prayerful.

Metal: Place one hand on the top of your head and the other across the front of your forehead. Look the overwhelming Earth in the eye, take a deep breath, and exhale softly making a "Ssssssssssss" sound, like the air leaking from a tire.

Repeat the process until you both feel a shift in the dynamics. If you stay with it, you might even forget what upset you.

CHAPTER 14

METAL WITH WATER: MR. SPOCK AND VAN GOGH, COMPARING STARRY SKIES

Keep up your bright swords, for the dew will rust them.
—Shakespeare

*I feel most at home in the water....
That's where I belong.*
—Michael Phelps

METALS AND WATERS RELATE VIA the Nurturing Cycle, which, as we know, gives a tendency of interdependence to their relationship dynamics. In nature, the minerals of metal enrich water, and water carries them away to nurture life. It's the same for people: Metals need to share their findings, or their distilled wisdom will be lost. Waters use the wisdom of Metals to create new ideas. It's a relationship of endings feeding beginnings. Perhaps Spock's tales of his travels would inspire Van Gogh. Like all Nurturing Cycle connections, relationships between Metals and Waters won't always be fantastic. But they will always be important.

METAL/WATER CONNECTIONS

Friendships: Metals are usually very disciplined people able to look back across the whole of a cycle and determine what was useful and should be carried forward, and what can be discarded. We've all known people who can make the complex seem simple, right? Those are usually Metals. Waters are inspired, imaginative people who can take the old and create something new. When the Metal and Water connect, they will probably recognize what they can do for each other. And it can be an easy connection. Metal provides Water with support and structure for creating the new, while Water provides Metal with dissemination of their work. They will be extra compatible, too, since both are loners who tend to live in their heads.

Work: The social connections between these two based on findings and ideas lend themselves to deep discussions. If these talks can move out of the range of concepts into synthesizing and planning, Metal and Water working together will be a thing of beauty, likely to create something greater than either could create separately. And this will be gratifying for both; Metals will adore that Waters want their conclusions for use in new ways, and Waters will be grateful for the seeds around which they can create their concepts. If their projects involve writing, so much the better, because Metals and Waters both love the written word.

Marriage: Metals' primary relationship focus is on connecting with information. Waters' primary relationship focus is on connecting with their inner selves and something greater than themselves. For both Metals and Waters, intimate connections are less important, so close personal relationships aren't going to be a top priority for either club. However, a Fire or Earth secondary in one or both will lend a motivating power for intimacy that can hold these two together.

Family: Will Metal/Water relationships create families? In a Metal/Water household, unless someone has a secondary Earth, the couple will likely not want children. It just isn't their focus. If they do have a family, the Metal could be slightly more engaged than the Water if they chose to approach having a family as the "right" thing to do.

Over the years, I've seen dozens of outstanding Metal/Water relationships:

» *Steve and Jolie, Husband and Wife*: He's a scientific researcher (Metal) and she teaches philosophy at a local college (Water). Together they developed a series of children's lectures called *And Then What?* The series highlights important discoveries from science and what could be done with the information going forward.

» *Tad and Troy, Writing Team*: Tad's the Metal, and Troy's the Water. Together they research and write space age fantasies. They're killer at it, too.

» *Jan and Brittany, Coworkers*: Jan (Water) and Brittany (Metal) created a line of hand-painted silk clothes. Jan does the painting, and Brittany makes the clothes to her exacting standards. The pieces are beautiful!

METAL/WATER RELATIONSHIP CHALLENGES

There are just three ways a Five Elements relationship can get into trouble. We're going to use those to explore potential challenges with Metal/Water connections.

I. We Don't Understand Ourselves or Each Other

When we understand someone's club, we understand them, which means that their bizarre or disturbing behavior might actually make sense. Of course a Metal is going to insist on going the speed limit in the middle of a vast expanse of empty desert. Of course a Water is going to occasionally forget about the date you planned. And when any of these behaviors aren't exactly appropriate, understanding their club will make it easier to talk to the Metal or Water in a language they will hear. Metal/Water relationships are pretty compatible because they're both such conceptual people. But as my Metal client Ted found out, that won't matter if you just don't understand your Water son. Their story is in the next CASE CORNER.

CASE CORNER
Ted and Brian, Father and Son

Ted is a member of the Metal Club, and his son Brian is a Water person. In high school, Ted played soccer, was on the gymnastics team, and was captain of the debate club. Ted majored in accounting in college and married a nice girl from the Earth Club. After graduation, he went to work and she stayed home, which made them both happy.

Brian was their first child and was always a bit of a loner. Content reading or drawing by himself, he was indifferent when his younger brother came along. In school, Brian excelled at art, was pretty good at music, but was late everywhere he went. And even though he would kick a soccer ball around with his dad when requested, sports didn't excite him.

When Brian was in high school, Ted couldn't understand why his oldest son wouldn't play ball, debate, or participate in anything involving competition. Brian wasn't interested in the car his father wanted to get him, either; he rode his bike to school, claiming it was environmentally friendly. Worried that he and his wife were raising a slacker, Ted began trying to toughen up his son.

The truth was that Brian thought sports and cars were a waste of time. Instead, he joined the astronomy club and took up photography. He also drew an occasional political cartoon for the school paper. But Ted's determination to get Brian to do all that he'd done in high school created stress in the family. Before long, Ted showed up at my office.

As we spoke, it became clear that Ted wasn't that out of balance himself; he just didn't understand how to parent a Water. I explained the differences between Metal and Water people, and Ted came to understand that Brian wasn't slacking off; he was just marching to the drum of the Water Club, which meant less structure and more "go with the flow." Ted also realized that it was his job to help Brian foster his own talents, not replicate anyone else's, and as he reframed his relationship with Brian, life in the household immediately improved.

By the time Brian graduated, he'd been accepted into the photography program at Brooks Institute with his father's blessing. These days, Brian's a professional photographer with his own wife and child. Want to guess which club his son belongs to? Right, he's a little Metal.

II. We Don't Understand Our Relationship Dynamics

Metal and Water relate on the Nurturing Cycle, which can have its highs and lows. Some nurturing is always good, but too much of anything is bad. For Metals and Waters, the energy flows from

Metal to Water, so Waters will probably feel more nurtured than the Metals, which might be a problem. Metals often feel entitled, so it's a good idea for the Water to express appreciation to the Metal when they think of it.

> *Example*: George (Water) discovered the value of understanding the clubs and relationship dynamics too late. He'd hired a research assistant, Chris (Metal), who was all he could ask for in an assistant. The information and wise observations Chris sent George were brilliant, exceedingly well organized, and just what he needed. For the first time in a long time, George felt supported. This was understandable given the fact that Metal not only feeds Water but also provides much-needed structure. But the happiness didn't last. George rarely gave Chris positive feedback or showed his appreciation, which didn't meet Chris's Metal need to be acknowledged for his wisdom. Eventually, Chris took a different job. This wouldn't have happened if George had understood what matters to Metals.

REMINDERS FOR METAL/ WATER CONNECTIONS

If you find yourself in a Metal/Water relationship that isn't going the way you'd like, take a moment to remind yourself what's important to the other person. If you're the Metal, remember that Waters need flexibility and flow; don't take it personally when they show up late or don't follow the rules. If you're the Water, remember that Metals need process and protocol in their lives to honor the wisdom of the past. If they insist on following the recipe instead of "winging it," or want everything put back where it belongs, relax—that's normal for a Metal. And if things get stressed, reach for the Metal and Water Quick Tips covered earlier.

III. We're So Stressed We Create Stressed Relationships

It's not always easy to get along, even if we understand our clubs and relationship dynamics. That's because for most people, life these days includes stress. Knowing what a stressed Metal/Water relationship looks like will help you recognize problematic aspects of your own Metal/Water relationships and fix them. It's not hard. As we've seen, when stress is a factor, the clubs can only go one of two places: an excess or deficient version of normal. Metals first.

Metal Out of Balance

» *Deficient*: A Metal with too *little* Metal energy will be unable to sort and process as they normally do, and the decisions that used to come so easily will be difficult. Disorganization will set in, as will confusion, and the Metal person will distance themselves even more from almost everyone. The Water will miss the attention and input as the Metal holds back, but will probably not make a big deal about it. They will also miss the structure the Metal once provided, a structure that supported Water's inner quest. That will hurt, but just for a while.

Example: Stacy (Metal) prided herself on her ability to keep an orderly yet comfortable house. She'd even managed to convince Josh, her Watery husband, to keep the "public" areas of the house presentable. But when Stacy's mother suffered a stroke, the almost constant attention she gave her mom depleted Stacy's Metal. The house rapidly became disorganized as Josh, lacking Stacy's Metal structure, left things wherever they dropped while flowing around the house. Eventually, he retreated to his study and waited for Stacy to return to normal, which she did as her mother recovered and needed her less.

» A Metal with too *much* Metal energy will develop an exaggerated sense of importance. They'll hold on to significant discoveries, unwilling to share them, and become even more disciplined and dismissive of the people they deem to be less brilliant than they are. Again, the Water will miss the attention and input they were used to receiving from the Metal. But they will refuse to conform to what they perceive to be unreasonable demands and structure. If things don't change soon, the Water will just ignore the Metal.

Example: Kirk (Water) was a student in Mr. Lane's (Metal) drafting class. Kirk loved the artistic aspect of drafting and appreciated the structure Mr. Lane brought to the class. The week after Mr. Lane received a teaching award, he started requiring markedly greater accuracy from his students. He also began bragging about the award and other accomplishments he'd had that the students would probably never obtain. Eventually, Mr. Lane's excessive structure and dismissiveness got to be too much for Kirk and he transferred to a different class.

» *Result:* Whether the relationship is suffering from too much or too little Metal, the Water will initially miss the Metal's input. Too little Metal will remove some of the structure that served the Water. Too much Metal will cause the Water to feel restricted. But Waters are loners and will eventually flow away from anything that doesn't serve their purpose. To save relationships where this is happening, the Metal needs to be brought back into balance.

Water Out of Balance

» *Deficient*: A Water with too *little* Water energy will find their inspiration drying up and will be unable to do anything with what Metal gives them. If Metal questions this, the Water will become fearful and disconnect themself even more than usual. This will leave the Metal temporarily confused and sad about that lack of flow for its wisdom, but they will quickly compartmentalize the event and focus on any number of other projects.

Example: Joe (Water) was in his forties. He worked as a short-order cook, but his passion was playing guitar. He tried but never made it in the music business, so focused less and less on his guitar. Eventually, his Water depleted; he lost hope and gave up. A few years later he met Carole, a Metal who liked his cooking. They started dating, and the presence of her Metal fed his Water. His hope returned, but instead of going for the music full time, he was encouraged by Carole to try something more practical. Enthused, Joe went back to college and trained for a job in renewable energy. He and Carole play music and sing on the weekends.

» *Excess*: A Water with too *much* Water energy will demand more from the Metal because, in their mind, it's all about what they're doing for the Metal. If the Metal argues with them, the Water will become uncharacteristically belligerent and then paranoid that the Metal is up to something. The Metal will initially feel pressured by Water, but they will soon refuse to be bullied and, if necessary, leave. Sadly, the beginnings of this dynamic became apparent to my client Gwen when her father became a widower. Their story is featured in the next CASE CORNER.

» *Result*: Whether the relationship is suffering from too much or too little Water, the Metal is going to question the value of a connection with the Water. Too little Water will confuse the Metal and make them wonder why their valuable information isn't being used. Too much Water will rust the Metal, threatening its all-important structure. Since Metals excel at detaching themselves from unpleasantness, they will retreat to their ivory tower and pursue other projects. To save relationships where this is happening, the Water needs to be brought back into balance.

CASE CORNER
Excess Water: Samuel and Gwen, Father and Daughter

Samuel (Water) was a military man most of his life. It wasn't his first choice but soon became the best option, so he relied on his strong secondary Metal to get by. And he did. When he retired, he and his wife traveled and enjoyed life for several years. His Water came back full force, and they went wherever they wanted (and could afford), whenever they wanted. It was a wonderful time. But then his wife fell ill and passed on. This left Samuel depressed and bitter. He did fine on his own for several years but eventually began acting out, either challenging his daughter Gwen (Metal) when she tried to help him or shifting to paranoid behaviors, fearful that something bad would happen to someone else he loved. That's when Gwen called me.

Gwen had been checking in on him since her mom passed. The occasional presence of her Metal brought some degree of structure to Samuel's aimless ways, and she had hoped that he could remain independent for a long time. However, little by little, his calls to her accounting office increased. Initially, Gwen resented having her work time interrupted and refused to take more than one call from him a day. Eventually she realized that wasn't the proper way to approach the issue, so gave in and took all of his calls.

But when Samuel started calling day and night, she knew she had a problem. He called at midnight one night sure someone was breaking into his house. Another time he called during dinner concerned that an approaching storm was going to damage his house. Another call, late at night, was to make sure Gwen's oldest daughter had gotten home from a date; he'd heard sirens in the distance.

When Gwen and I talked, it was clear that her father was in an excess Water state bordering on paranoia. I asked if she thought he needed professional help or might need to be relocated to an assisted living arrangement, but she balked. She believed he was just alone too much. She decided it was best for him to move in with her and her family so she could get a better idea of what was going on.

It turned out to be a great idea. Gwen's Metal gave Samuel the structure he needed, and her strong secondary Earth helped guide his Water (Earth controls Water) in a comfortable way. Soon, Samuel was happy reading and painting alone in his room most days, but grateful for the family connection and discussions over dinner. He lived seven more years and then passed away peacefully in his sleep.

METAL/WATER RELATIONSHIPS: THE BOTTOM LINE

Personal relationships aren't a high priority for either Metal or Water Clubs. Metals care about creating wisdom from the past. Waters care about creating something greater than themselves. If these two clubs connect by using knowledge to create something new, it will be a heady start. Going forward, if they can address their differences in structure and tidiness, a relationship between these two clubs could be stable. But if stress is part of the picture, without intervention a troubled Metal/Water relationship will likely see the Metal and the Water preferring time alone in different rooms—or cities.

If you find yourself in a Metal/Water relationship that's having trouble, ask yourself the following questions:

- » Do you understand the priorities and needs of your club and your partner's? Are your expectations for the relationship realistic?

- » Do you understand the tendencies of relating on the Nurturing Cycle? Is this helping or hurting what you want from the relationship?

- » Are either or both of you stressed? If so, start using the Quick Tips for Metals and Waters at the ends of Chapters 7 and 3.

A QUICK WAY TO DEFUSE METAL/WATER PROBLEMS

In the middle of an argument or fight, Metals and Waters might well be able to detach. For this reason, Metals and Waters in relationships probably won't have huge fights (unless they draw on energy from their secondary elemental affinities). But here's a quick way to balance the energy between the two if times get tense.

Metal: Place one hand on the top of your head and the other across the front of your forehead. Look the impossible Water in the eye, take a deep breath, and exhale softly making a "Ssssssssssss" sound, like the air leaking from a tire.

Water: Put one hand across the back of your head at the base of your skull and the other across your forehead. Look the dismissive Metal in the eye, take a deep breath, and exhale a soft "Whooooooo." If there's a little energy behind it, so much the better.

Repeat the process until you both feel a shift in the dynamics. If you stay with it, be careful—you might start smiling.

CONTROLLING CYCLE RELATIONSHIPS

MY WAY OR THE HIGHWAY!
I GUESS EXIT 17 WILL DO.
S.
CartoonStock.com

CHAPTER 15

WATER WITH FIRE: VAN GOGH AND THE MAD HATTER, A MOODY, WILD TIME

Water is the driving force of all nature.
—Leonardo da Vinci

You don't extinguish fire by adding more fire, you need water.
—Pope Shenouda III

WATERS AND FIRES RELATE VIA the Controlling Cycle of the model. As expected, connections on this cycle can have a slight sense of control or even opposition at times. But as we discussed in Chapter 2, that isn't necessarily bad. In nature, fire left to its own devices will eventually burn itself out. But some water flowing to that fire helps keep it in check and therefore alive. Controlling Cycle relationships with people can work much the same way. They don't have to be automatically oppositional. In fact, they can feel very supportive. Van Gogh and the Mad Hatter could end up best friends! A Fire person can burn a bit brighter knowing that there's a Water person around to help manage their energy. Controlling Cycle relationships can offer glimpses of completely different worlds, too.

WATER/FIRE CONNECTIONS

Friendships: Waters are philosophic people who value inner focus and quiet time. The person obsessed with knowing "Why?" is usually a Water. Fires are engaging people who love social gatherings and need connections outside of themselves. The person excited about a party is usually a Fire. If a Water and a Fire connect, it could be a compelling relationship for both: the joining of pure opposites, the deeply contracted inner world of Water's full yin with the completely expanded outer world of Fire's full yang. The Water will be fascinated by the Fire's passion and heat, and the Fire will be intrigued by the Water's depth and stillness. Opposites can attract and create stable relationships.

Work: Neither Water nor Fire has much structure, so the possibility of them working well together will really depend on the kind of work that's involved. The outgoing Fire person would be perfect for promoting the artistic accomplishments of the creative Water person. They can be seen as the proverbial doer (Fire) and thinker (Water), so would do well together in a situation requiring both. But if things get out of balance, given the directional energy of the Controlling Flow, the Fire is going to feel like the Water is raining on their parade. And they well could be.

Marriage: Waters' primary relationship focus is on connecting with both their inner selves and something greater than themselves. Fires' primary relationship focus is on intense connections outside of themselves that tend to be brief. If they gave each other lots of space, a marriage between Water and Fire could work, though it might be rather mercurial given both have so little structure. But opposites attract: The Water will experience the heat of the sun it never sees from its depths. The Fire will experience the cool of the depths it can never access. They can complete each other—if they can stand each other.

Family: In a Water/Fire household, unless one (or both) has a strong secondary Earth, the couple will likely not want children. It just isn't their focus. If they do have a family, the Fire will usually be more engaged than the Water.

Over the years, I've seen many first-rate Water/Fire relationships:

- » *Rip and Lynn, Husband and Wife:* Rip (Water) wrote his first book several years ago and decided to self-publish it. Lynn (Fire) agreed to help him promote it by setting up book signings. She went with him and connected with people by talking about the book. Rip answered questions and signed his book. It worked great!

- » *Harrison and Franco, Research Partners*: Harrison (Water) and Franco (Fire) run research focus groups for marketing companies. During each group, Franco's ability to speak rapidly and stay upbeat keeps the participants engaged while Harrison uses his prodigious imagination to throw out possibilities and ideas for reaction. They must be good; they're certainly busy.

- » *Alice and Roberta, Flea Market Sisters*: Alice (Water) and her sister Roberta (Fire) have a business selling old books at flea markets. Alice loves to scour shops all over the state for hidden treasures, and Roberta, as an outgoing Fire, could sell snow to penguins. They're a great team and love working together.

WATER/FIRE RELATIONSHIP CHALLENGES

As was true in the section on Nurturing Cycle relationships, when applying the Five Elements model to people and their relationships on the Controlling Cycle, there are still only three ways a relationship can get into trouble. We're going to use those to explore potential challenges with Water/Fire connections.

I. We Don't Understand Ourselves or Each Other

A person's club affiliation is determined by their energetic wiring, and it's the same wiring every other member of that club possesses. When we understand this wiring, their apparent bizarre or perturbing behaviors can make total sense. Of course a Water in the grasp of the muses will paint through the night. Of course a Fire will accept invitations from people they don't even know. And when these behaviors aren't exactly desirable, understanding their club will make it easier to talk to the Water or Fire in a language they will hear. But first, we have to understand each other.

> *Example*: Lisa (Fire) was a vivacious, fun-loving teen. She didn't get into heavy drama but was flighty in a cute way. Her junior year, she had Mr. Jackson (Water) as her philosophy teacher. If she laughed or giggled in class, he frowned at her. If she spontaneously asked a slightly off-topic question, he pointed out how irrelevant it was. His teaching style was slow, thoughtful, and rambling. Not surprisingly, Lisa found Mr. Jackson a "total downer" and the class pretty boring, so she wasn't doing well in it.

I tried to help Lisa see that as a Fire, she was naturally outgoing and lively, but Mr. Jackson was probably a Water. That meant he valued quiet, inner-directed time and expected everyone in his class to be that way. This simple reframing helped Lisa manage herself better in Mr. Jackson's class. She didn't have fun, didn't like the class or him that much, but at least she passed.

II. We Don't Understand Our Relationship Dynamics

Water and Fire relate on the Controlling Cycle, which can be both helpful and difficult. Someone controlling you feels bad, but someone keeping you from getting out of control is good. And since in the Five Element model the energy flows from Waters to Fires, it's the Fires who will likely feel a sense of being controlled in a Water/Fire connection. And while the Fire may never send the Water a *Thank You* card, they can learn to appreciate it as my friend's son, Marty, found out in the next CASE CORNER.

CASE CORNER

Chase and Marty, College Roommates

The cosmic roommate lottery paired Chase (Water) and Marty (Fire) together their freshman year of college. They were both from the Midwest, but their similarities ended there. Chase dressed in gray sweats, socks, and sandals most of the time. Marty wore bright shirts with his jeans and loafers. Chase studied late into the night, but Marty hung out at local haunts with his group of new friends. Chase thought Marty was shallow and glib. Marty found Chase to be somber and morose.

One night well past midnight, Chase was asleep when Marty came back to the room with two friends. They'd obtained a bottle of rum, but since all three were underage, they were going to drink it in the privacy of Marty and Chase's room. Upset at the disturbance, Chase cussed out Marty, which really doused Marty's Fire. After that, even though they had several classes together, the guys rarely spoke.

At the end of their first semester, Chase received excellent grades, but Marty barely passed his classes. When Marty returned from holiday break, in a characteristically Fire gesture of spontaneous goodwill, he brought Chase a winter hat his grandmother had knit. Chase, who in *his* characteristically Water way had very few friends, was deeply touched. The boys started sharing a few dinners after that and soon became friends.

One evening, the topic of grades came up, and Marty grew agitated. When pressed, he admitted to Chase that he probably wasn't going to pass their philosophy class; so many of the concepts made absolutely no sense to him. An "essential universe"? What the heck was that? Chase offered to help him, but Marty would have to toe the line in terms of study time.

For the rest of the semester, Chase "controlled" the ratio of Marty's social time to study time. That meant Marty spent less time partying with friends and more time in the library with Chase. It was hard on Marty; his Fire wanted connections with people, not books. But he gained a new respect for the importance of balance and was also pleased to see that he *could* do well in classes if he applied himself.

Not surprisingly, Marty made passing grades on his homework assignments and scored a B on the final. And even though he began the school year sure that being assigned Chase as a roommate was a total disaster, he ended the year grateful for the control Chase's Water exercised over his Fire.

> **REMINDERS FOR WATER/ FIRE CONNECTIONS**
>
> *If you find yourself in a Water/Fire relationship that isn't going the way you'd like, take a moment to remind yourself what's important to the other person. If you're the Water, remember that Fires need to connect with people and things outside of themselves. If they run out to a party rather than watching a movie with you, that's normal for a Fire. If you're the Fire, remember that Waters need quiet time alone to connect inside; don't take it personally when they don't want to go out with you, or entertain your friends. And if things get rocky, reach for the Water and Fire Quick Tips covered earlier.*

III. We're So Stressed We Create Stressed Relationships

As we've learned, even if we understand our clubs and relationship dynamics, it's not always easy to get along. The problems usually start when we get stressed. Knowing what a stressed Water/Fire relationship looks like not only helps you recognize problematic aspects in your own Water/Fire relationships, it also helps you fix them. It's not hard. As we know, Water and Fire can each only go one of two places when stress is a factor: an excess state or a deficient state of energy. Let's take a look, Water first.

Water Out of Balance

» *Deficient*: A Water with too *little* Water energy will disconnect from most things around them and turn inward. In their low-energy state, they will neither notice the Fire nor have the energy to attempt to control it. This means the Fire will burn hotter than usual and become panicked and hysterical, unable to figure out why the Water has gone icy and retreated. If things don't change, the Fire could burn itself out.

Example: Eddie (Fire) and Edith (Water) each had Earth as their secondary. They were a happily married couple with two children who grew up, married, and moved away. Five years before she was set to retire, Edith was laid off. This perceived rejection took her Water deep into depression, and she withdrew from everyone. Without Edith's Water to balance his Fire in the ways it always had, Eddie became anxious and restless. He loaded up his schedule with meetings and connections. And he still tried to spend time at home with Edith, even though she mostly read and barely acknowledged him. Eddie literally worked himself sick and suffered a minor heart attack. This brought their adult daughter (an Earth) home, and she made sure both got the care they needed to recover completely. Once recovered, Eddie retired so he and Edith could travel the world.

» *Excess*: A Water with too *much* Water energy will focus solely on what they want. What other people think, feel, or need will seem less important, so the Water will become much more aggressive about forcing their ideas and beliefs on others. This flood of Water will douse the Fire's flames, leaving them scattered and overwhelmed. If this lasts, the Fire will become emotionally unstable and depleted, their characteristic joy snuffed out.

Example: Sol (Water) played a mean guitar and wrote soulful songs. Kris (Fire) was very social and knew everyone in town. She took a strong liking to Sol's music when she heard him play at a local club and offered to help him land other gigs. He accepted, and for several months it worked well for both of them. But as Sol became better known, his Water sense of self inflated, and he soon decided that the

Controlling Cycle Relationships

partnership with Kris was working solely because of him. His overly Watery attitude confused Kris and doused her enthusiasm when she pitched him. Eventually, the partnership ended because Kris just couldn't get bookings for Sol the way she had in the beginning.

» *Result:* Whether there is too much or too little Water in the relationship, the Fire is going to suffer. Too little Water will leave the Fire burned out; too much Water will leave the Fire snuffed out. Yet the pull of opposites here may make it very hard for the Fire to leave, unless they meet another Water who can help modulate, support, and balance them. To save relationships where this is happening, the Water needs to be brought back into balance.

Fire Out of Balance

» *Deficient:* A Fire person with too *little* Fire energy will lack joy, humor, and spontaneity. They will feel alone and try desperately to connect, often in clumsy or inappropriate ways. The Water person will miss the Fire's brightness and warmth, and might even feel a bit abandoned, a testament to the impact the Fire made on the Water. To help the Fire, the Water might even pull back its energy so as not to over-control it.

Example: Grace (Water) and Lizzie (Fire) ran a small auction house. They mostly handled estate liquidations; it was a living, and both were pleased. Grace evaluated the merchandise, and Lizzie ran the auctions. When their auction house burned down, Grace took it philosophically—that's what insurance is for—but Lizzie was devastated. Her enthusiasm for rebuilding never kicked in, and whenever Grace wanted her to look at the plans for the improved setup, Lizzie was scattered and found the whole thing too overwhelming. Grace managed the rebuilding on her own and was pretty miserable without Lizzie's "sunshine" around. But when the time finally came to celebrate the finished construction, Lizzie's Fire had rebuilt, and she laughed and danced at the grand reopening.

» *Excess*: A Fire person with too *much* Fire energy will laugh too loud and could appear flustered, anxious, or panicked. This will likely either annoy the quiet-loving Water into retreating, or overwhelm them with hopelessness as they try to keep the overly dramatic Fire calmed down. The downward spiral of this became apparent to my client Jessica, as seen in the next CASE CORNER.

» *Result*: Whether the relationship is suffering from too much or too little Fire, the Water is going to be miserable. Too little Fire will leave the Water feeling cold and abandoned; too much Fire will leave the Water overwhelmed with trying to calm the Fire. But the pull of opposites may make it very hard for the Water to leave, unless they meet another Fire who can warm them. To save relationships where this is happening, the Fire needs to be brought back into balance.

CASE CORNER
Excess Fire: Jessica and Doug, Sister and Brother

When a client of mine broke her foot, she couldn't serve as chaperone on her youngest son's high school band trip to Florida. Her twenty-five-year-old daughter, Jessica (Water), agreed to step in for her mother. Jessica hadn't lived at home for several years, so it would be great to have time with her brother, Doug. She loved the music, and Doug (Fire) was excited she was going, so how tough could one week be with a group of high school students?

Doug played percussion in the band and was really looking forward to the trip. But when it arrived, the sheer excitement of the adventure, coupled with tropical heat and the rousing receptions at their performances, put Doug's Fire into overdrive. After the first performance, he and several other guys from the percussion section took their drumsticks back to their rooms and paraded up and down the halls at 2:00 a.m. drumming on the walls. Jessica was horrified. She yanked Doug back into the room and told him what an idiot he was being. But Doug couldn't stop laughing about it, so she locked herself in the bathroom until he calmed down.

The next day, he and several friends hid the conductor's score before a rehearsal and were almost sent home. When Jessica found out about that, she threatened to tell their mother all that Doug was doing unless he pulled himself together. That managed to tone down his flames for a few more days, but he still cracked silly jokes, staged mock food fights with friends, and was generally almost out of control by Jessica's standards. It was all she could do to keep him focused and well behaved.

The band tour was a huge success, but Jessica returned from the trip completely exhausted. She swore she would never do anything like that again, and so far, she hasn't.

WATER/FIRE RELATIONSHIPS: THE BOTTOM LINE

Long-term relationships aren't a priority for either the Water or the Fire Club. Waters need quiet time to ponder life's mysteries. Fires need fun and excitement. Given their opposing natures, a connection between Water and Fire might seem doomed, but don't count them out. The lure of interacting with the unknown and mysterious sometimes holds these relationships together longer than anyone might expect. But if stress is part of the picture, without intervention a troubled Water/Fire relationship will likely see the Water hunkered in their quiet room and the Fire out painting the town.

If you do find yourself in a Water/Fire relationship that's having trouble, ask yourself the following questions:

» Do you understand the priorities and needs of your club and your partner's? Are your expectations for the relationship realistic?

» Do you understand the tendencies of relating on the Controlling Cycle? Is this helping or hurting what you want from the relationship?

» Are either or both of you stressed? If so, start using the Quick Tips for Waters and Fires at the ends of Chapters 3 and 5.

A QUICK WAY TO DEFUSE WATER/FIRE PROBLEMS

In the middle of a fight, we all know it's difficult to pull back (Metals are usually the only ones who can do it). For Waters and Fires in combat, here's a quick way to take down some of the intensity.

Water: Put one hand across the back of your head at the base of your skull and the other across your forehead. Look the frantic Fire in the eye, take a deep breath, and exhale a soft "Whooooooo." If there's a little energy behind it, so much the better.

Fire: Put one hand across the back of your head directly behind your eyes and the other across your forehead. Look the withering Water in the eye, take a deep breath, and exhale a soft "Heeeeeeeee." Emphasize the sighing aspect of this sound.

Repeat the process until you both feel a shift in the dynamics. When that happens, you'll probably become amused instead of upset.

CHAPTER 16

FIRE WITH METAL: THE MAD HATTER AND MR. SPOCK, FUN AND GAMES IN SPACE

The finest steel has to go through the hottest fire.
—Richard Nixon

Poor is the power of the lead that becomes bullets compared to the powerof the hot metal that becomes types.
—Georg Brandes

FIRES AND METALS RELATE VIA the Controlling Cycle, which means their connections will have a slight sense of control or opposition to them. But as we discussed, that isn't necessarily bad. In nature, too much metal can become overly rigid and lack flexibility. The Tin Man from *The Wizard of Oz* comes to mind here. Fire energy warming metal helps keep metal pliant. And it works the same way with people. The Metal will feel warmed and enlivened by the Fire, possibly even freer to explore structure and control knowing that the Fire will help keep alive a sense of flexibility and fun. Someone else in control can be freeing, especially for the Metal. The Mad Hatter might even get Spock to smile!

FIRE/METAL CONNECTIONS

Friendships: Fire people are lively, upbeat people who can uplift ordinary experiences with their enthusiasm and passion. The person excited about anything is usually a Fire. Metals are wise people able to synthesize information and develop protocol. The person insisting on the right way to do something is usually a Metal. If Fire and Metal meet up, they will certainly intrigue each other with their differences. Metal is the most solid of the elements. Fire isn't really solid; it's simply heat made visible. Fire will experience a sense of structure it has never known, and Metal can experiment with being flexible and perhaps even spontaneous. A relationship between these two will surprise a lot of people. And it might last.

Work: Fires are playful and gregarious; Metals are often deadly serious. Working together may not go over well unless they are involved in something where both Fire's charisma and Metal's deep wisdom are needed. Teaching seminars would be an excellent example. But if things get out of balance, given the directional energy of the Controlling Flow, the Metal is going to feel like the Fire is hogging the spotlight. And they likely are.

Marriage: Fire's primary relationship focus is on intense connections outside of themselves that tend to be brief. Metal's primary relationship focus is on connecting with information. If the Fire spends time connecting with others while the Metal works, this could be an excellent relationship. It would really help if one or both had a secondary Earth, too. But their mutual intrigue with each other and the chance to experience vicariously an existence they'll never have themselves might make these two inclined to stick it out for the long haul. Through the marriage, the Fire will love the structure of Metal, and the Metal will usually appreciate the spontaneity of the Fire.

Family: A Fire/Metal connection with even a little Earth will likely have children. The Metal will think it the right thing to do, and the Fire will enjoy the adventure. If they do have children, they will both be involved, although the Fire probably more so.

Over the years, I've seen many exceptional Fire/Metal relationships:

» *Brad and Laura, Husband and Wife:* Brad (Metal) is an architect; Laura (Fire, secondary Earth) is a mom. Brad is developing a computer program that creates "to scale" floor plans with furniture. So while he works late in his home office, Laura uses the time to go out for drinks with her girlfriends.

» *Kent and Trisha, Accountant and Receptionist*: Kent (Metal) hired Trisha (Fire) three years ago when his clients complained about his dreary office. He repainted, but also brought in Trisha's sunny personality to brighten things up. It worked; his clients are happier.

» *Joyce and Cara, Fundraisers:* Joyce (Metal) is an attorney who runs a charity supporting people with multiple sclerosis. Cara (Fire) is a childhood friend whose father died of MS. Cara manages the fundraisers, and Joyce makes sure the right people are invited. Together they provide valuable support for an important cause.

FIRE/METAL RELATIONSHIP CHALLENGES

As we know, when applying the Five Elements model to people and their relationships on the Controlling Cycle, there are only three ways a relationship can get into trouble. We're going to use those to explore potential challenges with Fire/Metal connections.

I. We Don't Understand Ourselves or Each Other

A person's club affiliation is determined by their energetic wiring. Members of the same club possess the same basic wiring; that's why they have similar likes, dislikes, and tendencies. When we understand this wiring, their apparent bizarre or perturbing behaviors can make total sense. Of course a Fire is going to say yes to something one minute but then change their mind several times. Of course a Metal is going to say yes once, remember that they said yes, and never budge from that position (unless given clear, logical reasons to change).

And when these behaviors aren't exactly desirable, understanding their club membership will make it easier to talk to the Fire or Metal in a language they will hear. But first, we have to understand each other.

> *Example*: A Metal friend wrote me about his widowed brother, Reese, marrying a woman named Sherry (Fire). My friend was thrilled that Reese was happy for the first time in years, but was concerned that Sherry wasn't fitting into the family. Sherry and Reese were hosting Thanksgiving, but it seemed the family's usual traditional Thanksgiving dinner was out the window. At Sherry's encouragement, she and Reese were planning a party for fifty with no turkey and a live band. I explained to my friend that Fires don't usually like too much structure, so a staid, formal dinner would not be their cup of tea. Fires also like to change things up—they get bored

easily. I encouraged him to try it and see if he liked it. To his credit he went, but not surprisingly, he didn't like the change from tradition. Metals rarely do.

II. We Don't Understand Our Relationship Dynamics

Fire and Metal relate on the Controlling Cycle, which can be both helpful and difficult. Being controlled by someone feels bad, yet having someone keep you from getting out of control can be good. And since the energy flows from Fire to Metal in this relationship, there's going to be a big dance around the issue of control. Being in control is a primary need of a Metal, so if the Fire tries to shift them too far away from their own sense of control, it won't be good. But if the Fire prevents them from getting too controlling, they will come to appreciate it, as my client Claire found out in our next CASE CORNER.

CASE CORNER
Graham and Claire, Dating

Claire (Metal) was a serious, quiet, systematic software programmer. She loved her job and how everything always worked out if she just followed the programming protocols. In her personal life, she'd never really thought of marriage because the whole idea seemed so messy: no privacy, other people's things scattered all over, noise, and the like. None of it appealed to her. Rarely lonely, Claire got a cat and decided that was enough.

To humor an Earth friend who was concerned about her, Claire agreed to a blind date. That was how she met Graham (Fire), a wonderfully funny and outgoing guy. Claire was intrigued by his unabashed enjoyment of life and laughed more than she had in years that evening, so agreed to see him again, and then again. Time with Graham became a whirlwind of activity and he rocked her well-organized, stable world.

As they settled into as much of a dating "routine" as Claire could create with the gregarious and spontaneous Graham, many of her well-ordered, quiet ways were upset. While part of her found the change exhilarating, another part of her was afraid of losing who she was. She told him they needed to stop seeing each other. Graham argued, but Claire was resolute.

Within the first month of no Graham, Claire realized how dull her life really was. She was all work and no play, an easy place for a Metal person to go. Claire and I talked about it, and I explained how Fires can keep Metals from becoming too fixed and set in their ways. Shaking things up now and then can be good for a Metal. She acknowledged that Graham certainly had done that for her.

It took Claire some time (Metals rarely do anything quickly), but eventually she agreed that she liked who she was better with Graham than without. She called him and asked him to dinner. He said yes.

> **REMINDERS FOR FIRE/METAL CONNECTIONS**
>
> *If you find yourself in a Fire/Metal relationship that isn't going the way you'd like, take a moment to remind yourself what's important to the other person. If you're the Metal, remember that Fires have little patience for long, boring discussions, so if they decline to attend a lecture on Hominid evolution with you, that's normal for a Fire. If you're the Fire, remember that Metals need time to process information to determine what is worthy of keeping and what should be discarded. If they decline to go to the exciting new fluff movie you're dying to see, that's normal for a Metal. And if things get stressed, reach for the Fire and Metal Quick Tips covered earlier.*

III. We're So Stressed We Create Stressed Relationships

As we know, even if we understand our club affiliation and relationship dynamics, it's still not easy to get along all the time. Stress changes everything, right? Knowing what a stressed Fire/Metal relationship looks like not only helps you recognize problematic aspects in your own Fire/Metal relationships, it also helps you fix them. It's not hard. Fire and Metal can each only go one of two places when stress is a factor: an excess state or a deficient state of energy. Let's take a look, Fire first.

Fire Out of Balance

» *Deficient*: A Fire with too *little* Fire energy will lose their joie de vivre, excitement, and spontaneity. They become confused and unstable, and then make poor decisions. Without the warmth of the Fire to keep them pliant, the Metal will become overcontrolling and dismissive, and will judge the Fire harshly.

Example: My client Jorge (Fire) was pursuing acting and landed the lead in a local production. The reviews of his performance were thoughtful and insightful, but decidedly unkind. This Watery deluge not only dampened Jorge's passion for performing, it also doused his usual Fire enthusiasm, which affected his performance as head bartender at work. His boss, Alexi (Metal), was patient with Jorge for a while, but the humor and congeniality Jorge brought to his job was key to the tone of the restaurant. Soon, not only was Jorge subdued, he started making mistakes on his drinks and beverage orders. Without Jorge's fun-loving style to keep her relaxed, Alexi became more controlling and demanding. Eventually she gave Jorge an ultimatum: Snap out of it or leave. He left.

» *Excess*: A Fire with too *much* Fire energy will insist on more connection than the Metal is willing to give. They will laugh too loud for the attention, and then panic when it isn't forthcoming. The Metal will be surprised by the change and become either unforgiving or judgmental. But if the Fire keeps burning hot, the Metal will detach to protect itself from what appears to be inevitable destruction.

Example: Several years ago, a client told me about a high school student named Franklin (Metal) who petitioned the court to live with his father instead of his mother. No one could figure out why Franklin would do that because his mother, Becca (Fire), was one of the coolest people around. She was outgoing and fun, and everyone wanted to be her friend. But according to my client, Franklin was an extremely serious, studious boy who Becca believed was

Controlling Cycle Relationships

ignoring life. She encouraged Franklin to drink at home, attend parties where alcohol was served, and go out with kids who were more "fun" than the few close friends he had. It didn't surprise me that Franklin wanted to leave; Becca's Fire was likely extremely threatening to him.

» *Result*: Whether the relationship is suffering from too much or too little Fire, the Metal is going to be affected. Too little Fire will leave the Metal feeling momentarily confused by the lack of warmth, but they will cover any hurt with a rigid display of dismissiveness and detachment. Too much Fire will threaten Metal's survival, and they'll detach to avoid a complete meltdown. To save relationships where this is happening, the Fire needs to be brought back into balance.

Metal Out of Balance

» *Deficient*: A Metal with too *little* Metal energy will cling to their opinions and self-image like a life raft. As their structure weakens and falls apart, their ability to let go will desert them. The Fire will be frustrated by the missing structure and process in life and bored by the same old, same old going on yet again.

Example: Jana (Fire) and Della (Metal) were business partners who ran training seminars on spirituality in the twenty-first century. Jana brought the transcendent experience, and Della brought the rational explanations. When Della's husband died, the Earthy home environment that had fed her Metal disappeared. Time went by, and Della couldn't clear out her husband's things or get herself back into the orderly daily rhythm she'd had for decades. Jana understood Della's loss, but she and the business needed Della's structure. Della tried to come back to work but was confused and kept repeating herself. Jana hung in there, but seriously considered closing things down. Fortunately, an Earth friend of Della's moved in with her for a while and helped her sort through her husband's things. This nurturing flow of Earth energy built Della's Metal, and very soon she was able to bring her full self back to the business.

» *Excess*: A Metal with too *much* Metal energy will lose their characteristic reasonableness. They will become inflexible, rigid, and insistent on strict adherence to their normal routines and protocol. This will constrict the Fire, and they will either jump away from the Metal to avoid confinement or burn brighter to try to soften the overly structured Metal. An interesting twist on a Fire's ability to help a Metal is featured in the next CASE CORNER.

» *Result:* Whether the relationship is threatened by too much or too little Metal, the Fire is going to suffer. Too little Metal will leave the Fire scattered without the structure Metal usually provides. Too much Metal will confine the Fire, who will either leave or burn hotter to melt the restrictive Metal. To save relationships where this is happening, the Metal needs to be brought back into balance.

CASE CORNER

Excess Metal: Kylee and Ron, Tutor and Student

Ron (Metal) was an eighth grader I knew who was having trouble at school. His home life was unpredictable—there was a special-needs younger sister, plus his parents were divorced—and Ron had ramped up his Metal to try to stabilize life around him. That meant, in search of structure, Ron had become controlling and demanding at school, as well as verbally judgmental of several fellow students who weren't as mentally capable as he was. He wasn't overtly cruel, but his words and attitude stung the few friends he still had.

Ron's grandmother hired Kylee (Fire) to work with him. Kylee knew Ron's background and suspected that in spite of his bravado, he was probably hurting inside. She tutored him three times a week and with her naturally sunny disposition, she brought fun and giggles with her smarts. She had contests instead of tests for Ron. She built on the fact that he was an excellent researcher (Metals usually are) and assigned him "homework" to find trivia and facts that she knew he'd enjoy. Kylee made studying fun and easy for Ron, which gave him a sense of control over that part of his life.

It took several months, but the warming energy Kylee's Fire brought, along with her wisdom regarding how best to deal with Ron, did soften his Metal. Soon his teachers noticed that he wasn't as aloof as he'd been and even had a few new friends. Kylee worked with Ron off and on through high school. During that time, his mother remarried and his home life stabilized. Ron graduated from high school with honors and a full scholarship to the college he wanted to attend. And Kylee was front row center at his graduation.

FIRE/METAL RELATIONSHIPS: THE BOTTOM LINE

Long-term relationships aren't a priority for either the Fire or the Metal Club. Fires need the energy of spontaneity and fun. Metals need the quiet, controlled order of study. Yet the interaction of structure and order with warmth and passion often holds these two together in spite of their dramatic differences. But if stress is part of the picture, without intervention a troubled Fire/Metal relationship will likely see the Fire breaking free and the Metal ensconced in their ivory tower.

If you do find yourself in a Fire/Metal relationship that's having trouble, ask yourself the following questions:

» Do you understand the priorities and needs of your club and your partner's? Are your expectations for the relationship realistic?

» Do you understand the tendencies of relating on the Controlling Cycle? Is this helping or hurting what you want from the relationship?

» Are either or both of you stressed? If so, start using the Quick Tips for Fires and Metals at the ends of Chapters 5 and 7.

A QUICK WAY TO DEFUSE FIRE/METAL PROBLEMS

In the middle of a fight, the Metal might be able to detach, but not the Fire. For Fires and Metals in combat, here's a quick way to take down some of the intensity.

Fire: Put one hand across the back of your head directly behind your eyes and the other across your forehead. Look the unreasonable Metal in the eye, take a deep breath, and exhale a soft "Heeeeeeeee." Emphasize the sighing aspect of this sound.

Metal: Place one hand on the top of your head and the other across the front of your forehead. Look the panicked Fire in the eye, take a deep breath, and exhale softly making a "Ssssssssssss" sound, like the air leaking from a tire.

Repeat the process until you both feel a shift in the dynamics. Don't be surprised if you become relieved instead of disturbed.

CHAPTER 17

METAL WITH WOOD: MR. SPOCK AND THOR, BRAINS AND BRAWN FACE OFF

*Wood is much harder to produce than metal.
And metal is recyclable, while wood isn't.*
—Helmut Jahn

Be like a tree and let the dead leaves drop.
—Rumi

METALS AND WOODS RELATE VIA the Controlling Cycle, which I can tell you from personal experience means these connections will have a slight feeling of control or opposition. But I can also tell you that this isn't necessarily bad. In nature, too much wood grows thick and dense, making it impossible for the sunlight so necessary for life and sustenance to penetrate. If this happens, the wood dies. Metal pruning wood trees keeps them alive and vibrant. Controlling Cycle relationships with people can work much the same way. Wood people can go a bit farther "out there" knowing that the Metal person is around to help keep them in check. Hopefully Spock, in his wisdom, would appreciate Thor's assistance.

METAL/WOOD CONNECTIONS

Friendships: Metals are wise people who can look back across a whole cycle and determine what's worth keeping and what should be discarded. The person telling you what matters is probably a Metal. Woods are productive people who can usually get any job done. The person shouting, "I'll do it!" is probably a Wood. Metal and Wood are the two most structured elements, so a connection between them will thrive on organization and the ability to glimpse unknown territory: Metal is new yin, the energy of contraction; Wood is new yang, the energy of expansion. This is another example of opposites supporting each other. The Metal person will appreciate being involved in making things happen. The Wood person will appreciate Metal's understanding of what has and has not worked in the past.

Work: Metals and Woods are both structured, focus-oriented people. But their focuses are diametrically opposed. Metals look to the past, while Woods look to the future. Yet when they can appreciate this about each other, they can accomplish anything. Wood brings planning and the energy to manifest the plan. Metal brings structure, process, and an analysis of the plan. The biggest challenge will be who gets the credit. Wood needs personal success; Metal needs acknowledgment. But with the two of them working together, there should be enough of both to go around.

Marriage: Metal's primary relationship focus is on connecting with information and synthesizing it. Wood's primary relationship focus is on connecting with outer accomplishments. They aren't going to spend a lot of personal time together unless one or both have a secondary Earth. They will thrive on their individual and joint accomplishments though, and just need to remember to make time for romance.

Family: A Metal/Wood connection may or may not have children. Both may think they "should" have a family, but neither will be especially interested unless there's some Earth energy in the mix. If they do have a family, they will probably hire nannies. Family vacations, however, will be extravagant.

Over the years, I've seen many tremendous Metal/Wood relationships:

- » *Les and Randy, Coauthors:* **These guys are writing an incredible novel. They came up with the plot together, and both love to write. Les (Metal) is doing most of the research, and Randy (Wood) makes sure things keep moving.**
- » *Roger and Maya, Husband and Wife*: **Roger (Metal) and Maya (Wood) have been married for twenty years. He's an architect, and she runs a construction business. You should see their house!**
- » *Grady and Holly, Road Rally Team*: **These two are a boatload of fun. Grady (Wood) drives the car, and Holly (Metal) manages the maps. It's a weekend hobby that keeps them happy, excited, and engaged. They both especially like it when they win.**

METAL/WOOD RELATIONSHIP CHALLENGES

As stated, there are only three ways a Five Elements relationship can get into trouble. We're going to use those to explore potential challenges with Metal/Wood connections.

I. We Don't Understand Ourselves or Each Other

A member of the Metal Club possesses the same wiring as every other Metal Club member. The same is true of any single Wood person and the whole of the Wood Club. And when we understand this wiring, their apparent bizarre or perturbing behaviors can make total sense. Of course a Wood is going to proactively offer thirty reasons a project should begin immediately. Of course a Metal is going to reactively respond with their own thirty reasons the project should wait. And when these behaviors aren't exactly desirable, understanding their club will make it easier to talk to the Metal or Wood person in a language they will hear. But first, we have to understand each other.

> *Example*: Maria (Wood), a client of mine, worked as a brand manager at a packaged goods firm. She was excellent at conceiving and launching brand improvements as well as product spin-offs. As a Wood, she had a real hands-on approach to her job that management appreciated. So when Lee (Metal), the division manager, became ill, Maria was asked to step into his role for the three months he would be out. Maria agreed and was excited to show what she could do. But the hands-on approach that had worked so well for her as brand manager became a liability as head of the division. Lee's job was supervising a mature and very functional group made up of innovative managers using the tried-and-true process and protocol already in place. Maria tried to "improve" the process and was seen as interfering.

When Lee returned, Maria was very happy to go back to the excitement of innovation.

II. We Don't Understand Our Relationship Dynamics

Metal and Wood relate on the Controlling Cycle, which brings a special dynamic between these two because both have issues around control. Metal wants to be in control; Wood wants to avoid being out of control. It's a subtle difference, but trust me, an important one. It's not made any easier by the fact that Metal's wiring really does think it's their job to make sure Wood doesn't get out of control. My client Melody became a pro at this dynamic while raising two boys: one a Metal, the other a Wood. Her story is in the next CASE CORNER.

CASE CORNER

Trevor and Timmy, Brothers

When they were young, Trevor (Metal) and Timmy (Wood) got along famously. They were each other's best friend and even shared the same room. But about the time Trevor turned sixteen and Timmy was twelve, they began fighting. Trevor often came off like a know-it-all, which wasn't hard because he really was a smart guy. But smart or not, Timmy didn't like Trevor correcting him or telling him what to do. It was especially embarrassing for Timmy if Trevor corrected him in front of the rest of the family, even though sometimes the corrections were appropriate. Their mom, Melody, tried to tell Timmy that Trevor was just trying to help, but Timmy didn't care.

The family lived with the arguing for a year, but Melody finally called me after a particularly disturbing fight. She had separated the boys before things got physical but was worried what might happen if she wasn't around to step in. I explained to her that while some fighting and competition was natural in siblings, and the older brother usually does have the upper hand, there was something bigger than either of these going on, something that would be part of the boys' relationship for the rest of their lives.

I helped her understand the Five Elements model and the Controlling Cycle that defined Trevor and Timmy's relationship. Not only was Timmy at a disadvantage being the youngest, but Trevor's Metal would always feel controlling to Timmy's Wood. Both could make him feel stuck and "less than" much of the time—bad places for the "need to succeed" Wood.

Once Melody understood what was happening, she went home and had private talks with both boys. Trevor agreed to let Timmy make his own mistakes so he could learn from them. He also agreed to quietly facilitate opportunities for Timmy to succeed at something and was instrumental in Timmy's science fair project making it to the state level. For his part, Timmy begrudgingly agreed that Trevor probably had more experience than he did so might have sound advice to offer.

Both boys tried, and things did get back to a more peaceful place at home. But Melody continues to believe that the change that made the biggest difference was when the family started calling Timmy by the name of Tim. And she could be right.

> **REMINDERS FOR METAL/WOOD CONNECTIONS**
>
> *If you find yourself in a Metal/Wood relationship that isn't going the way you'd like, take a moment to remind yourself what's important to the other person. If you're the Wood, remember that Metals focus on the past, so if they don't want to spend hours discussing possible destinations for a vacation two years away, that's normal for a Metal. If you're the Metal, remember that Woods need to accomplish their goals, so if they would rather work on their own projects than listen to you explain yours, that's normal for a Wood. And if things get stressed, reach for the Metal and Wood Quick Tips covered earlier.*

III. We're So Stressed We Create Stressed Relationships

Even if we understand our clubs and relationship dynamics, it's still not easy to get along all the time. Stress can change everything. Knowing what a stressed Metal/Wood relationship looks like not only helps you recognize problematic aspects in your own Metal/Wood relationships, it also helps fix them. It's not hard. Metal and Wood can each only go one of two places when stress is a factor: an excess state or a deficient state. Let's take a look, Metal first.

Metal Out of Balance

» *Deficient*: A Metal with too *little* Metal will lose their grip on the perfectionism that drives them and become hopelessly disorganized. The Wood will become frustrated by the Metal's inability to provide the necessary process and protocol, and missing the Metal's controlling influence, they will probably get angry and out of control themselves.

Example: Rhonda (Wood) and Jasper (Metal) ran a business specializing in African artifacts. Jasper managed the office and was especially brilliant with the detailed paperwork necessary to import from a foreign country. Rhonda was a fantastic salesperson (Woods frequently are) and racked up excellent sales at the trade shows she attended. But when the IRS audited their company, the stress of the experience took its toll on Jasper. Nonstop worry that his records weren't going to pass muster depleted his Metal, and he started making mistakes on the import documents necessary to land the goods needed to fill Rhonda's orders. Deeply frustrated, Rhonda ranted about Jasper to her husband (also a Metal), who offered to help Jasper get organized. He did, and once the audit was over without penalty, Jasper was soon back to his lovable, picky self.

» *Excess*: A Metal with too *much* Metal energy will find their normal reasonableness deserting them. They will become domineering, dismissive, and controlling. They will work almost constantly. When this happens, the Wood will feel overcontrolled, which will likely make them frustrated and angry. A whopper of a fight could be on the horizon.

Example: My friend Amanda (Wood) hired an interior designer to help her decorate her new house. Clara (Metal) came highly recommended for her excellent taste and attention to detail. But when Amanda started working with her, there wasn't any room in Clara's world for what Amanda wanted. They started with the living room, and when Amanda said she wanted to include her grandmother's coffee table in the room, rather dismissively Clara informed her that it didn't "go" with the look they were creating and had to be removed. Amanda felt controlled and stopped in her tracks, not a good feeling for a Wood. Soon it was Clara who was removed.

» *Result:* Whether the relationship is suffering from too much or too little Metal, the Wood is going to be angry and frustrated. Too little Metal will leave the over-energized Wood working overtime to pick up the slack and questioning the benefit of the Metal's partnership. Too much Metal will find the Wood dreaming of freedom under the weight of process and control. To save relationships where this is happening, the Metal needs to be brought back into balance.

Wood Out of Balance

» *Deficient:* A Wood with too *little* Wood energy will lose their drive and ability to accomplish anything. The Wood's indecisiveness and lack of results will displease the Metal, but the kindness of the Metal might cause them to pull back some of their energy to allow the Wood space to grow. On the other hand, the Metal's need for perfection might cause them to question the Wood's value and necessity.

Example: Many years ago, two teenagers decide to put on a small musical for our neighborhood. Nancy (Metal) was an accomplished classical guitarist, and Gina (Wood) was passable on flute. The idea was that Nancy would arrange the venue (folding chairs under a lovely oak tree), and Gina would sell tickets to the neighbors. At the first house Gina visited, the neighbor berated her quite sternly for being so pushy as to ask that everyone pay five dollars to attend an amateur show. It took the wind out of Gina's sails—and sales. Her poor little Wood shriveled up, and the sad outcome was that she failed miserably as a salesperson. Nancy was initially disgusted with Gina's inability to deliver an audience, but her kind feelings toward her friend kicked in and her balanced Metal let it go.

» *Excess*: A Wood with too *much* Wood energy will become impatient and reckless, and the results they obtain will be compromised. The Wood's aggressive behavior and lack of productivity will initially sadden the Metal, but the obvious need for the Wood to be controlled will cause them to step up. A battle over control is likely, which will probably cause the Metal to detach. An interesting twist on this dynamic is featured in the next CASE CORNER.

» *Result*: Whether the relationship is suffering from too much or too little Wood, the Metal is going to be displeased. Too little Wood will leave the Metal questioning the value of the Wood, but the wise Metal might realize what's happening and pull back a bit. Too much Wood will likely bring out the Metal's pruning shears, which will lead to a battle over control. To save relationships where this is happening, the Wood needs to be brought back into balance.

CASE CORNER

Excess Wood: Wilson and Roland, Life Partners

Wilson (Wood) and Roland (Metal) have been together for twenty-five years. Wilson had his own construction business, and Roland managed the house and worked as a freelance accountant. When Wilson retired, his Wood energy had nowhere to go, so he went off the deep end envisioning, planning, building, and completing projects for the couple's yard. He built new decks, laid out new gardens, and constructed new trellises. He created deadlines for himself, too, as if *this* was his new job. There were few conversations between the two of them that did not include Wilson's ongoing ideas for their property.

Finally, Roland called me. He was worried that Wilson was overdoing it, but he was also feeling controlled, not a good feeling for a Metal. Before Wilson retired, Roland had been in charge of the gardening; it was his world. But Wilson had taken it over, and now he even watered Roland's plants. Roland was concerned that Wilson seemed to be making a division—his world would be outside, and Roland's would be inside. But Roland wanted none of that. What could he do?

It was clear that in retirement, Wilson probably had no idea what to do with all the Wood energy he'd put into his successful business, so was looking for projects. Unfortunately, Roland's garden was an easy target. I explained the Five Elements model to Roland and told him that as a Metal, he was the perfect person to help "prune" Wilson's excess Wood. We discussed strategies, all of which included *not* telling Wilson "no." A Wood stopped in their tracks is like a car hitting a brick wall—it's ugly for all. Finally, we developed a plan that Roland liked.

First, Roland expressed to Wilson how he missed his time in the garden and asked if there was a way he could help with what was being done. Wilson was happy to have Roland help him, which at least got Roland back outside. Next, as they were working on the garden one day, Roland expressed his gratitude for all that Wilson was doing, which made Wilson feel good. Then Roland mentioned he had a few ideas to add to Wilson's list of projects and wondered if they could discuss them sometime. Wilson just needed to be productive, so was happy to do those, too. Several months later, Roland was back to "owning" the garden while Wilson built the new garage they both wanted.

METAL/WOOD RELATIONSHIPS: THE BOTTOM LINE

Personal relationships aren't a high priority for either the Metal or the Wood Club. Metals care about understanding the past, and Woods care about creating the future. Yet the lure of joint success and acknowledgment from using the past to create the future can be intoxicating for both. Going forward, if they can address their individual issues around control and who gets to be right, a relationship between a Metal and a Wood can be pretty stable. But if stress is part of the picture, without intervention a troubled Metal/Wood relationship will likely split so each can do things their own way.

If you do find yourself in a Metal/Wood relationship that's having trouble, ask yourself the following questions:

» Do you understand the priorities and needs of your club and your partner's? Are your expectations for the relationship realistic?

» Do you understand the tendencies of relating on the Controlling Cycle? Is this helping or hurting what you want from the relationship?

» Are either or both of you stressed? If so, start using the Quick Tips for Metals and Woods at the ends of Chapters 7 and 4.

A QUICK WAY TO DEFUSE METAL/WOOD PROBLEMS

In the middle of a fight, the Metal might be able to detach, but not the Wood. For Metals and Woods in combat, here's a quick way to take down some of the intensity.

Metal: Place one hand on the top of your head and the other across the front of your forehead. Look the insensitive Wood in the eye, take a deep breath, and exhale softly making a "Sssssssssssss" sound, like the air leaking from a tire.

Wood: Put your thumbs at the outside edges of your eyes and rest your fingers across your forehead. Look the finicky Metal in the eye, take a deep breath, and exhale a sharp "Shhhhhhhhh." Push that sound out vigorously at the end.

Repeat the process until you both feel a shift in the dynamics. That means you're ready to get back to work.

CHAPTER 18

WOOD WITH EARTH: THOR AND DOROTHY GALE, THE GALACTIC MEANING OF HOME

A tree falls the way it leans.
—Bulgarian Proverb

Service to others is the rent you pay for your room here on Earth.
—Muhammad Ali

WOODS AND EARTHS RELATE VIA the Controlling Cycle, but their experience of a Controlling Cycle relationship will be slightly different from the three we just covered. Water/Fire, Fire/Metal, and Metal/Wood all use oppositions to create balance: Water/Fire balances yin against yang, Fire/Metal balances least structure against most structure, and Metal/Wood balances new yin against new yang. The Wood/Earth relationship involves a supportive, rather than oppositional, balancing mechanism because Earth doesn't anchor a polarity. Instead, it's the element of balance for the whole system. In nature, wood "controls" earth by stabilizing it, not decreasing it. This means Dorothy and Thor could be best friends forever!

As we have said, Controlling Cycle relationships will have a slight feeling of control or opposition, and the Wood/Earth connection is no exception. Wood stabilizing Earth when it needs it may mean toning down caring and compassion. But it can also mean that the Earth can help more people knowing that the Wood is there to keep them from overdoing.

WOOD/EARTH CONNECTIONS

Friendships: Woods are dynamic and grounded people who stand up for the underdog. The person who cares passionately about fairness is usually a Wood. Earths are deeply compassionate people who love helping others and making a difference. The person asking, "Can I help you?" is usually an Earth. Wood and Earth have a symbiotic relationship: Wood stabilizes Earth with its root structure; Earth nourishes Wood with its nutrients. This dynamic will lend a nurturing quality to this Controlling Cycle friendship. Earth will appreciate Wood's stability, and Wood will appreciate Earth's caring and altruism.

Work: Woods are forward-thinking, decisive people. They know the goal and can envision how to get there. Sadly for Woods, the ends can often justify the means. Earth people are slower to move because they take time to ponder before acting. They care about the effect their actions have on others and want all to be well for everyone. If these two can honor what each brings to the table, they will create a wonderfully comfortable and productive work environment. If not, the Wood will probably think the Earth slow, and the Earth will probably find the Wood harsh.

Marriage: Wood's primary relationship focus is on connecting with outer accomplishments. Earth's primary relationship focus is on deep, lasting relationships with others. A connection between the two will look like the stereotypical 1950s marriage: The Wood person will go to work, and the Earth person will stay home with the children. And that can be great for both! The Wood will focus on achievement and the financial gains that provides, and the Earth will create a home and develop deep connections with a family. And as long as both equally value what the other contributes, this will be a rock-solid marriage.

Family: In almost any home relationship with an Earth, children are a given. Family matters deeply to Earths. And the Wood will be fine with that, see it as their legacy, and trust the Earth to manage things well.

Over the years, I have seen many, many exceptional Wood/Earth relationships:

- » *Ned and Anita, Husband and Wife:* Ned (Wood) and Anita (Earth) have been best friends since first grade. They married right after college and have three adorable children. She stays home with the children and he goes to work every day. It's a dream marriage for both.
- » *Connie and Mike, Attorney and Paralegal:* Connie (Wood) is a high-powered trial attorney. Mike (Earth, with a secondary Metal) is her right-hand guy and knows exactly what she needs to win a case. They've been a team long enough that Mike frequently has material for Connie before she even asks.

» *Denise and Leah, Restaurateurs:* Denise (Wood) and Leah (Earth) opened a small restaurant in the Fulton Market area of Chicago. Leah's an inventive whiz in the kitchen, and Denise is a brilliant manager. Things are looking pretty rosy for this duo.

WOOD/EARTH RELATIONSHIP CHALLENGES

As we know, there are only three ways a Five Elements relationship can get into trouble. We're going to use those to explore potential challenges with Wood/Earth connections.

I. We Don't Understand Ourselves or Each Other

All members of the Wood Club are wired the same as every other Wood Club member. The same is true of any single Earth person and the whole of the Earth Club. Understanding this wiring means their apparent bizarre or perturbing behaviors can make total sense. Of course a Wood will want attention when they come home at night. Of course an Earth will think feeding the baby is a good reason not to meet them at the door. And when these behaviors aren't exactly desirable, understanding their club will make it easier to talk to the Wood or Earth person in a language they'll hear. But first, we have to understand each other.

Example: Ronnie (Earth), a friend of mine, and her older brother, Rick (Earth), come from a whole family of very Earthy teachers. About two years after Rick was widowed, he started dating Peggy (Wood), who he thought was the most "together" woman he'd ever met. He raved on and on about Peggy, so his family invited her for Thanksgiving dinner. Well, Peggy's Wood was a total shock. She questioned Ronnie's mother about when to start cooking a casserole and disagreed with their older sister's opinion of a movie. The whole family was flummoxed, and Rick finally took Peggy home early. The good news is that I explained the difference between

Earths and Woods to Ronnie so she was able to help the family understand that Peggy wasn't really rude, she was just opinionated. Last I heard, Peggy and Rick are still together.

II. We Don't Understand Our Relationship Dynamics

Wood and Earth relate on the Controlling Cycle. And while that does bring a sense of control, as we said earlier, it's also about support, which is a good thing. Since the energy flows from Wood to Earth, it's the Earth who will feel the constraints of control more than the Wood. If a Wood relating to an Earth remembers to think in terms of support instead of control (not an easy mission for a Wood given their dislike of being out of control), all will be well. This is a lesson my client Nick found out the hard way.

CASE CORNER
Nick and Susie, Executive and Administrative Assistant

Nick (Wood) was a very successful marketing executive in almost every way possible. He was brilliant at his work and rose up the ranks quickly. His salary improved annually. He earned awards and accolades from his superiors. His clients adored him. Nick's only real problem was that his administrative assistants kept quitting. He often went through one a year. But rather than wonder if it was something about him, he complained loudly that he just couldn't get good help anymore.

After the resignation of his third administrative assistant in two years, he brought the issue up with me. I asked him what he looked for in an assistant, and he rattled off a rather perfect description of an Earth. He wanted them to be kind and caring, good with people, willing to get him food or coffee, and able to help others with problems so that he didn't have to deal with them. Of course there were additional business skill sets, but the personality was clearly Earth.

I pulled out my trusty Five Elements model and explained how it worked. I also described the tendencies of Wood (easy for me), and Nick agreed that within the confines of the model, he was certainly a Wood. Next, I described Earths and asked if they sounded similar to his requirements for an assistant. He had to agree with me there, too. Finally, I pointed out that even if he never opened his mouth, his Wood was probably going to feel a little controlling to any Earth assistant he hired.

This concerned him because he didn't want to change his requirements for an assistant—he wanted that kind of person. I countered that he didn't need to change the assistants; he needed to change how he related to them. We had a lively discussion about support vs. control, tone of voice, and temper. I suspect Nick was somewhat overwhelmed when he left. But he did try, and the last assistant he had (Susie) lasted three years. The only reason she left was to start a family.

REMINDERS FOR WOOD/EARTH CONNECTIONS

If you find yourself in a Wood/Earth relationship that isn't going the way you'd like, take a moment to remind yourself what's important to the other person. If you're the Earth, remember that Woods can find socializing frivolous—that's normal for a Wood. If you want them to attend a family party, give them a role. If you're the Wood, remember that Earths value peace and harmony, so if they don't want to watch the Super Bowl with you because of the violence, that's normal for an Earth. And if things get stressed, reach for the Wood and Earth Quick Tips covered earlier.

III. We're So Stressed We Create Stressed Relationships

Sometimes it's still not easy to get along all the time, even if we understand our clubs and relationship dynamics. Stress can change everything. Knowing what a stressed Wood/Earth relationship looks like not only helps you recognize problematic aspects in your own Wood/Earth relationships, it also helps fix them. It's not hard. Wood and Earth can each only go one of two places when stress is a factor: an excess state or a deficient state. Let's take a look, Wood first.

Wood Out of Balance

» *Deficient*: A Wood person with too *little* Wood energy loses their initiative. They become indecisive and unable to do much of anything. When their productivity drops off, they'll feel humiliated and withdraw from people, especially those closest to them who they know they're letting down. The Earth will feel lost without the support, worry that they've done something wrong, and try harder. But this will only make the Wood feel worse and possibly lash out in frustration.

Example: Todd (Wood) and Sharine (Earth) had a lovely home with two adorable little girls. Todd was doing well managing a high-end restaurant right up until the time the chain was sold and the restaurants consolidated. His restaurant was closed, and the new owners made it clear that—nothing personal—there was no other restaurant for him. They gave him a great severance package, so the family finances were secure for a while, but Todd was shaken to his core and his Wood tanked. Sharine was supportive, but that only made Todd feel worse. He started drinking (easy for a Wood to do) and couldn't get his act together to look for work.

Fortunately, a good friend asked Todd and a few other guys on a weeklong fishing trip, and Sharine encouraged him to go. Completely removing Todd from the situation (and the people he felt he was letting down) helped him put things in perspective, and he returned from the trip ready to tackle the job search. Months later he landed an excellent position with an up-and-coming restaurant in town.

» *Excess*: A Wood person with too *much* Wood energy becomes aggressive and determined to get what they want no matter the obstacles. The ends will justify the means, and Wood will put any necessary structure in place to accomplish their goal. The Earth will feel completely overwhelmed, possibly restricted, and worried that they have done something wrong. If they reach out to the Wood, the Wood will brush them aside in pursuit of their success.

Example: This is a funny story that came to me via the blog I write on using the Five Elements to help relationships. A woman we'll call Missy (Earth) wrote in about a neighbor (clearly a Wood) who, during the heat of the summer, frequently invited herself and her two ill-behaved children over to use Missy's inground pool. The neighbor's children splashed water all over, ran around the pool when they were told to walk, and were generally rude. It ruined the pool time for Missy's whole family when they were there, but Missy's Earth felt trapped in the face of this overabundance of Wood. She didn't want to be rude or hurt feelings, but did ask the neighbor not to come over uninvited. The neighbor ignored her request and continued to drop in. Finally, Missy's Metal husband went over and spoke to the neighbors. I thought of it as an act of kindness: his Metal pruned the neighbor's clearly overabundant Wood.

» *Result*: Whether the relationship is suffering from too much or too little Wood, the Earth is going to worry that they've done something wrong. Too little Wood will leave the Earth lost and unsupported, trying harder to please the Wood. Too much Wood will cause the Earth to feel overstructured and unsure how to bring things back to normal. To save relationships where this is happening, the Wood needs to be brought back into balance.

Earth Out of Balance

» *Deficient*: An Earth person with too *little* Earth energy becomes clingy and wants assurance from others that everything is okay, even though they're sure it's not. Any kind of separation from loved ones will make the Earth anxious and more needy. The Wood will be confused and frustrated by this behavior, as it will slow their momentum. The Earth will sense the Wood's displeasure and feel abandoned.

Example: Nadia (Earth) and Weston (Wood) had a son named Drake who was autistic. Weston worked long hours, so the care of little Drake fell to Nadia. In true Earth style, she gave her all to her son and refused help from Weston or their friends. But as her Earth depleted, Nadia began calling Weston at work more frequently just to make sure he was okay. Soon, she was interrupting his meetings, worried that he hadn't returned her call from an hour earlier. Weston finally told Nadia that she either got help with Drake or he was leaving. Fortunately, Nadia had a sister who was in between jobs and could move in for a time. The loving attention she gave to Nadia, plus the help with Drake, allowed Nadia's Earth to rebuild. By the time her sister left for a new job in Europe, Nadia had hired a trained assistant and life for her, Weston, and Drake was happy again.

Controlling Cycle Relationships

» *Excess:* An Earth person with too *much* Earth energy obsessively worries that they aren't doing enough. To feel needed, they will meddle and insert themselves in an interfering way. An Earth in excess is often looking for people with whom they can bond, which often leads to codependency. The Wood will feel suffocated and irritated by the Earth's intrusions and pull away. This will only make the Earth more worried and less supported. How this dynamic unfolded in an interesting way is featured in the next CASE CORNER.

» *Result:* Whether the relationship is suffering from too much or too little Earth energy, the Earth is going to be needy and worried. Too little Earth will leave the Wood frustrated by the added attention the Earth requires and the amount of time that takes away from their personal pursuits. Too much Earth will find the Wood irritated by the Earth's meddling and interference, which moves them off task. To save relationships where this is happening, the Earth needs to be brought back into balance.

CASE CORNER

Excess Earth: Ed and Paulo, Coworkers

Ed (Wood) and Paulo (Earth) both worked for the same software firm. The offices at the firm weren't really offices; it was an "open concept" setup that basically meant everyone but upper management worked in semi-open cubicles. Ed did marketing and forecasting for the firm and took his job very seriously. He was there to work and when done, he headed home to his wife. He'd been with the company three years and had already indicated that he had his eye on a private office.

Paulo, my client, was an upbeat, single guy who'd been hired two years earlier to help with promotions. But his Earth needed to connect with people, so he was very social with the people on his floor. Paulo was on a budget, so took his lunch every day, as did several of the other employees. They all shared lunch together outside (if the Chicago weather was nice) or in the break room. Over time, Paulo became friends with many of the other employees.

About a year ago, Paulo was leaning over the edge of a friend's cube checking in on her sick brother when Ed walked by and rather harshly asked him to keep his voice down. Paulo felt badly, and when he was done talking to his friend, he went to Ed and apologized. Ed snapped that this was an office, not a dorm, and stomped away. This made Paulo feel even worse.

Whenever their paths would cross, Ed made it very clear that he had no use for Paulo, which upset Paulo's need to be connected. To feel needed, Paulo started inserting himself more frequently into the affairs of the other employees. Some found him caring, but most felt he was borderline nosey, perhaps even meddling. At the point someone from human resources spoke with him, Paulo set up his first appointment with me.

During that first session, Paulo explained that he'd moved to this country just three years ago, leaving his mother, father, and siblings behind. He'd been close to his father, who I gathered was a Wood, and missed the advice his father used to give him. It seemed likely that without his father's Wood to help keep Paulo stable, his Earth had become excessive. Using many of the Earth Quick Tips from Chapter 6, we worked to bring Paulo's Earth back into balance. As he mellowed, not only did he get along better with his fellow employees, including Ed, he lost thirty pounds because he was no longer eating the sweets his excessive Earth craved.

WOOD/EARTH RELATIONSHIPS: THE BOTTOM LINE

The Wood Club doesn't emphasize long-term connections. Conversely, relationships are everything to the Earth Club. Yet just as nature has shown, where wood anchors earth and earth feeds wood, these two clubs often create stable, mutually beneficial relationships. Woods create success; Earths support the process. And this works as long as they can maintain the balance between independence and dependence, autonomy and connection. But if stress is part of the picture, without intervention a troubled Wood/Earth relationship will see the frustrated Wood leave while the caring Earth tries harder.

If you do find yourself in a Wood/Earth relationship that's having trouble, ask yourself the following questions:

» Do you understand the priorities and needs of your club and your partner's? Are your expectations for the relationship realistic?

» Do you understand the tendencies of relating on the Controlling Cycle? Is this helping or hurting what you want from the relationship?

» Are either or both of you stressed? If so, start using the Quick Tips for Woods and Earths at the ends of Chapters 4 and 6.

> ## A QUICK WAY TO DEFUSE WOOD/EARTH PROBLEMS
>
> *In the middle of a fight, a Metal might be able to detach, but not a Wood or Earth. For Woods and Earths in combat, here's a quick way to take down some of the intensity.*
>
> *Wood: Put your thumbs at the outside edges of your eyes and rest your fingers across your forehead. Look the needy Earth in the eye, take a deep breath, and exhale a sharp "Shhhhhhhhh." Push that sound out vigorously at the end.*
>
> *Earth: Place the thumbs of each hand on your cheekbones directly below your eyes and rest the fingers of each hand across your forehead. Look the warrior Wood in the eye, take a deep breath, and exhale softly making an "Aummmmm" sound, like the OM. Make the sound prayerful.*
>
> *Repeat the process until you both feel a shift in the dynamics, which means that life can get back to normal.*

CHAPTER 19

EARTH WITH WATER: DOROTHY GALE AND VAN GOGH, GOING IT ALONE, TOGETHER

The Earth has its music for those who listen.
—Reginald Vincent Holmes

If there is magic on this planet, it is contained in water.
—Loren Eiseley

EARTHS AND WATERS RELATE VIA the Controlling Cycle. But just like the Wood/Earth relationship discussed in the last chapter, the Earth/Water aspect of a Controlling Cycle relationship is also more supportive than oppositional because it involves Earth. In nature, a lack of structure will allow water to spread too thin and evaporate. Earth is what supports and contains water as it flows. The same is true with Earth/Water relationships. Earth doesn't decrease Water; it gives structure by guiding it. This means that the Water can allow itself to go deeper and flow faster because the

Earth is there to keep it safe. Dorothy could be just the person Van Gogh needs!

EARTH/WATER CONNECTIONS

Friendships: Earths are caring people who can be counted on to be there when needed. They love lots of time with their closest friends and family. Waters are deeply introspective people who love to ponder the mysteries of the universe. The people happiest alone are usually Waters. If Earth and Water meet up, an automatic attraction might not seem likely given Water's loner status and Earth's need to connect. But even loners need nurturing, so don't rule out a stable connection between these two. Water might actually enjoy time with Earth if it means they can go slightly further into the depths of discovery. And Earth, as always, will be thrilled to help.

Work: Earth people are usually a stabilizing influence wherever they are. An Earth in the workplace can bring a sense of comfort and ease. Waters need time alone at work to do what they do best, which is think, ponder, and imagine the new. Waters also have very little structure, so an Earth supporting them in some way will be a happy connection for both. But if things get out of balance, given the directional energy of the Controlling Flow, the Water is going to feel like the Earth is holding them back. And they could be, but for their own good.

Marriage: Earth's primary relationship focus is on deep, lasting connections with others. Water's primary relationship focus is on connecting with their inner selves and something bigger. Given Earth's tendency to support

Water, a marriage between the two might last as long as the Earth gives the Water plenty of space, and the Water plugs into the family now and then. The Water will be fine giving the Earth the space they need to create a home, although the Water's study will probably be off limits.

Family: Children are a given in most relationships with an Earth person because family matters deeply to Earths. The Water probably won't care either way, but if love is involved, and the Earth really wants a family, the Water will acquiesce. The care of the children will be strictly in the Earth's hands, however, which will be fine with them.

Over the years, I've seen many strong Earth/Water relationships:

- » *Ellen and Greg, Artist and Assistant*: Ellen (Water) is a promising young artist, and her best friend, Greg (Earth), helps her around the studio. They have fun together.
- » *Cam and Callie, Chef and Artist*: Cam (Earth) is an awesome cook who has developed a cookbook based on her Native American heritage. Callie (Water) is helping her illustrate the book. It looks awesome!
- » *Kip and Donna, Husband and Wife*: Kip (Water) teaches philosophy at the same high school where Donna (Earth) is a counselor. The commute together is fun.

EARTH/WATER RELATIONSHIP CHALLENGES

As stated, there are three ways Five Elements relationships get into trouble. We're going to use those to explore potential challenges with Earth/Water connections.

I. We Don't Understand Ourselves or Each Other

Earth Club members are all wired the same. The same is true for Water Club members; they are all alike, too. This means if we understand the wiring of a particular club, we can understand the club members. And hopefully their apparent bizarre or perturbing behaviors will make total sense. Of course an Earth will want the whole family to sit down together for dinner every night. Of course the Water will forget about dinner if they're deeply involved in reading a book. And when these behaviors aren't exactly desirable, understanding their club will make it easier to talk to the Earth or Water in a language they'll hear. But first, we have to understand each other.

> *Example*: A friend of mine needed a sitter for her six-year-old son, Bruce (Water). Their usual sitter was on vacation, so they hired Kim (Earth), who came highly recommended. When Kim arrived that Saturday night, she seemed pleasant and grandmotherly. My friend and her partner had a wonderful dinner out, but when they arrived home, Kim was very flustered. The more she'd tried to engage Bruce by playing games together or doing easy puzzles, the more withdrawn he became. Finally, in a gloomy voice, he asked if he could just go to bed. My friend apologized for not explaining that Bruce did better if supervised rather than engaged. Later, she and I had a good laugh over the fact that the more Kim tried, the more Bruce would have felt overwhelmed by her Earth. My friend swore she'd explain Waters to every sitter from then on. And she has.

II. We Don't Understand Our Relationship Dynamics

Earth and Water relate on the Controlling Cycle. And while that does bring a sense of control, it's also about support. But because the energy flows from Earth to Water, it's the Water who will feel the constraints of containment more than the Earth. If an Earth relating to a Water remembers to think in terms of support instead of control (which shouldn't be hard for the Earth), that's great. Waters always do better with guidelines to ensure they don't flow all over the place. This is a lesson my client Don found out the hard way.

CASE CORNER
Don and Taylor, Father and Daughter

Don (Earth) was a single father of a twelve-year-old daughter, Taylor (Water). They'd been on their own together since Taylor's mom died six years earlier and had settled into a pretty stable routine. Don ran a small restaurant and his hours allowed him to get Taylor off to school before going to work. The school bus dropped Taylor at the restaurant after school, where she studied in his office, read, or played games on his computer. She grabbed dinner with her dad, and they were home by 8:00 p.m. Taylor's Watery nature enjoyed the alone time, and all was well.

But as Taylor grew, the stable routine became less stable. There were school clubs to join (she loved astronomy), school orchestras to join (violin was her instrument), and a few close friends to hang out with after school. When she turned thirteen, Don agreed to let Taylor spend her after-school time as she wanted, but she had to be at the restaurant by 6:00 p.m. so he could make sure she had a good dinner.

At first Taylor was happy flowing wherever she wanted. She had stories to tell her dad over dinner, and it warmed his heart to see her so happy. Over time, however, Taylor became somewhat withdrawn with little to say or share. If Don questioned her, she asked why he wanted to know. And if she wanted something, she would fixate on it until he lovingly gave in. Eventually, she hardly spoke to Don at all. When he called me, Don said it was like she was frozen.

I suggested that what had probably happened was that Taylor was suffering from too much Water. The guiding containment of Earth is supposed to keep Water balanced. And without that coming from Don, Taylor had gone with the flow a little too far. My suggestion was to spend more time with Taylor so that his Earth was a greater presence in her life. Nothing too heavy; Waters still need to flow, but some structure is always good. Don agreed with my suggestions and slowly began connecting with Taylor more and more. They went on a few weekend trips to places she chose, took a French cooking class together (nothing says Earth like food), and began cycling. They had a great time together, and by the end of the school year, Taylor was back to her flowy self and Don was one relieved dad.

REMINDERS FOR EARTH/WATER CONNECTIONS

If you find yourself in an Earth/Water relationship that isn't going the way you'd like, take a moment to remind yourself what's important to the other person. If you're the Water person, remember that Earths need time together to feel connected. If they want to have dinner with you every night of the week, that's normal for an Earth. If you're the Earth person, remember that Waters are focused on big issues. If they want to discuss existential realism over dinner yet again, that's normal for a Water. And if things get stressed, reach for the Earth and Water Quick Tips covered earlier.

III. We're So Stressed We Create Stressed Relationships

It's still not easy to get along all the time, even if we understand our clubs and relationship dynamics. Stress can and will change everything. Knowing what a stressed Earth/Water relationship looks like not only helps you recognize problematic aspects in your own Earth/Water relationships, it also helps fix them. It's not hard. Earth and Water can each only go one of two places when stress is a factor: an excess state or a deficient state. Let's take a look, Earth first.

Earth Out of Balance

» *Deficient*: An Earth with too *little* Earth energy becomes flighty and concerned that they just aren't doing enough for those around them. They will worry obsessively and try to make connections but will eventually not have the energy to reach out. At that point, the Water may wonder why they aren't getting the attention they deserve, but when they seek out the Earth, they will find a sluggish, withdrawn person craving sweets.

Example: Sylvester (Water) and Stella (Earth) had been dating for a year when Stella took a new job as executive secretary to the CEO of a manufacturing firm. About that same time, Sylvester began writing his PhD dissertation. For the first few months of Stella's new job, the couple still went out, but Sylvester was distracted by his thesis and bored with Stella's increased calls worrying about him and complaining about her demanding boss (who turned out to be a Wood). Stella asked if she and Sylvester could go away for a weekend to connect, but Sylvester didn't want to take the time. Over the following weeks, Stella stopped calling Sylvester, and it finally dawned on him that she might leave.

He called, but it was too late. Stella was dating a new guy (a Fire) who fed her Earth and wanted to connect with her.

» *Excess*: An Earth person with too *much* Earth energy inserts themself as often as possible in the Water's life in an attempt to take the relationship to a place where the Water can't live without them. Unfortunately, constant meddling will have the opposite effect; the Water will be overwhelmed and resent the interruptions. The more the Earth tries to connect with the Water, the more constrained the Water will feel.

Example: Torren (Water) and Hayward (Earth) were friends in college. They met up again years later when Torren's paintings were just starting to sell. He was receiving requests from around the country for showings but didn't want to be bothered with the logistics of emails, setting up shows, and the like. Hayward had recently quit a stifling corporate job, so offered to help Torren get organized. Initially, it was a good match: Torren could focus on painting, and Hayward loved the freedom from the structured corporate life. But Hayward soon found that working in an isolated job made him lonely, so he started dropping in more often at Torren's studio with lists of ways he could help. The constant flow of ideas and interruptions overwhelmed Torren and made it hard for him to work. Eventually, Torren had to ask Hayward to leave.

» *Result:* Whether the relationship is suffering from too much or too little Earth energy, the Earth person is going to be worried and clingy. Too little Earth will leave the Water bothered by the lack of attention when they want it. Too much Earth will find the Water irritated by the Earth's constant presence and meddling ways. To save relationships where this is happening, the Earth needs to be brought back into balance.

Water Out of Balance

» *Deficient*: A Water person with too *little* Water energy becomes gloomy and depressed, then isolates themselves further by insisting on even more alone time than usual. The Earth will worry that they've done something wrong and ramp up their efforts to please the Water. The added Earth attention will feel more constraining to the Water and might even diminish their energy further. An interesting twist on this dynamic is featured in the next CASE CORNER.

» *Excess*: A Water person with too *much* Water energy fixates on their goal and loses their normal go-with-the-flow ease toward obtaining it. The Earth person will perceive the need to contain the Water and try harder, but the Earth who gets in the Water's way will find it isn't always easy to stop a runaway flood. Waters are tenacious. No matter what the Earth tries, the Water will likely have its way.

Example: Riley (Earth), a high school student, took a class called *Aesthetics* her junior year that dealt with appreciating the arts. Her teacher, Dr. Johnson (Water), loved the arts and had no end of symphonies, paintings, and dramas he thought they should experience. But there was no structure—no suggestions or rules for what might make something more, or less, aesthetically pleasing. Class was a flood of Watery input with no container. Riley frequently stopped by Dr. Johnson's office and asked for guidelines, but he wouldn't hear of it. Art was to be met and appreciated as it was. The abundance of Water was making mud of Riley's Earth, and she started skipping class. She ended up in my office, and I gave her the Quick Tips for Earths. She used them and managed to make it through the class. And fortunately, Dr. Johnson believed all art was sacred and couldn't be judged, so gave everyone in his class an A.

» *Result*: Whether the relationship is suffering from too much or too little Water energy, the Earth is going to worry that they've done something wrong and do everything they can to help the Water. Too little Water energy causes the Earth to overwhelm the Water with attention in an attempt to fix things. Too much Water energy will find the Earth doing all they can to provide guidance in the face of a flood. To save relationships where this is happening, the Water needs to be brought back into balance.

CASE CORNER
Deficient Water: Cate and Elise, Sisters

"Worried Sister," who we'll call Elise (Earth), wrote to my *ASK VICKI* blog on using the Five Elements model to help relationships because she was concerned about her sister, Cate (Water). In her youth, Cate was generally an optimistic girl who trusted that things would always work out for the best. Cate married young, and the couple joined a philosophic organization where they felt they were doing something big and important. After several years, Cate's husband became disenchanted and left the group, but Cate stayed.

The tension between Cate and her husband over Cate's continued involvement with the group eventually led to divorce. Ten years later, the group leader was caught embezzling cash from the coffers. He was quietly imprisoned and the group disbanded. Cate, who had been working in the group's office, was devastated. Elise reached out to Cate, but she wanted time alone to adjust.

Cate eventually found a job as caregiver for an elderly lady on a farm and spent fifteen years with her. When she died, the woman left Cate her six cats and enough money to buy a small place of her own. Elise offered to help her move, and Cate didn't resist. But Elise was shocked at how different Cate had become. She had not a drop of hope or optimism left and no longer trusted anyone or anything (except her six cats). She also appeared overly frightened about current events in the world. Elise wrote me to ask if there was a way to help Cate return to her true Watery, optimistic self.

After reminding her that Cate might well need professional assistance, I helped Elise understand that years of disappointment and disillusionment had probably created a state of deficient Water in Cate. Then, years of taking care of someone else had brought up Cate's secondary Earth to the degree that it was now overcontrolling what little Water Cate had left. Taking care of six cats was building her Earth even more, keeping her Water chronically depressed. I gave Elise several suggestions for building Cate's Water from the Quick Tips in Chapter 3 and also reminded her that the gift of Water is imagination. Elise helping Cate imagine or rediscover a purpose to her life, and a way to connect to it, could help a lot.

EARTH/WATER RELATIONSHIPS: THE BOTTOM LINE

The Water Club doesn't emphasize long-term personal connections; they value time alone. The Earth Club, however, lives for the deep, lasting relationships that mean the world to them. Yet sitting at the start of the cycle as they do, the childlike side of Waters will often accept a certain amount of nurturing from the ever-ready Earth. And this works as long as the Earth person can be patient while the Water is "away at sea" for extended periods. But if stress is part of the picture, without intervention a troubled Earth/Water relationship could see the Water floating away for good while the Earth waits onshore.

If you do find yourself in an Earth/Water relationship that's having trouble, ask yourself the following questions:

» Do you understand the priorities and needs of your club and your partner's? Are your expectations for the relationship realistic?

» Do you understand the tendencies of relating on the Controlling Cycle? Is this helping or hurting what you want from the relationship?

» Are either or both of you stressed? If so, start using the Quick Tips for Earths and Waters at the ends of Chapters 6 and 3.

A QUICK WAY TO DEFUSE EARTH/WATER PROBLEMS

In the middle of a disagreement, a Metal might be able to detach, but not an Earth or Water. For Earths and Waters in a tiff, here's a quick way to bring back the harmony.

Earth: Place the thumbs of each hand on your cheekbones directly below your eyes and rest the fingers of each hand across your forehead. Look the aloof Water in the eye, take a deep breath, and exhale softly making an "Aummmmm" sound, like the OM. Make the sound prayerful.

Water: Put one hand across the back of your head at the base of your skull and the other across your forehead. Look the worried Earth in the eye, take a deep breath, and exhale a soft "Whooooooo." If there's a little energy behind it, so much the better.

Repeat the process until you both feel a shift in the dynamics. When that happens, you'll feel movement instead of mud.

SAME-ELEMENT RELATIONSHIPS

"LOOKS LIKE THEY WERE REALLY MEANT FOR EACH OTHER."

CHAPTER 20

WATER WITH WATER: VAN GOGH AND EEYORE, MAYBE A GOOD DAY

We forget that the water cycle and the life cycle are one.
—Jacques-Yves Cousteau

IT'S NOT UNCOMMON FOR PEOPLE from the same club to end up in relationships. Like absolutely can attract like. And similar to Nurturing Cycle and Controlling Cycle relationships, there are pros and cons with Same-Club relationships. Certainly no one will ever understand a Water better than another Water. But for people who relate on the Nurturing and Controlling Cycles, energy is exchanged via the big circle and the big star. Same-Club relationships don't have that dynamic, which means there can be less movement and counterbalancing energy in these connections. This will impact some relationships more than others. For Waters, movement isn't usually a problem, but they can face other issues in their Same-Club connections. Would Van Gogh and Eeyore ever see the bright side of anything?

WATER/WATER CONNECTIONS

Friendships: Waters are usually self-sufficient loners content with few friends and minimal social events. If they decide to make another Water one of their friends, it should be a compatible relationship. They'll have an abundance of ideas and will take their discussions to the furthest reaches of reality (people passionate about debating realism versus empiricism are likely Waters). But they might have trouble if they want to make something happen with their great ideas. Waters usually aren't good at getting things done.

Work: Depending on the type of work, two Waters can work well together. If they are artists, philosophers, idea people, or in some other role that isn't required to manifest anything other than a product of their imagination, Waters will be fantastic together. And if one of the Waters has a secondary Wood or Metal, that little bit of structure will really help. Otherwise, two Waters at work won't be good at meeting deadlines, or even getting to work on time.

Marriage: The primary relationship focus for Waters is connecting with both their inner selves and something greater than themselves. This means intimate connections with people matter less, so close personal relationships aren't going to be a top priority for the Waters of the world (unless they have a secondary Earth). However, if love finds them, they'll understand when the other doesn't want to go to the party; they won't want to go, either. Staying home together reading, philosophizing, debating, or watching a movie will be preferred instead. But paying bills on time and buying everything on a grocery list could be another story altogether.

Family: Will Water/Water relationships create families? Not likely, unless one (or both) has a strong secondary Earth. Raising children usually isn't a priority or a focus for Waters. If they do have a family and can afford it, they will probably hire an Earth nanny.

Over the years, I've seen several first-class Water/Water relationships:

- » *Rocky and Corky, Graphic Designers*: These guys share an office and an assistant. They toss ideas back and forth and keep each other's Water flowing.
- » *Tish and Kay: Friends and Volunteers*: They both help out at a local homeless shelter and are deeply touched by the experiences they share together.
- » *Patrick and Dyllis: Brother and Sister*: They run a religious reading room (along with another brother who's a Wood) and love the connection with something bigger than themselves.

WATER/WATER RELATIONSHIP CHALLENGES

Throughout this book we've stated that when applying the Five Elements model to people and their relationships there are really only three ways a relationship can get into trouble. When dealing with Same-Club relationships, two of those three aren't really issues. No one will understand you better than a member of your own club, so not understanding each other is unlikely with a Same-Club relationship. And there's no relationship dynamic between Same-Club relationships, so not understanding that won't be a problem, either. But stress is another story.

> **REMINDERS FOR WATER/ WATER CONNECTIONS**
>
> *If you find yourself in a Water/Water relationship that isn't going the way you'd like, take a moment to remind yourself that what's important to you is just as important to the other person. Remember that other Water people need alone time to read and ponder just like you do, but it might not be at the same time. Don't take it personally if the other Water refuses to attend a scintillating lecture on astrophysics because they would rather stay home and read* The History of Truth. *And if things get really stressed, reach for the Water Quick Tips covered earlier.*

We're So Stressed We Create Stressed Relationships

Same-Club relationships are just as vulnerable to stress as Nurturing and Controlling Cycle relationships, maybe even more so. Without the dynamics provided by the cycles, there can be less cohesion in a Water/Water connection because Waters are such loners. And that's on a good day! If either or both of the Waters are stressed, things can go downhill pretty fast because, short of tapping into their secondary affiliations, neither partner brings a different perspective to help counter the stress.

Under stress, Water's primary need to connect with their inner self will distort. Knowing what a stressed Water/Water relationship looks like not only helps you recognize problematic aspects in your own Water/Water relationships, it also helps you fix them. Just like any other Five Elements connection, stressed Waters in a relationship can each only go one of two places: an excess state or a deficient state. And it will look different depending on whether one or both Waters are stressed.

Same-Element Relationships

» *Deficient*: Because a Water's energy is fed by connecting with their inner self, if anything blocks their ability to do that, their energy can go into a deficient state. However, with an abundance of Water in the relationship, and a Watery partner who also needs alone time, they may not stay there long. If they do stay in a deficient state, they'll have a poor sense of self and feel disconnected and isolated. As the stressed Water loses focus, their partner will probably wonder why they aren't as fascinating to be around as they used to be. It's possible the stressed Water will move back toward balance just by being around their partner in the flow of normal Water life. If this doesn't happen, the stressed Water will slide downhill and become absentminded, pessimistic, and boring. Eventually, their Water partner will flow away.

Example: Harold and Baylor met while philosophy majors in college. They bonded slowly over coffees, beers, and late-in-to-the-night discussions. After graduation, they moved to Chicago, got jobs at different libraries, and each began writing a book. Harold's was a semi-biographical novel; Baylor's was his thoughts on humanity's future. All was well until Harold shared his partially written book with a coworker who found it "boring and dull." Devastated, he lost all inspiration for the book and sunk into a funk. Baylor left him alone to process, but that only made matters worse. Finally, Baylor called me for help, and I suggested that he and Harold put down their books for one week and do things together near water, even if that was just sharing ideas as they had during college. It worked. Being around his Water partner and physical water was enough to get Harold's inspiration, and Water, flowing again.

» *Excess*: It is much more likely that a stressed Water in a Same-Club relationship will have excess Water energy. When one of the Waters has too *much* Water, they can become narcissistic and intolerant of their partner's views and ideas. Everything will become all about them, which will be a total turnoff to the unstressed Water because all Waters are naturally a little narcissistic. As the stressed Water becomes more demanding and stuck, the other Water will probably figure life's too short for this kind of thing and flow away.

Example: Annette and Jasmine were artists who shared the same large loft studio. They both had keys and came and went as their muses dictated. One day, Annette arrived at the studio to discover that Jasmine had moved her work area from her end of the studio up closer to Annette's area. When Annette asked why, Jasmine said that she'd received a huge commission from a wealthy couple in town and the light was better at Annette's end of the studio. Annette was surprised but decided to go with the flow. The following week, Annette arrived to find Jasmine looking through several of her sketches. When asked what she was doing, Jasmine replied that she suspected Annette was copying her work and was looking for proof. Annette assured her that she wasn't, and let it slide. But when Jasmine didn't pay her half of the rent and accused Annette of having taken the money, Annette decided it was time to move on. She found her own little garret and was much happier alone.

» *Result*: When one of the Waters in the relationship is suffering from too much or too little Water energy, the other Water is going to be only so tolerant. Waters don't care about deep personal relationships; they care about connections with their inner selves and something bigger than themselves. If a Water partner stays out of balance for too long, the other Water will probably philosophically figure there are always more fish in the sea and float away. To save relationships where this is happening, the stressed Water needs to be brought back into balance.

Two Waters Out of Balance

» *Deficient*: If both Waters have too *little* Water energy, it will be a gigantic downer—the ultimate pity party. And it can also be dangerous because there's no one from a different club to help balance them out. When both Waters are deficient, the best they can hope for is that a kind Metal shows up, either as counselor or friend, and helps them build their Water with inspiration, ideas, or a trip to the lake. With both Waters deficient, it's unlikely that either will have the gumption to leave.

» *Excess*: If both Waters have too *much* Water energy, it will be a battle of egos and paranoia. They'll both be fixated on what they want, and if it's not the same thing, that will be a problem. They'll constantly blame each other for everything that goes wrong, and there *will* be a lot going wrong. They'll be demanding and unforgiving, and probably sneak around to be the first one to leave. Before that happens, if they're lucky, a sweet Earth friend or counselor will show up and guide their Waters toward safe and productive channels to bring both Waters back into balance.

Mixed: If one Water has too *little* Water energy and the other has *too much* Water energy, even though it seems as though they should balance each other out, that isn't likely because Water people don't usually create strong personal connections with others. As each Water stays focused on their own stress issues, they could quickly disgust each other with their morbidity (too little Water) and belligerence (too much Water), if they're around enough to notice. If nothing changes, they'll probably each float their own way. To save relationships where this is happening, both Waters need to be brought back into balance. Stan and Reba found this out as you will see in the next CASE CORNER.

CASE CORNER
Too Little/Too Much Water: Stan and Reba, Husband and Wife

You met both Stan and Reba in Chapter 10 on Water/Wood relationships. Stan is the college physics professor who wrote the book with a Wood colleague, and Reba is the librarian who asked her Wood sister to help design a private library for a patron. They're wonderful people.

Stan and Reba went through a rough time early in their marriage while he was working on his PhD. Reba had just gotten her job at the library and thought she'd died and gone to heaven. So many books and so little time! She read before work, during her lunch break, and after work while Stan was studying. She also joined three separate book clubs and loved each one for different reasons. But she missed the long walks and talks she had with Stan, and as her Water increased, she started blaming him for the loss of those times and pushed aside the fear that it was about her. Reba reminded herself that it would all be better when Stan's dissertation was done, but she wasn't sure she was going to make it that long. She wasn't happy, and with her excess Water making it all about her, drifting away was tempting.

For his part, Stan was writing. And reading. And discussing options with his professors. Things flowed along well, and Stan was guardedly optimistic about

Same-Element Relationships

the reception his work on particle astrophysics would receive. But about the time Reba joined her third book club, Stan stumbled. His advisor mentioned an article that appeared to question the main thesis of Stan's dissertation. Stan quickly obtained a copy, and sure enough, the author made several points that argued against Stan's work. Deflated and terrified that he'd just wasted two years chasing a crazy idea, Stan lost his way and the connection to his big idea. For the first time in his life, he felt alone and hopeless. His confidence disappeared. Reba had been so testy the last few times they'd spoken that he didn't want to reach out to her. So he sat for hours every day staring at an empty computer screen.

Eventually, Stan's advisor figured out what was happening with Stan and suggested a meeting. They discussed other possibilities and this helped build back some of Stan's Water. He found an obscure article in a little-known journal that supported his thesis, and once his advisor agreed it was credible, Stan's Water flooded back and he was good to go. But he realized Reba wasn't happy, so he used his reclaimed optimism to suggest that they take a walk and talk about *them*, not books or physics. The talk was successful, and Reba resigned from two of the book clubs. Stan made time for walks and talks every weekend, plus they both started doing three things daily from the Water Quick Tips I'd given them. And slowly but surely, their Water/Water connection moved back into balance and has stayed there ever since.

WATER/WATER RELATIONSHIPS: THE BOTTOM LINE

Members of the Water Club have very little structure, value time alone, and don't emphasize deep connections with others, so a relationship between two Waters might not look like much of a relationship. Their togetherness, however, will take this into account, and two Waters can create a stable, if not very dynamic, relationship. But if stress is part of the picture, without intervention a troubled Water/Water relationship can easily drift apart and be over before anyone notices.

If you find yourself in a troubled Water/Water relationship, check to see if either or both of you are stressed. If so, use the Water Quick Tips at the end of Chapter 3.

A QUICK WAY TO DEFUSE WATER/WATER PROBLEMS

In the middle of a fight, we all know it's difficult to pull back. For two Waters in combat, here's a quick way to take down some of the intensity.

Both Waters: Put one hand across the back of your head at the base of your skull and the other across your forehead. Look your Water cohort in the eye, take a deep breath, and exhale a soft "Whooooooo." If there's energy behind it, so much the better.

Repeat the process until you both feel a shift in the dynamic. You'll know that's happened when you start feeling ridiculous instead of irritated.

CHAPTER 21

WOOD WITH WOOD: THOR AND KATNISS EVERDEEN, WINNING 101

A tree does not move unless there is wind.

—Afghan Proverb

AS MENTIONED, IT'S NOT UNCOMMON for people from the same club to end up in relationships. And just like any combination of clubs, there are pros and cons with Same-Club relationships. Someone from your own clubhouse will certainly understand you. But the energy exchange via the big circle or the big star will be missing in Same-Club relationships, which means there can be less movement and counterbalancing energy in these connections. Fortunately, Woods have an intrinsic sense of outward movement, but they face other issues in their Same-Club connections. For Thor and Katniss, who gets to win?

WOOD/WOOD CONNECTIONS

Friendships: Woods are serious individuals who rarely make time for social events unless they have a role to play or it furthers a goal. If one Wood decides to befriend another Wood, it will probably be based on shared goals. Two Woods in a relationship will be phenomenally productive and will have well-planned and ordered lives. But they'll have to be careful to share the credit and the glory in whatever they do, which isn't easy for a Wood. They'll also need to remember to chill out now and then.

Work: Most Wood/Wood relationships will have a work vibe to them anyway, since Wood is all about accomplishment. The challenge with two Woods working together is going to be deciding who gets to lead. If that isn't clearly delineated, there could be real problems. When a Wood leads, they know that things won't be out of control. They can't guarantee that if someone else is calling the shots. Separating responsibilities so each can lead in their own area will be key.

Marriage: Woods' primary relationship focus is on individualization and personal accomplishments, not lasting personal relationships. So unless either (or both) has a secondary Earth, a marriage between two Woods could well be a marriage of companionship and productivity, not romance and family. They will pursue their individual plans and happily celebrate together each time a goal is accomplished and the next one undertaken. In this marriage, the home will be important as a place where they are rooted and a symbol of success, but just like in the office, make sure each has their own area of responsibility. They'll need to remember to have fun sometimes, too.

Same-Element Relationships

Family: Will Wood/Wood relationships create families? Not likely, unless one (or both) has a strong secondary Earth. Raising children usually isn't a priority for Woods. If they do have a family, like Water people, they will probably hire an Earth nanny if they can afford it.

Over the years, I've seen many impressive Wood/Wood relationships:

» *Jenn and Louise, Organizers*: These girls have a great business helping organizationally challenged people clear out clutter. They're really in demand!

» *Rand and Hannah, Fundraisers*: This married couple helps not-for-profit companies throw fundraising events. They are top drawer and in high demand.

» *Adelle and Jock, Brother and Sister*: They run the family import business. They get to be the bosses, travel all over, plus wheel and deal. Perfect!

WOOD/WOOD RELATIONSHIP CHALLENGES

Throughout this book we've stated that when applying the Five Elements model to people and their relationships, there are only three ways a relationship can get into trouble. However, when dealing with Same-Club relationships, two of those three aren't really issues. No one will understand a Wood better than another Wood, so not understanding each other is unlikely. And there's no relationship dynamic between Same-Club relationships, so not understanding that won't be a problem, either. But as we said in the last chapter, stress is another story.

> **REMINDERS FOR WOOD/WOOD CONNECTIONS**
>
> *If you find yourself in a Wood/Wood relationship that isn't going the way you'd like, take a moment to remind yourself that what's important to you is just as important to the other person. Remember that other Woods need accomplishment and success as much as you do, so share the reins and the glory. When your partner succeeds, celebrate like it's your success, too. It is! And if things get really stressed, reach for the Wood Quick Tips covered earlier.*

We're So Stressed We Create Stressed Relationships

Same-Club relationships are likely to be even more vulnerable to stress than Nurturing and Controlling Cycle relationships. Without the dynamics provided by the cycles, there can be less togetherness in a Wood/Wood connection because Woods are so focused on individualization. And if either or both of the Woods are stressed, things can be even more challenging because, short of tapping into their secondary affiliations, neither partner brings a different perspective to help counter the stress.

Under stress, Wood's primary need to accomplish something will distort. Knowing what a stressed Wood/Wood relationship looks like not only helps you recognize problematic aspects in your own Wood/Wood relationships, it also helps you fix them. Just like any other Five Elements connection, stressed Woods in a relationship can each only go one of two places: an excess state of energy or a deficient state. And it will look different depending on whether one or both Woods are stressed.

Same-Element Relationships

One Wood Out of Balance

» *Deficient*: Because a Wood's energy is fed by personal accomplishment, if they're underperforming, it's easy for a stressed Wood to go into a deficient state. If and when they do, they'll have difficulty concentrating or making decisions. They will be humiliated by their lack of productivity and pull away from their Wood partner. It's likely that their partner will know exactly what's happening, too. Competition is natural to Woods, which means they keep track of each other. If the non-stressed partner has a secondary Earth, they will step in and try to help. If not, they may pronounce themselves the winner and move on to more worthy opponents.

Example: Kurt and Nellie were an awesome Wood couple and very successful: He was a partner in a Chicago law firm, and she had been elected alderman for their neighborhood. He felt set in his career path, but Nellie had political aspirations. She enjoyed public service and the visibility it provided, so when congressional elections approached, she decided to run. Kurt bankrolled her, and she campaigned hard. But in the end, she lost, and it really took her down. Her Wood depleted, and she refused to leave the house, humiliated that she had lost and sure that anyone she saw was labeling her a loser. Kurt grew concerned when she wouldn't go to the social functions he needed her to attend. He gave her a stern talking-to, and she ended up in my office. The Wood Quick Tips helped, as did brainstorming new career opportunities for her to work toward.

» *Excess*: In a Wood/Wood connection, a stressed Wood is more likely to go into a state of excess Wood energy than a state of deficient energy. Woods often bring out the competitive nature in each other. And when challenged, Woods ramp things up. But that comes with a price. Too much Wood will find the out-of-balance partner impatient and reckless. They will push too hard and take action before it's time. The inevitable failure will bring on bursts of rage that even their Wood partner will fear. These outbursts, along with the blame that will be leveled at them by the excess Wood, will probably cause the Wood partner to run for their life.

Example: Shira and Micca were best friends and partners running a small restaurant in a Chicago suburb. They offered mostly healthy sandwiches and salads, and the idea caught on. Soon they opened a second place in a neighboring town. Shira managed one spot, and Micca the other. They had a friendly competition regarding customers and sales, and it was all in good fun until Shira's Water sister came to help her. The sister pumped Shira full of grand ideas of what could be done with the restaurant, and pretty soon all those Water ideas built Shira's Wood to excess. Without telling Micca, Shira took over the storefront next to her and expanded her shop. But when Micca questioned her, Shira told her to butt out, sure that Micca was trying to hold her back. Shira made several poor decisions in her haste to prove her worth, and it came back to haunt her. Micca's restaurant grew slowly and made modest profits that year. Shira's place closed.

» *Result*: When one of the Woods in the relationship is suffering from either too much or too little Wood energy, the other Wood is only going to be so tolerant for so long. Woods don't care about personal relationships; they care about personal success and accomplishment. If a Wood partner stays out of balance for too long, the other Wood will likely decide they are better off alone and move on.

Same-Element Relationships

To save relationships where this is happening, the stressed Wood needs to be brought back into balance.

Two Woods Out of Balance

» *Deficient*: If both Woods have too *little* Wood energy, neither lion will be able to roar. They'll have trouble accomplishing anything, alone or together. Despondent over their joint lack of productivity, they'll withdraw from each other and hate themselves inside. When both Woods are deficient, the best they can hope for is that a wise Water shows up, either as counselor or friend, and helps them build their Wood by offering enthusiasm, inspiration, and suggestions. If not, with both Woods deficient, it's unlikely that either will notice if the other one leaves.

» *Excess*: If both Woods have too *much* Wood energy, it will be an ugly battle for bragging rights. They'll both be short-tempered, angry, and impatient. Obsessed with winning at any cost, they'll epitomize the old saying that the ends justify the means and go to extraordinary lengths to win. But they won't leave, not until *they* are the winner (or have come to harm). Before that happens, if they're lucky, a rational Metal friend or counselor will show up and prune their Woods to bring both back into balance. How Janine and Laura dealt with this is covered in the next CASE CORNER.

Mixed: If one Wood has too *little* Wood energy and the other has *too much* Wood energy, it could be a bloodbath. The under-energized Wood will be erratic, anxious, and unable to concentrate, easy prey for an over-energized, combative Wood. However, though the partner with excess Wood will obsess about making things happen, they probably won't be very successful given their lack of organization. Full of themself, the over-energized Wood will likely decide they're worthy of better and leave in a flourish of ugliness and blame. To save relationships where this is happening, both Woods need to be brought back into balance.

CASE CORNER
Dual Excess Wood: Janine and Casey, Board Members

A good friend of mine, Janine, was a married mother of one working in Chicago. For three years, she'd also served as president of her condo association. Under her guidance, they had a congenial board with pleasant but efficient meetings. All that changed when Casey joined the board. She was cheery, but very opinionated. Productive, but overly assertive. Upbeat, but a little reckless. Janine and Casey clashed almost immediately. For every suggestion Janine made, Casey loudly offered an alternative. If Janine suggested having something signed by Friday, Casey said she thought Monday was soon enough. If Janine had paint samples for the laundry area, Casey suggested the colors should be a darker beige. Janine was beginning to feel very competitive toward Casey, so she gave me a call.

It didn't take long to figure out that Casey was also a Wood, and both ladies were in a state of excess Wood. I pointed out to Janine that most people would be happy to have a Wood serve on their board because Woods are great problem-solvers and can see the way out of almost any difficult situation. They are also very goal-oriented and are happy to step up and lead the way, which is what Casey was trying to do even though the board already had a very competent leader in Janine. Casey's excess Wood had created a competi-

Same-Element Relationships

tion around the leadership position, and she was doing her best to outperform Janine.

I helped Janine see that as the current leader of the board, there were several reasons she found Casey threatening, but most important was that she was challenging Janine's command. Woods thrive on individual accomplishment and success, so when Janine's board did something great for their condo, Janine gave the whole board credit but privately gave herself extra credit for leading the way. It's natural and understandable, and it's one of the things that juice Woods about leadership. And Casey was out for the juice. In fact, in her excess state, she *needed* the juice.

Other than recommending Casey seek professional help, which Janine wasn't comfortable doing, I suggested her best course of action was to give Casey a chance to prove herself. It was possible Casey's Wood was in an excess state because she hadn't had an outlet for expressing it; an opportunity to shine on the board could help balance it. And if she failed, Janine would have the board's support in removing her.

I also reminded Janine that while Wood/Wood relationships can be exceedingly productive, the challenge will always be deciding who gets to lead. For now, Janine was leading the whole board, but letting Casey lead on selected projects would be a great solution and take some of the work off Janine's plate. Janine took my advice, and luckily, having an outlet for her Wood was all Casey needed to balance it. And once Casey wasn't threatening her, Janine's Wood settled back down, too. Years later, the two are still friends.

WOOD/WOOD RELATIONSHIPS: THE BOTTOM LINE

Members of the Wood Club need personal accomplishments, success, and acknowledgment. They don't necessarily need deep connections with others; they need to be productive. If they want the connection and are willing to work together, two Woods can create a stable, and intense, relationship. But if stress is part of the picture, without intervention a troubled Wood/Wood relationship can deteriorate quickly into a state of acrimony and ruin.

If you find yourself in a troubled Wood/Wood relationship, check to see if either or both of you are stressed. If so, use the Wood Quick Tips at the end of Chapter 4.

A QUICK WAY TO DEFUSE WOOD/WOOD PROBLEMS

In the middle of a fight, we all know it's difficult to pull back, especially for Woods. For two Wood people in combat, here's a quick way to take down some of the intensity.

Both Woods: Put your thumbs at the outside edges of your eyes and rest your fingers across your forehead. Look your fellow Wood in the eye, take a deep breath, and exhale a sharp "Shhhhhhhh." Push that sound out vigorously at the end.

Repeat the process until you both feel a shift in the dynamic; you'll probably start feeling silly instead of angry.

CHAPTER 22

FIRE WITH FIRE: THE MAD HATTER AND THE JOKER, OVER THE TOP

One of the strongest characteristics of genius is the power of lighting its own fire.

—John W. Foster

AS WE'VE SAID, IT'S NOT uncommon for people from the same club to end up in relationships. And there are pros and cons with Same-Club connections, just like with any combination of clubs. Certainly, someone from your own clubhouse is really going to get you. But the energy exchange via the big circle or the big star will be missing in Same-Club relationships, which usually means there can be less movement and counterbalancing energy in these connections. However, since Fires are always active, lack of movement probably won't be an issue they'll face. Instead, other issues pop up in their Same-Club connections. For the Mad Hatter and the Joker, who burns out first?

FIRE/FIRE CONNECTIONS

Friendships: Fires are upbeat people who like to keep moving and are always ready to celebrate. Fires need intense, short-term connections, so it won't be hard for two Fires to find each other and connect. And when they do, it will be a joyful and amazing relationship, but probably just for a while. Nothing lasts forever in a Fire's world.

Work: Most Fire/Fire relationships centered on work will involve something Fires do well. Perhaps acting, public speaking, comedy, or motivational presentations. Two Fires doing "Fire" things will be great together as long as they share the spotlight. Fires like to be the star of the show, but they'll have to take turns to get along. Two Fires will also have to be mindful not to whip each other into a frenzy.

Marriage: Fires' primary relationship focus is on intense connections outside of themselves, not lasting personal relationships. If either (or both) has a secondary Earth, a marriage between two Fires might last. They will absolutely adore each other initially, but their strong need for something new, or to see what's next, could make it hard for Fires to stay tied down. Think of your stereotypical "movie star" couple. They need to move. If it does last, they will have to remember to schedule downtime with each other.

Family: Will Fire/Fire relationships create families? Without a secondary Earth, probably not; children imply permanence and Fires don't automatically go there. If they do have a family, they will likely hire a nanny to provide stability for the children.

Over the years, I've seen many phenomenal Fire/Fire relationships:

- *Parker and Kramer, Comedians*: These two guys are hysterically funny and have a great thing going. They play at several local clubs.

- *Greg and Kelly, Speaker and Clown*: Greg is a motivational coach for executives. Kelly's a professional clown who does children's parties. They're married because both have a secondary Earth.

- *Gracie and Lana, Daycare Team*: These ladies are always on the go, which makes them perfect for running a daycare center.

FIRE/FIRE RELATIONSHIP CHALLENGES

Throughout this book we've stated that when applying the Five Elements model to people and their relationships there are really only three ways a relationship can get into trouble. But when dealing with Same-Club relationships, two of those three aren't really issues. No one will understand a Fire better than another Fire, so not understanding each other is unlikely. And there's no relationship dynamic between Same-Club relationships, so not understanding that won't be a problem, either. But stress is another story. It can absolutely be a problem in Same-Club relationships.

REMINDERS FOR FIRE/FIRE CONNECTIONS

If you find yourself in a Fire/Fire relationship that isn't going the way you'd like, take a moment to remind yourself that what's important to you is just as important to the other person. Remember that other Fires need attention and accolades as much you do, so share the spotlight. When your partner is passionate about something, anything, acknowledge that passion. It's part of what connects you! And if things get really stressed, reach for the Fire Quick Tips covered earlier.

We're So Stressed We Create Stressed Relationships

As we've said, Same-Club relationships are just as vulnerable to stress as Nurturing and Controlling Cycle relationships. And without the dynamics provided by the cycles, there can be less downtime in a Fire/Fire connection because Fires are so focused on action. If either or both of the Fires are stressed, things will be even more challenging because neither partner brings a different perspective to help counter the stress.

Under stress, Fire's primary need for spontaneous connection with someone or something distorts. Knowing what a stressed Fire/Fire relationship looks like not only helps you recognize problematic aspects in your own Fire/Fire relationships, it also helps you fix them. Just like any other Five Elements connection, stressed Fires in a relationship can each only go one of two places: an excess state or a deficient state. And it will look different depending on whether one or both Fires are stressed.

One Fire Out of Balance

» *Deficient*: A Fire's energy is fed by connecting with someone or something. If that isn't happening in a Fire's life, it's easy for a stressed Fire to get into a deficient energy state. If they do, they'll appear scattered and overwhelmed. The joy will vanish from their life; they'll be down and out of it. If their Fire partner notices this, they should be able to cajole them back into a good space. But if the depleted Fire stays down too long, and their partner isn't able to elicit a change in them, the balanced partner will miss the fun and likely move on to happier grounds—especially since Fires don't emphasize long-term relationships.

Example: Doyle and Benson, both Fires, were business partners in a charity that held quarterly auctions as fundraisers. Their auctions were very popular because Doyle and

Same-Element Relationships

Benson were both funny, charismatic guys who put a great deal of effort into their events. Several local celebrities were usually persuaded to attend, too, so the turnout was always excellent. But two months before the auction, Doyle's sister became seriously ill, and he took temporary custody of her seven-year-old daughter. Taking care of his niece, plus the fear that his sister might die, completely drained Doyle's Fire. He became scattered and unfocused, and lost his usual sense of humor. As the event approached, Benson did everything he could think of to get Doyle revved up, but nothing worked. Benson eventually hired another Fire to help him out that year.

» *Excess*: In a Fire/Fire connection, it's more likely that one (or both) will go to a state of *too much* Fire. Fires are great at bouncing off of each other and escalating the energy. The phrase "whipping each other into a frenzy" comes to mind here. Usually, they stabilize when exhaustion sets in, but sometimes a Fire person can end up stuck in a place of too much Fire. They'll become anxious, restless, and panicked by everyday events. They'll try to do too much and overschedule themselves, seeking the high that comes from exciting connections. Their Fire partner will feel the heat rising and join in for the fun, but when the inevitable burnout approaches, they will distance themselves in self-defense. The overheated Fire will keep going and going to feed the need for excitement but will eventually crash and burn.

Example: Patrice and Janka were a new comedy team trying to break into the business. They'd gone to college together and had been successful in school talent shows, so decided to give show business a try. They had a great routine, so got bookings around the city and at private parties. As business picked up, Janka wanted to double-book some evenings, but as much as Patrice loved the attention, she thought two jobs a night was too much. Yet Janka needed more, so without telling Patrice, she began taking solo jobs at late-night clubs. Things were fine for a while, but soon Janka became more manic than usual in her routines with Patrice. She also became agitated and harsh offstage. For Patrice, working with Janka became a job instead of a high, and the franticness of Janka's delivery was wearing her down. Patrice finally confronted Janka, who admitted she was working solo gigs, too. Patrice quit on the spot; she was going to try acting.

» *Result*: When one of the Fires in the relationship is suffering from either too much or too little Fire energy, the other Fire is only going to be so tolerant for so long. Fires don't care about long-term connections; they care about quick connections with someone or something fun. If a Fire partner stays out of balance for too long, the other Fire will likely head off in search of new and exciting possibilities. To save relationships where this is happening, the stressed Fire needs to be brought back into balance.

Two Fires Out of Balance

» *Deficient*: If both Fires have too *little* Fire energy, life will lose its trademark joy. Both Fires will be scattered and feel isolated, even in the same room. Spontaneity will disappear, as will any sense of togetherness. In an attempt to feel a connection, either or both may reach out to other people, but probably with little success. When both Fires are deficient, the best they can hope for is that a wise Wood shows up and helps build their Fire by offering reasons to celebrate. If not, as the gap widens between them, they'll probably look elsewhere for sparks and flames.

Same-Element Relationships

» *Excess*: If both Fires have too *much* Fire energy, it will be an ugly battle for center stage. Irrational and anxious about everything, they'll both overload their schedules for the buzz and excitement, but not together. They will go it alone because each will want to be the star of the show. The typical joy and enthusiasm associated with Fire will flame out of control and scorch anything nearby with hysteria and excess. Hopefully, before the inevitable burnout happens, a Watery friend will show up and gently douse their flames back into balance with serious advice. How Liza and Skip managed this experience is covered in the next CASE CORNER.

Mixed: If one Fire person has too *little* Fire and the other has *too much* Fire, it could quickly drive them apart. The under-energized Fire will be scattered and overwhelmed, lack joy and spontaneity, and be unable to connect. The hysteria and manic behaviors of the over-energized Fire will add to their partner's overwhelm and deplete them even more because, counterintuitively, a Fire with too little Fire handles external flames poorly. Their Fire needs to grow from within. Because neither partner will feel sparks between them, both will set off in desperate search of new connections. To save relationships where this is happening, both Fires need to be brought back into balance.

CASE CORNER
Dual Excess Fire: Liza and Skip, Dating

Liza was an engaging and dynamic waitress at a high-end restaurant in Chicago. She made great money and loved her job. Connecting with her customers was always enjoyable, but she could leave them when the restaurant closed and there were always new ones to meet the next day. She never dated any customers, but not for lack of invitations. She did date some of the guys from the restaurant, but she just wasn't ready to settle down. There was too much of life left to live! Then she met Skip.

Skip's band was hired to play at a private party at the restaurant. Liza was one of the waitresses, and they hit it off immediately. Two Fires flirting are electric, so when he asked for her number, she gave it to him. They dated steadily for three months, and Liza admitted it was the best time she'd had in years. They had no shortage of places to go, and pretty soon they were seeing each other every night. Their lives became almost nonstop activity. Nights Skip didn't have a job, he hung out at the bar until Liza was off and they'd go dancing. Nights Skip had a job, Liza would go along if she was free. Liza admitted she knew the pace couldn't last, but she was having so much fun!

One night while they were out with friends, Liza realized that Skip often interrupted her stories to tell a story of his own. She also realized that she was doing the same to him. At first it was a cute and friendly competition between them, but as their frantic lives grew busier and busier, their competition for the spotlight grew more serious. Skip would describe a job playing for the governor. Liza mentioned a celebrity who dined at the restaurant and often asked for her.

For Valentine's Day, Skip showed up at the restaurant with a suitcase. He'd arranged for her to get off early and they were flying to Paris. Liza's excited coworkers waved them off as they grabbed a cab for O'Hare. Yet the trip was anything but romantic. The

Same-Element Relationships

pace of their four months together had elevated both of their Fires to the point that they were scattered and slightly frenzied. They talked too loudly on the overnight flight and the attendant had to ask them to be quiet multiple times. Skip was restless and had to walk the aisle. Liza was aware she was anxious about the flight crashing.

In Paris, Liza and Skip disagreed on almost everything. Liza found Paris slow, so suggested a quick trip to London. When Skip called the idea absurd, she exploded at him. The hotel manager was called to quiet them. Frazzled and almost hysterical, Liza left the hotel and flew back to Chicago on the first flight she could get. Once home, she called in sick to work and slept for two days. Then she called her mother who arranged for us to talk. It was easy to see that Skip and Liza were two Fires out of control. Sadly, without anyone to help control them, their crash was inevitable.

FIRE/FIRE RELATIONSHIPS: THE BOTTOM LINE

The Fire Club doesn't emphasize lasting relationships with others. Fires need intensity and the excitement of connecting with people in spontaneous ways. If a short-term connection lasts longer than usual, two Fires can create a stable relationship provided they can agree to share the spotlight. But if stress is part of the picture, without intervention a troubled Fire/Fire relationship can explode, rupture, and go down in flames.

If you find yourself in a troubled Fire/Fire relationship, check to see if either or both of you are stressed. If so, start using the Fire Quick Tips at the end of Chapter 5.

A QUICK WAY TO DEFUSE FIRE/FIRE PROBLEMS

In the middle of a fight, we all know it's difficult to pull back, especially with manic Fires. For two Fires in combat, here's a quick way to take down some of the intensity.

Both Fires: Put one hand across the back of your head directly behind your eyes and the other across your forehead. Look your Fire accomplice in the eye, take a deep breath, and exhale a soft "Heeeeeeee." Emphasize the sighing aspect of this sound.

Repeat the process until you both feel a shift in the dynamic. By then, you'll probably have forgotten why you were fighting.

CHAPTER 23

EARTH WITH EARTH: DOROTHY GALE AND MOTHER THERESA, DOUBLE THE COMPASSION

The earth is what we all have in common.
—Wendell Berry

WHEN PEOPLE FROM THE SAME club end up in relationships, as they can, it will be just like any combination of clubs: pros and cons will abound. Someone from your own clubhouse is absolutely going to understand you. But the energy exchange via the big circle or the big star in the Five Elements model will be missing in Same-Club relationships, which means there can be less movement and counterbalancing energy in these connections. For Earths, who are all about dynamic balance, Same-Club connections can become pretty static if they aren't careful. Dorothy and Mother Theresa could get deeply bogged down in simply appreciating each other!

EARTH/EARTH CONNECTIONS

» *Friendships:* Earths are caring, compassionate people who like to help others. Earths need deep, lasting connections, so when two Earths find each other, a relationship between them could be very happy and last a long time. It will be a cozy, comfortable, supportive connection, maybe even best friends for life. But it could also get too comfortable and move toward stuck.

» *Work:* Most Earth/Earth relationships centered on work will involve supporting themselves and/or others. Earth people love harmony and making a difference, and take pride in their ability to help others. But sometimes their need to be needed can cause them to meddle in issues that aren't theirs to address. At work, two Earths will have to be mindful about boundaries between business and private relationships.

» *Marriage:* Earths' primary relationship focus is on deep, lasting relationships with others. A marriage between two Earths will likely last forever because Earths rarely leave relationships. Their bond will be tight and enduring, although their need to be needed could create fertile ground for codependency if they aren't careful. In a marriage, Earths will have to remember to step out of their comfort zones now and then to keep things moving.

» *Family:* Will Earth/Earth relationships create families? Absolutely! Family is the most important part of life for Earths. They will want to have children, potentially lots of them. They are also likely to adopt children from high-risk situations. Earths exist to help anyone and everyone, and that starts with family. You can always count on an Earth to be there when you need them. Period.

Over the years, I've seen many fantastic Earth/Earth relationships:

- » *Francis and Fred, Chefs*: They are two amazing culinary masters who run a farm-to-table restaurant. The food is outrageous!
- » *Forest and Larkin, Gardeners*: These ladies create and maintain edible gardens in senior centers. The residents are able to help plant and care for the veggies, and even help harvest them.
- » *Rona and Teri, Play Center Owners*: These two run a local play center that offers healthy, organic snacks. It's amazing how many parents appreciate this.

EARTH/EARTH RELATIONSHIP CHALLENGES

Throughout this book we've stated that when applying the Five Elements model to people and their relationships there are really only three ways a relationship can get into trouble. But when dealing with Same-Club relationships, two of those three aren't really issues. No one will understand an Earth better than another Earth, so not understanding each other is unlikely. And there's no relationship dynamic between Same-Club relationships, so not understanding that won't be a problem, either. But stress is another story. It will absolutely be a problem in Same-Club relationships.

> **REMINDERS FOR EARTH/ METAL CONNECTIONS**
>
> *If you find yourself in an Earth/Metal relationship that isn't going the way you'd like, take a moment to remind yourself what's important to the other person. If you're the Earth, remember that Metals thrive on order and discipline. Of course they'll expect everything to be shipshape all of the time! If you're the Metal, remember that Earths use mementos to remind themselves of their lasting connections with the people who gave them the mementos. Of course they'll want them scattered all over the house so they can see them! And if things get stressed, reach for the Earth and Metal Quick Tips covered earlier.*

We're So Stressed We Create Stressed Relationships

As we've said, Same-Club relationships are just as vulnerable to stress as Nurturing and Controlling Cycle relationships. And without the dynamic movement and balance provided by the cycles, there can be less excitement in an Earth/Earth connection because Earths are so focused on comfort. If either or both of the Earths are stressed, things will be even more challenging because neither partner brings a different perspective to help counter the stress.

Under stress, Earth's primary need to help others distorts. Knowing what a stressed Earth/Earth relationship looks like not only helps you recognize problematic aspects in your own Earth/Earth relationships, it also helps you fix them. Just like any other Five Elements connection, each stressed Earth in a relationship can only go one of two places: an excess state or a deficient state. And it will look different depending on whether one or both Earths are stressed.

Same-Element Relationships

One Earth Out of Balance

» *Deficient*: Because an Earth's energy is fed by helping others, if that isn't happening in an Earth's life, it's easy for a stressed Earth to go into a deficient energy state. If they do, they'll become clingy. Their need to feel a connection will manifest as excessive—almost obsessive—concern for others. This will most likely be directed at their Earth partner who, if they are aware what is happening, will easily balance them with an infusion of gentle Earth support. If left unaddressed, the deficient Earth will continue their downward slide and become a guilt-ridden person sure they just haven't done enough for someone. Eventually, this may get bad enough that their balanced Earth partner will step in and arrange for help. Earths don't often leave a relationship (unless they have a strong secondary Wood or Metal).

Example: My client Addie was concerned about her sister, Sunny. Sunny's dog had recently died, and Sunny missed him terribly. Addie had encouraged her to adopt a puppy, but Sunny said she couldn't take the pain of losing another pet. As weeks went by, Sunny started stopping by Addie's house to see if she needed anything at the store. Or she'd ask her to have coffee then spend the time bemoaning all she hadn't done for her dog. Addie let this continue for another few weeks, and then she went to a local shelter and adopted a puppy for Sunny. It was a good move, too. With a new puppy to love, Sunny's Earth energy built up quickly and she was back to her old self in no time.

» *Excess*: In an Earth/Earth connection, it's more likely that one (or both) will go into a state of *too much* Earth energy. If this happens, the over-energized partner will meddle and insert themselves where they really aren't needed. They'll worry that they aren't doing enough and be deeply upset when their unneeded help is turned away. If the balanced Earth partner doesn't take the bait and move into a codependent relationship with them, the smothering energy coming from their over-energized partner will likely cause them to seek help. Again, Earths rarely leave.

Example: Terence (Earth), a twenty-four-year-old Chicago culinary graduate, landed a job in LA and was excited about the change. Everyone was happy for him except his mom (Earth). She didn't want her "baby" so far away. Terence promised she could come to visit once he was settled, but this was a big chance for him. His mother let him go but called almost daily to see how he was. Did he eat breakfast? Was he staying warm enough? Had he seen anyone famous? Terence told me he considered turning off his cell, but then worried that his family wouldn't be able to reach him in an emergency. The final straw was when his mother showed up in LA to surprise him. He let her stay for a long weekend, but then sent her back to Chicago. Privately, he called his father and encouraged him to get some support for his mother. She started counseling and it went well.

» *Result*: When one of the Earths in the relationship is suffering from either too much or too little Earth energy, the other Earth will likely tolerate it for a while. When the balanced Earth partner realizes what's happening, they might be able to help, or they might get caught in the quicksand of Earth codependency. Either way, the partner is going to stick it out with them unless they have a strong secondary in a structured club like Wood or Metal. To help improve relationships where this is happening, the stressed Earth needs to be brought back into balance.

Same-Element Relationships

Two Earths Out of Balance

» *Deficient*: If both Earths have too *little* Earth energy, they will become clingy and needy. But no matter how hard they reach out or how strong their need, it's likely neither will feel a deep connection coming from their under-energized partner. This will cause separation anxiety to build for both. Fearing they've been abandoned, both could reach out to others to fill their need to be needed, even as they feel deeply guilty doing so. At this point, they can hope that their wise Fire friends will show up bringing joy and connection to help build their Earth together. If not, the fabric of the relationship might be sufficiently weakened that one, or both, could develop new relationships and leave.

» *Excess*: If both Earths have too *much* Earth energy, it could be a slippery slide into codependency. Needing to be needed, they will insert themselves into each other's affairs even as they worry that they aren't doing enough. To manage their life, each will lean on the other as their sense of personal autonomy weakens. Hopefully, before it's too late, their Wood friends will show up and gently balance their Earth with serious advice. If not, once a full codependent relationship is established, they'll be unable to function without the other, and outside assistance in breaking the cycle will probably be needed. How Steph and Paula managed this experience is covered in the next CASE CORNER.

Mixed: If one Earth person has too *little* Earth energy and the other has *too much* Earth energy, it could go one of two ways. If this is a close relationship, being around the excess Earth could help balance the deficient Earth because the excess Earth's meddling might actually offer good advice for the under-energized Earth. But if this doesn't happen, a codependent relationship could likely develop between the two, driven by the over-energized Earth doing too much for the under-energized Earth, and the under-energized Earth liking the sense of connection. To save relationships, and possibly people, where this is happening, both Earths need to be brought back into balance.

CASE CORNER

Dual Excess Earth: Steph and Paula, Sisters

If this hadn't gone a little overboard, it would have been a cute story. Steph is a friend of mine, and Paula is her sister. They're both Earths, really sweet women in their forties, and normally pretty balanced. But they went through a short period where both of them got a little crazy. It all started when they found out that Steph's husband was being honored as man of the year by a local charity at a black-tie gala. Steph made sure that Paula and her husband were invited, and then the two of them started the all-important search for the perfect dress. They had a full month before the event.

Given their full lives and schedules, the first week they shopped separately. Each bought three gowns and met at Paula's on Saturday for opinions. Paula didn't think Steph had gotten anything that did her figure justice, and Steph didn't think anything Paula bought was fancy enough. They returned the dresses and tried again the following week. When they met at Paula's the next Saturday, it was pretty much the same story: Paula didn't think anything Steph had chosen was good enough, and Steph found something "not quite right" about all of Paula's dresses.

Same-Element Relationships

Worried about time, the sisters decided to take a day off work and go into the city together to look for gowns, since the last two weeks had proven that neither could possibly find the right dress without the other. The trip was moderately successful in that each of them came home with a few dresses, but that weekend when they tried them on again, each sister still believed the other deserved better.

With just a week to go, they went back to the city to a very expensive dress shop. There, the Wood salesperson assured them that the dresses they each selected were perfect. Plunking down four times what they'd expected to pay, the ladies came home relieved, each sister sure that she'd prevented the other from disaster should they have settled for any of the previous twelve dresses they'd tried.

When the day of the gala arrived, Paula and Steph did their hair together and helped each other with the jewelry they'd picked out together. It was a fantastic time, and they were all proud of Steph's husband.

But the following week, when Steph was getting ready for work, she called Paula to ask whether the blue blouse or beige blouse would look better with her tweed skirt. Paula told her the blue was absolutely the only good choice, and then asked which shoes would look best with her slacks. As Steph hung up, it occurred to her that something was probably off balance; needing Paula's opinion on everything wasn't normal.

She gave me a call, and I suggested that they both might have a little too much Earth energy going. Steph laughed and agreed. And fortunately for her, she knew just what to do. Steph used the Earth Quick Tips to bring stability back to her own Earth. And once Steph's Earth didn't rise to match Paula's, hers settled down, too.

EARTH/EARTH RELATIONSHIPS: THE BOTTOM LINE

The Earth Club is all about lasting relationships of any and every kind. Earths need to love and be loved. They need to help and be needed. Their lives exist around the permanence of hearth and home, where connection rules. Two Earths will naturally create a stable relationship and will revel in the joy of the experience. But if stress is part of the picture, without intervention a troubled Earth/Earth relationship will likely continue in a dysfunctional state; it takes a lot to end an Earth/Earth connection.

If you find yourself in a troubled Earth/Earth relationship, check to see if either or both of you are stressed. If so, start using the Earth Quick Tips at the end of Chapter 6.

A QUICK WAY TO DEFUSE EARTH/EARTH PROBLEMS

While two Earths usually won't fight loudly, it can happen. In the middle of a tiff, when all of the cajoling and pleading isn't working, here's a quick way to stabilize the connection.

Both Earths: Place the thumbs of each hand on your cheekbones directly below your eyes and rest the fingers of each hand across your forehead. Look your Earth partner in the eye, take a deep breath, and exhale softly making an "Aummmmm" sound, like the OM. Make the sound prayerful.

Repeat the process until you both feel a shift in the dynamic. That's when you'll want to kiss and make up.

CHAPTER 24

METAL WITH METAL: MR. SPOCK AND SHERLOCK HOLMES, IT SHOULD BE CLEARLY OBVIOUS

*An excellent man, like precious metal,
is in every way invariable.*

—John Locke

WHEN PEOPLE FROM THE SAME club end up in relationships, which isn't uncommon, there are pros and cons just like any combination of clubs. One Metal is certainly going to understand another Metal. But the energy exchange via the big circle or the big star will be missing in Same-Club relationships, which means there can be less movement and counterbalancing energy in these connections. Metals have an intrinsic sense of inward movement but face other issues in their Same-Club connections. It sure won't be fun for Spock and Sherlock should they ever disagree!

METAL/METAL CONNECTIONS

Friendships: Metals are serious individuals who would rather work and study than socialize. If Metals form friendships, they will probably be based on common intellectual interests. Two Metals in a relationship will be wise and kind and give each other plenty of space. They will follow rules and schedules, and keep everything in order, but will need to be reminded that some spontaneity can be fun, even if a bit messy.

Work: Most Metal/Metal relationships will have an intellectual work vibe to them since Metal is all about obtaining knowledge and creating the best ways to use it. The challenge with two Metals working together is going to be who gets to create the rules they follow. Perfection matters deeply to Metals, and each can have their own idea of what is "right." If these issues get ironed out, Metals will work quite well together. But they'll likely need separate offices.

Marriage: Metals' primary relationship focus is on connecting with information and processing it. To do this, they need time alone to study. This means that, similar to Woods, unless either (or both) of the Metals have a secondary Earth, a marriage between them could well be a marriage of intellectual compatibility, not passion. They will pursue their individual studies and share their individual insights. Metals dislike clutter, so a shared home will need to be minimalistic and kept in meticulous shape. Their marriage will be very orderly, but they'll need to be careful of becoming inflexible and dull.

Family: Will Metal/Metal relationships create families? Not likely, unless one (or both) has a strong secondary Earth. Raising children usually isn't a priority or a focus for Metals. If they do have a family, like Waters and Woods, they'll probably want to hire an Earth nanny.

Over the years, I've seen many remarkable Metal/Metal relationships:

- *Gil and Hope, Husband and Wife*: He's an architect, and she's an accountant. They golf (a Metal activity) together most weekends nine months of the year and take annual winter vacations in golf-friendly locations.
- *Jackson and Ralph, Tour Owners:* They run a small tour company that offers "travel and learn" packages around the world. At every locale the guys offer loads of information about the destination, and people love it.
- *Ruth and Jan, Sisters*: Both girls joined the army and love the structure of the military environment. Their Earth parents are shocked, plus a little bit amazed.

METAL/METAL RELATIONSHIP CHALLENGES

Throughout this book we've stated that when applying the Five Elements model to people and their relationships there are really only three ways a relationship can get into trouble. But when dealing with Same-Club relationships, two of those three aren't really issues. No one will understand you better than a member of your own club, so not understanding each other is unlikely. And there's no relationship dynamic between Same-Club relationships, so not understanding that won't be a problem, either. But stress is another story. It will absolutely be a problem in Same-Club relationships.

Same-Element Relationships

> ### REMINDERS FOR METAL/ METAL CONNECTIONS
>
> *If you find yourself in a Metal/Metal relationship that isn't going the way you'd like, take a moment to remind yourself that what's important to you is just as important to the other person. Remember that other Metals need time alone to study and discern wisdom as much you do, so if the exact time you were hoping to share your great discovery doesn't work for them, select a different time. It isn't in your nature, but practice flexibility! Most importantly, when they share, give them the same rapt attention you'd want from them. And if things get really stressed, reach for the Metal Quick Tips covered earlier.*

We're So Stressed We Create Stressed Relationships

Same-Club relationships are just as vulnerable to stress as Nurturing and Controlling Cycle relationships. Without the movement and balancing effect of the cycles, there can be less flexibility in a Metal/Metal connection because Metals are so structured. And if either or both of the Metals are stressed, things can be even more challenging. Unless they tap into their secondary affiliations, neither partner brings a different perspective to help counter the stress.

Under stress, Metal's primary need to pursue perfection will distort. Knowing what a stressed Metal/Metal relationship looks like not only helps you recognize problematic aspects in your own Metal/Metal relationships, it also helps you fix them. Just like any other Five Elements connection, stressed Metals in a relationship can each only go one of two places: an excess state or a deficient state. And it will look different depending on whether one or both Metals are stressed.

One Metal Out of Balance

» *Deficient*: A Metal's energy is fed by intellectual study, so if they're underperforming or disorganized, it's easy for a stressed Metal to go into a deficient energy state. If and when they do, they'll be confused and have difficulty letting go of anything. The lack of new opinions will cause them to cling more dearly to previous opinions, and possibly even their Metal partner. It's likely the partner will notice that they haven't been as brilliant and pithy as usual, and because Metals are innately kind, they may even reach out to try to help. But as the deficient Metal sinks deeper into disarray at all levels, the Metal partner may decide the messiness is too big a distraction from their work and leave.

Example: Erin and Larry shared a loft on the west side of Chicago. Their joint Metal tastes contributed to a sleek, modern look that was always pristine and orderly. Both worked as freelance writers, and each had a desk in their joint home office. Of course, when not in use, both desks were completely cleared. A few years ago, Erin's career was going well, but Larry's stalled. He specialized in sports stories but was having trouble getting anything picked up. Demoralized, he stopped writing since he had a backlog of work to use. And because he was disorganized, he sent some of the same stories out twice, and the rejections he received were biting. As his Metal depleted even more, he became disheveled, and his spaces grew cluttered. Erin was patient for a while but finally couldn't take the disorder. She put her foot down and demanded Larry get help, which he did. It was a nice Earthy counselor, too, which helped bring his Metal energy back.

Same-Element Relationships

» *Excess*: In a Metal/Metal connection, it's more likely that one (or both) will go into a state of *too much* Metal energy. Unlimited, reinforced time alone for intellectual study can create excess Metal. The out-of-balance partner will become domineering and controlling. They'll insist that theirs is the only correct opinion or way to do things and become dismissive of all others. Their balanced partner won't like this because they'll be rather attached to their own opinions. As the excessive Metal becomes more formal and prejudiced, even their partner will be put off. If things don't change soon, the excessive Metal will be deemed a demanding boor, and the partner will leave.

Example: Fran and Essie opened a small accounting firm together. They specialized in managing retirement funds and became especially good at helping seniors. While they had comparable credentials and were both great with their clients, Fran's secondary Earth made her the more compassionate of the two. Unfortunately, it wasn't long before Fran's exaggerated Earth around the seniors overfed her primary Metal. Sure she was the only one who understood their clientele, Fran began demanding that she do most of the initial consultations. She designed new forms and insisted that they be used exclusively. She also redid the filing system, claiming it was vastly superior to what Essie had put in place. To her credit, Essie took this for almost six months, but she finally decided life was too short and left the business.

» *Result*: When one of the Metals in the relationship is suffering from either too much or too little Metal energy, the other Metal will only endure the discomfort for so long. Personal relationships usually aren't a top priority for Metals; they usually care more about intellectual study and perfection. If a Metal partner stays out of balance for too long, the other Metal will likely find the whole thing a big distraction and move on. To save relationships where this is happening, the stressed Metal needs to be brought back into balance.

Two Metals Out of Balance

» *Deficient*: If both Metals have too *little* Metal energy, they'll become confused and clingy, both to each other and their own opinions. Ironically, this may bring them temporarily closer, but if their dearly held opinions clash, neither will have the flexibility to be reasonable. This will drive a wedge between them, and grief could swamp them. When both Metals are deficient, the best they can hope for is that a caring Earth shows up, either as counselor or friend, and helps them build their Metal through nurturing and support. If not, with both Metals deficient, it's likely one or both will feel unfairly judged and leave.

» *Excess*: If both Metals have too *much* Metal energy, inflexibility will be the name of the game. They'll both become formal, prejudiced, and obsessed with strict adherence to their own disciplined routines. If their routines are compatible, they might last for a while. If not, they will judge each other harshly and cruelly. They will make uncompromising demands for change, and when they are ignored, one or both will leave. Before that happens, if they're lucky a joyful Fire friend or counselor will show up and soften their Metals back toward balance. How the excess Metal problems for Boris and Allen were managed is covered in the next CASE CORNER.

Mixed: If one Metal has too *little* Metal energy and the other has *too much* Metal energy, they will likely sink into a battle of control. The under-energized Metal will be confused and cling desperately to previous opinions while the over-energized Metal dismissively lobbies for their clearly more brilliant ideas. Being judged as harshly as they have judged will take the under-energized Metal to a place of deep grief, while the over-energized partner moves in for the intellectual kill to claim dominance. To save relationships where this is happening, both Metals need to be brought back into balance.

CASE CORNER
Dual Excess Metal: Boris and Allen, Twins and Attorneys

Twins Boris and Allen graduated from the same law school on the same day. They both moved to Manhattan, where they shared an apartment but worked for different law firms specializing in corporate law. Both brothers were dead serious about their careers, worked late hours, and brought work home over the weekends. Their mother, Jean, a friend of my mother, constantly expressed concern that the twins' lives were all work and no play. I told her that wasn't completely out of character for Metals.

For several years, neither boy took time off to come home for Christmas. When they finally did, Jean was concerned. Both brought a lot of work and missed several holiday events to take conference calls. When they left, they promised they'd make it home again sooner, but didn't. After three years without a visit, Jean finally announced that she was going to Manhattan to see them. They argued—what attorney doesn't—but she was resolute and arranged her flight and a hotel near the new condo the twins had purchased together the previous year.

The first evening Jean was there, the twins met her for dinner and she was stunned by their attitudes. Both seemed stiff and formal. They didn't hug her and offered just a peck on the cheek. When she asked how things were going, both boys jumped in with how well they were doing at work, but then stopped, clearly upset that the other was talking. She could feel tension in the air, so asked Boris how things were. He gave her a clipped review of the dozens of cases he'd successfully litigated—more than most in his firm, he added, shooting his brother a glance. Allen retorted with a dismissive comment regarding numbers being worthless compared to the size of the judgments. Boris glared.

Poor Jean couldn't believe how condescending her boys had become. If one ordered his steak medium rare, the other commented that the only way to order a good steak was rare. One thought mushrooms were evil; the other believed blue cheese was the only dressing worth having. They both made unreasonable demands of their poor waiter, questioning everything from the quality of the wine to the cleanliness of the glassware. They even argued over the tip as they split the bill. Before they left, Jean finally asked what was going on, but both completely dismissed her. Heartbroken, she went back to her room and called me, wanting to know what she could do. It seemed clear to me that their "all work, no play" approach to life had intensified the very aspect of their personalities that made them great attorneys: Both had too much Metal energy.

The following week, when Jean and I met for coffee, I shared with her a bizarre plan. I knew both boys had been devoted to their younger sister, Risa (a Fire), who happened to be graduating from college in a few months. Risa had accepted a job in Chicago but didn't start until August. I suggested Jean consider sending Risa to NYC to live with her brothers for a month. It was a long shot, but since they were too aloof to admit they had a problem, it was possible that living with Risa's Fire energy for a month might be enough to melt their Metal back into balance. Jean liked the idea since it meant she could go visit Risa often. Risa *loved* the idea.

The plan was positioned to Boris and Allen as a graduation gift for Risa. While both said they were too busy, they didn't say no, so the trip was arranged. And Risa had the time of her life! She went to museums, shows, and restaurants. Her best friend came for a few days, and Jean went every weekend. Within days of Risa arriving, the boys started coming home earlier and taking evenings off. But for Jean, the crowning glory was when she arrived for Risa's last weekend and both boys hugged her. She felt like she had her sons back. And she did.

METAL/METAL RELATIONSHIPS: THE BOTTOM LINE

Members of the Metal Club need time alone to distill the lessons of the past into the wisdom to be used going forward. They don't necessarily need deep connections with others; they need a stable and controlled environment in which to be brilliant. If they want the connection and are willing to work together, two Metals can create a stable, although potentially austere, relationship. But if stress is part of the picture, without intervention a troubled Metal/Metal relationship can easily fail when either or both Metals realize that life is easier, and less messy, alone.

If you find yourself in a troubled Metal/Metal relationship, check to see if either or both of you are stressed. If so, start using the Metal Quick Tips at the end of Chapter 7.

A QUICK WAY TO DEFUSE METAL/METAL PROBLEMS

In the middle of a disagreement, even Metals sometimes find it difficult to pull back. For two Metals locked in debate, here's a quick way to take down the intensity.

Both Metals: Place one hand on the top of your head and the other across the front of your forehead. Look your Metal colleague in the eye, take a deep breath, and exhale softly making a "Sssssssssssss" sound, like air leaking from a tire.

Repeat the process until you both feel a shift in the dynamic; you'll probably start feeling indifferent instead of dismissive.

CONCLUSION

MANAGING OURSELVES: WE ARE IN THE MODEL

Self-knowledge does not mean preoccupation with one's own thoughts; rather, it means concern about the effects one creates.

—The I Ching

CONGRATULATIONS! YOU'RE NOW AN EXPERT on relationships and can get along well with anyone! And when you *aren't* getting along with someone, you also know what to do for yourself, and the other person, to get the connection back on track.

If a relationship isn't doing well, stop and ask yourself why. Do you know their club affiliation? If not, observe them and find out. Then read about their club. Get to know their club. You will probably come to understand them better than they understand themselves. Honor their strengths. Excuse their weaknesses. And don't expect them to be something they aren't. I can tell you from experience, a Wood is never going to be a soft and caring Earth. Nor is a Metal going to be a go-with-the-flow Water. And that's okay. Everyone needs to be themselves.

Next, determine if you're relating to them on the Nurturing or Controlling Cycle. Or are they a member of your own club? As we've seen, all three types of relationships have their strengths and weaknesses. How you look at what's going on between you and this person should be based on your understanding of those relationship dynamics. A Nurturing Cycle relationship is going to feel nurturing, sometimes too much so. A Controlling Cycle relationship is going to feel controlling, but sometimes freeing. A Same-Club relationship is going to feel comfortable, although possibly a bit boring. What isn't working between the two of you? And what are you going to do about it?

START WITH YOU

I've learned the hard way that it's easier to change ourselves than to change other people. When Mark and I argue—we *do* relate on the Controlling Cycle—I may want to bite his head off, but the infinitely better approach is to give my Wood a chill pill. Or when I instantly don't click with someone I've just met, it's important for me to get a quick read on what they're doing that ruffles my Wood (being alive doesn't count). That usually tells me their club, and I can adjust my actions—and expectations—accordingly.

An excellent understanding of the clubs and how they relate will also help you understand yourself better, too. Remember how the wise folks in the Han dynasty determined that the five elements could describe the way all parts of any whole get along? Well, that includes the parts of any human. We have all five elements in us. A primary affiliation, then a second affiliation, then a third, a fourth, and a fifth. And while our third, fourth, and fifth affiliations usually don't necessarily impact us on a daily basis, our primary and secondary sure do. More importantly, the relationship between our primary affiliation and our secondary affiliation has a significant impact on how we express ourselves alone and with others. Here's how that works.

Conclusion

I know my main membership is in the Wood Club; that's where I hang out most days, especially when I'm stressed. But my secondary affiliation is the Earth Club. As I said earlier, that makes me kinder and gentler with clients, students, and Mark. If I want to put an assertive foot forward and get something done, I let my Wood lead. But if I want to stand in caring and compassion, I can nudge my Wood aside and let my Earth lead for a while. A primary affiliation isn't going to let a secondary affiliation lead forever, but when you need the shift, it's a short-term option. Honestly, I do this multiple times a day and my Wood is fine with it. Maybe it likes the rest.

What I do know is that my optimal functioning depends on how well these two parts of me get along. So, you might ask, how do these two parts of me relate? We all know the answer. Wood and Earth relate on the Controlling Cycle. Does that mean my own Wood can control my own Earth? Yes, it does. And what would that look like? Pretty much like any of the connections we discussed in the Chapter 18 on Wood/Earth relationships. Those same dynamics will play out inside of me. As long as my Wood is a happy camper and stays balanced, all will be well. But if it gets off balance, there are two things that can happen:

> *Option 1*: My Wood sends too much energy across the Controlling Cycle and suppresses my Earth. That means the times my Earth is supposed to show up and express caring and compassion, it won't be able to do a good job. Instead, when I tune into my Earth, I'll look like someone with *deficient* Earth. A bit clingy, needy, lonely, and overly concerned for others.

> *Option 2*: My Wood doesn't reach across the Controlling Cycle enough to keep my Earth stable and in balance. That means other times my Earth is supposed to show up and express caring and compassion, it won't be able to do a good

The Five Elements of Relationships

job for a different reason. When I tap into my Earth these times, I'll look like someone with *excess* Earth. Meddling, interfering, and needing to be needed.

When this happens, there is something I can do about it. I can harmonize the energy between my primary Wood and my secondary Earth the same way we harmonize energy between two club members in a relationship. Check out the nearby sidebar for a technique that works great! And it's also important that I take good care of my Wood and make sure it does right by my Earth. Managing my Wood helps guarantee not only that I'll get along better with others, but that I'll get along better with myself, too.

"I LIKE YOU, YOU REMIND ME OF SOMEONE"

CartoonStock.com

Conclusion

> ## A QUICK WAY TO HARMONIZE OUR PRIMARY AND SECONDARY AFFILIATIONS
>
> *When my primary Wood Club membership isn't working well with my secondary Earth Club connection, in addition to de-stressing, I can also use a modified version of the way to harmonize Wood/Earth relationships offered at the end of Chapter 18.*
>
> *To work with my own internal Wood/Earth relationship, I put my index and middle fingers at the outside edges of my eyes and rest each third finger on my cheekbones directly below my eyes. (If you look this up, you'll see that I'm on the first pair of Emotion Stabilizing Points from both Wood and Earth Quick Tips.)*
>
> *Holding all four places at once (two set of points around each eye) not only helps balance my Wood and Earth individually, it also harmonizes the relationship between them. When I do this, it always helps me express my Wood and Earth in beautifully balanced ways. No matter what your primary and secondary affiliations are, you can do this for yourself. Just use the first pair of Emotion Stabilizing Points for both your primary and secondary personalities and hold them in whatever way feels comfortable for you.*

MANAGING ANY PERSONAL STRESS

When really stressed, it's a given that I go to the anger and frustration of my Wood clubhouse. We all go to the stress of our primary affiliation; that's one of the best ways to know our main clubhouse. But the way we show stress isn't limited just to our primary club's expression. That would be too boring! In addition to the stress we encounter in our clubhouse, we all have multiple times a day that we may briefly dip into another club's stress. We all have times we worry, even if we aren't Earths. We all have fear, even if we aren't Waters. We all have Metal's grief, too, and Fire's panic. Even Wood's anger. The cool thing is that we now have a complete set of tools to use when this happens. Just look:

» If Mark is driving home in a terrible snowstorm, you'd better believe I'm worrying. How great to know what the worry professionals (Earths) do to manage their worry. It's all in the information about the Earth Club and the Earth Quick Tips. When I'm really worried, I sip lemon balm tea.

» If you're afraid that your son is going to fail a class, where do you go? The Water Club! Fear is the stress response of the Water Club. Grab the Water Quick Tips and conquer that temporary fear. Classical music does it for me.

» If your daughter is auditioning for a Broadway show, you're likely to be anxious for her. Anxiety hangs out in the Fire Club. Grab the Fire Quick Tips and zap that temporary anxiety. I have a blue shawl I throw around my shoulders.

» If someone cuts you off in traffic, welcome to *my* club! Grab the Wood Quick Tips (wait until you're home) and soothe that anger. Sipping lemon water is one of my favorites.

» If you hear sad news and grief lingers, reach for the Metal Quick Tips and help it move through. I especially love the Emotion Stabilizing Points for Metal and use them often by placing the palm of one hand on the top of my head and the other palm across my forehead. I usually hold this position for two to five minutes, breathing normally. It really helps!

The truth is that there are so many ways to use the information in this book. And now, more than almost any time in the history of our planet, is a great time to begin.

Conclusion

A FINAL THOUGHT

As a people, we are becoming more and more separated. Instead of the basic truth of our unified humanity, we emphasize our differences and often judge each other harshly for them. Yet we are all part of a singularly amazing whole! No other species on this wonderful planet has the capacity to love and think as we do. We should be the greatest hope for planet Earth, but the sad truth is that we're currently the greatest threat. We disagree with each other. We threaten, and are threatened by, each other. And these confrontations play out in an endless loop on a variety of media, which only reinforces them. Yet if we understood each other, I think it could be different.

In this book you have learned one way to better understand other people. Every person you meet will belong to one of the five clubhouses covered in this book. Every member of a clubhouse will have the tendencies specific to that clubhouse as I have covered them here. Remember that when you encounter your fellow humans. Remember what you know about their strengths and challenges given their club affiliation. Remember it all and be kind.

Waters will be inspired, philosophic humans. Don't expect them to be highly structured people or party animals, and then criticize them when they aren't. Appreciate Waters for who they are.

Woods will be assertive, visionary humans. Don't expect them to be deeply compassionate people or to go with the flow, and then criticize them when they aren't. Appreciate Woods for who they are.

Fires will be exciting, transformative humans. Don't expect them to be prim and quiet or to stay at home all the time, and then criticize them when they can't. Appreciate Fires for who they are.

Earths will be caring, compassionate humans. Don't expect them to make something happen at all costs or to lead the way, and then criticize them when they can't. Appreciate Earths for who they are.

Metals will be brilliant, wise humans. Don't expect them to be spontaneous or laid-back, and then criticize them when they aren't. Appreciate Metals for who they are.

Let's be grateful for our differences!

Several years ago, there was a commercial on television featuring the talented Ji-Yong Kim playing the 3rd Movement of Beethoven's "Moonlight Sonata" on a baby grand piano. The rapid pace and enchanting sounds of the chords and harmonies Ji played were mesmerizing. When finished, he paused briefly, then turned and played the same piece on a second piano that appeared identical to the first. But *that* piano had been tuned so that every key played middle C. With his fingers flying over the keyboard, the only sound was the same note over and over and over again. No harmony, no chords, no music.

We are the first piano. We are a group of five different clubs that can make beautiful music together. We just need to accept, respect, and understand ourselves and each other. When we do, I believe the music we will create will truly change the world.

> Blessings to all,
> Dr. Vicki Matthews
> Chicago, IL

Appendices

Nothing could go wrong!
There may be a small glitch or two.
First, the oceans will rise, then the sky will fall ...

APPENDIX I

PERSONALITY COMPARISONS: RESPONSE TO AN INVITATION

AN INTERESTING WAY TO HELP determine your primary elemental personality (and even possible secondary affiliation) is to ascertain your probable response to a specific situation, then compare it to the predictable responses from each of the elemental personalities. To do that, featured below is a quick demonstration of how each elemental personality would likely respond when invited to an out-of-town relative's party. Which one seems most like the way you'd respond?

The Water Personality

"That's curious. A letter? Who would write me? Oh, it's from Cindy. Is something wrong? You know what they say, 'no news is good news.' Well, better open it and see. [Opens letter.] Hmmm, she wants me to come visit for, oh God, their anniversary party. I hate parties! People crammed together, eating, drinking, and shouting. No, thank you. I'd rather stay home and read. I just started *The Philosophy of Truth* and still haven't finished that two-thousand-page tome, *The Meaning of Our Earthly Existence*. But I will get through it; persistence pays. What a bind. Go to a party when I'd much rather stay home. But she says she'd love to have me there; it would make the party if I would come. I'm trapped, but maybe it will be like when we were kids. A party? I'll consider it."

The Wood Personality

"How odd, a hand-addressed letter mixed in with all this correspondence. I'll get to it later. But wait, it's from Cindy; I wonder what's up. [Opens letter.] Ah, her anniversary party, and of course she wants me there. But darn, it's the same weekend as the Seattle Executives Conference! I was really looking forward to that. They appreciate my efforts on their behalf and should be asking me to sit on their board any time now. I will be good for them, too. Of course, my credibility in the industry will also go up, right on schedule. This is a very bad time to miss their conference, but family is family. I'll contact the chairman and make my apologies in person; that will look good. So, a party in Colorado next month? Maybe I can squeeze in some whitewater rafting while I'm there!"

The Fire Personality

"Wow, here's a letter from Cindy! No surprise, though. I've been thinking of her a lot lately. [Opens letter.] How exciting! They're planning a party for their anniversary and she wants me there! She wants me to sing at it, too! How fun! I wouldn't miss that for the world! Wow, what should I sing? Maybe I can sing a few songs. It's such an important event, and so many of the people we love will be there. I wonder if Ted will go with me. I'll bet I can talk him into it! He knows how much this will mean to me. Now, what will I sing? What will I sing? I should be working, but I think I'll take a quick peek through my music and see what inspires me. A party? Of course I'm going! This is just too exciting!"

The Earth Personality

"Oh, look, a letter from Cindy. Mother said she might write about their anniversary party. Apparently, it's a big deal for them. [Opens letter.] Yes, that's exactly what she's doing, bless her heart. Cindy's having a party! It says right here that they've been talking about this for months, and would I come? Absolutely! Maybe I'll even go down a week early and help out. Possibly pay for a few things, too; money is tight for them these days. Of course, I'll have to be careful not to embarrass them. But I'm sure we can make this just the most wonderful party ever. We'll have games for the children and special accommodations for people coming in from out of town. This will be a glorious family event, and everyone will have a fantastic time! I can't wait to help out!"

The Metal Personality

"Hmmm, a letter from Cindy. [Opens letter.] Well, well, she's having an anniversary party. Very appropriate; I will definitely attend. But I'm not going up early. The monthly reports are due the following Monday, and I must have the analysis done when I said I would. After all, that's the procedure. Procedures create order, and order is always our friend. I'll head up to the party right after work on Friday. I'm sure Cindy will understand. But I'm not taking Aunt Millie this time. She is just so emotional. And messy—I picked sunflower seeds out of my car for a month the last time I took her anywhere. It might be time to get rid of the car, anyway. I certainly don't use it that often since moving to the city. Well, well. A party for Cindy's anniversary? Absolutely perfect!"

The Five Elements of Relationships

Question: Did you see yourself in any these responses? Which response was most likely the one you would have had to the invitation? That could be your primary elemental personality!

"Finally, I've found myself."

APPENDIX II

ELEMENTAL PERSONALITY QUIZ

STILL NOT SURE OF YOUR primary elemental personality? Here's a short quiz that can help. But be warned, scores on quizzes can tend to show your elemental personality at the time you took the quiz. That means if you just finished cooking dinner, you might show a stronger Earth presence than at other times. Or if you just came home from a fun party (lucky you!), there might be a bit more Fire in your answers. But regardless, a quiz can certainly offer insight, especially if you are honest with yourself.

Instructions: Place a check mark next to each statement that applies to you.

_____ *I do all I can to avoid being alone. (1)*

_____ *A yes from me doesn't always mean yes. (1)*

_____ *I am excited about life. (1)*

_____ *I laugh and giggle a lot, sometimes too loudly or at the wrong time. (1)*

The Five Elements of Relationships

_____ *Difficult situations fluster me. (1)*

_____ *Noisy, busy places make me happy. (1)*

_____ *I can easily let bygones be bygones. (1)*

_____ *Secretly, I long for support and abundant praise; I often doubt myself. (1)*

_____ *I have a thin skin; what others say about me matters. (1)*

_____ *Sensual pleasures are important to me. (1)*

_____ *I am impulsive and need to act. (2)*

_____ *The ends often justify the means for me. (2)*

_____ *I come alive under pressure. (2)*

_____ *I am fiercely independent. (2)*

_____ *I enjoy planning and organizing everything. (2)*

_____ *Chaos brings me to my knees. (2)*

_____ *When people are treated unfairly, I stand up for them. (2)*

_____ *I am competitive and need to win, even with close friends and family. (2)*

_____ *Direct and straightforward, I sometimes come on too strong. (2)*

_____ *Taking risks is natural for me. (2)*

_____ *I love puzzles, riddles, and mysteries. (3)*

_____ *I put virtue and principles before having fun. (3)*

_____ *I enjoy tasks that require systematic, logical, analytical problem-solving. (3)*

_____ Life can feel sad and empty sometimes. (3)

_____ I am a perfectionist and can be extremely critical of myself. (3)

_____ Superficiality bores me. (3)

_____ I set high standards for myself and expect the same of others. (3)

_____ I often feel very inhibited. (3)

_____ I like to do more and be better than others, and I want people to notice. (3)

_____ Spontaneity frightens me. (3)

_____ I'm very suspicious of other people. (4)

_____ I tend to avoid intimate relationships. (4)

_____ I am patient and persevere even when the odds are against me. (4)

_____ Ideas stir me and ignite my imagination. (4)

_____ I can become deeply depressed for no apparent reason. (4)

_____ It takes time for me to trust someone. (4)

_____ I believe the world can be dangerous and I need to be cautious. (4)

_____ I will stand up for myself when others disagree, but I dread this happening. (4)

_____ I'm always curious about things. (4)

_____ I yearn for meaning in all aspects of my life. (4)

_____ I find myself in the middle a lot, but I'm only trying to help. (5)

_____ Feeling left out hurts me deeply. (5)

_____ I can easily mold myself into different people and situations. (5)

The Five Elements of Relationships

_____ *I am always accessible to my friends, day or night. (5)*

_____ *People say it's easy to tell me their secrets. (5)*

_____ *I love happy endings. (5)*

_____ *I find it difficult to ask others for help. (5)*

_____ *I love cooking, sewing, decorating, and everything about crafts. (5)*

_____ *I tend to obsess about problems if I'm upset. (5)*

_____ *Food, especially sweets, is often my best friend. (5)*

Scoring instructions are on the following page. An interactive 5E Personality Quiz is available at vickimatthews.com.

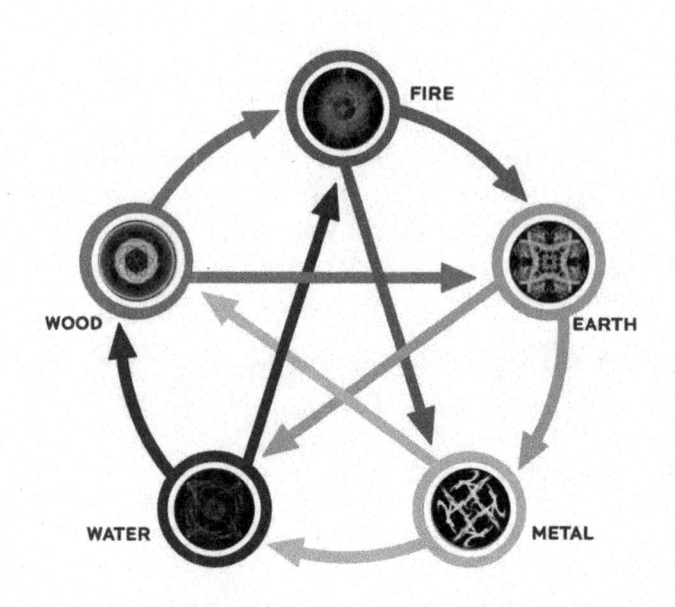

SCORING THE ELEMENTAL PERSONALITY QUIZ

The questions are categorized as a 1, 2, 3, 4, or 5 and grouped accordingly. Total the number of check marks you had for each group and enter those numbers in the chart below. The element with the highest number is likely your primary elemental personality. The second highest will be your secondary elemental personality, and so on.

Total # of 1s   Total # of 2s   Total # of 3s   Total # of 4s   Total # of 5s
_____   _____   _____   _____   _____
(Fire)   *(Wood)*   *(Metal)*   *(Water)*   *(Earth)*

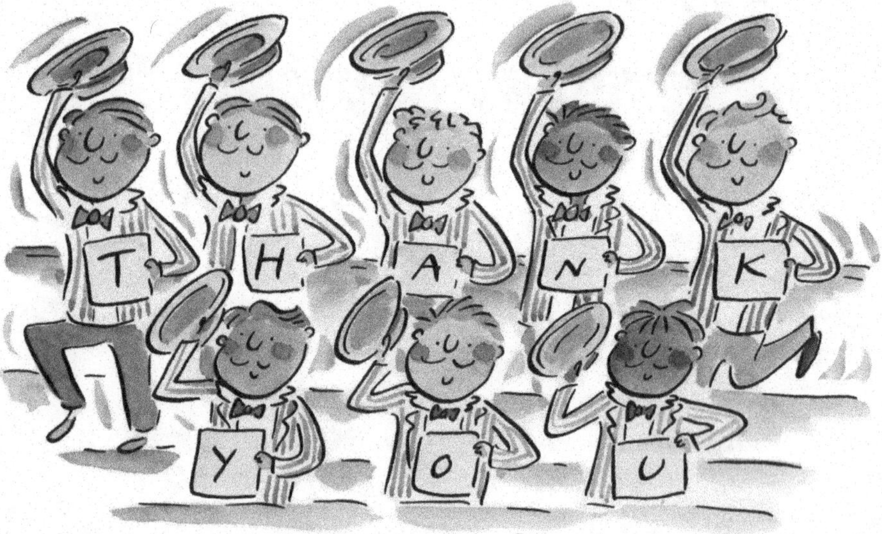
T
H
A
N
K
Y
O
U

ACKNOWLEDGMENTS

IT HAS BEEN SAID BY many authors that it takes the proverbial village to write and publish a book. I can tell you with certainty that it's true. This book would not be in your hands now if not for the loving support, encouragement, and diligent effort of the following people:

Lisa Hagan, my agent extraordinaire. Thank you for your enthusiasm regarding my work and this book.

Debra Englander, my editor, cheerleader, believer, and coach. Thank you! You make all the difference.

Heather King, production genius. Thank you for all the yeses, your skill, and your ongoing enthusiasm.

Mark, Cindy, Lori, Allee, and Jenny, my early readers. The book is definitely better because of your insights and input. Thank you!

Donna Eden, my teacher and friend. Thank you for supporting my passion for the Five Elements and giving me the opportunity to teach and practice my work in your world.

John Gray, author of *Men are from Mars, Women are from Venus*. Your book taught me that understanding is more important in a relationship than chemistry, and for that I will be eternally grateful.

And finally, to my classmates, fellow teachers, patients, family, and friends, thank you for the ways you have impacted my life. Each and every one of you has added an important piece to my understanding of the way the Five Elements affect our daily lives and relationships. It is a joy to walk this path together. Blessings to you all!

ABOUT THE AUTHOR

Photo by Kasia Vetter

DR. VICKI MATTHEWS is a naturopathic physician, relationship coach, and an outspoken voice for alternative healing and change. Vicki has appeared on Oprah's show twice and is the author of the award-winning novel, *The Goddess Letters*, which addresses cultural imbalances in our world.

Vicki has taught the material in *The Five Elements of Relationships* to thousands of people around the US and in Europe. She also blogs regularly at *Ask Vicki,* where she uses the Five Elements model from Traditional Chinese medicine to help people improve their lives, health, and relationships.

In addition to her Naturopathy degree, Vicki also has a BA in Psychology and an MBA in Consumer Behavior from the University of Chicago Booth School of Business. Vicki runs a private practice, consults globally, and writes, writes, writes.

FREE OFFER: *Manage Personal Stress: A Five Elements Guidebook*

Stress can be disastrous for people *and* their relationships. A good connection can always handle a little personal stress, but prolonged stress on people in a relationship can't help but impact that relationship. The sad truth is that our relationships are usually only as stable as we are.

Manage Personal Stress: A Five Elements Guidebook was created to help us keep ourselves—and therefore our relationships—happy, healthy, and stable during stressful times. Think of it as a quick reference guide for the times we are unsure exactly how to decrease our stress levels. The simple suggestions and techniques this mini book contains will help balance us personally so our relationships are less impacted by ongoing stress. And of course, each of these simple suggestions is based on the Five Elements model!

To claim your **free** copy of *Manage Personal Stress: A Five Elements Guidebook* as well as an 8½" by 11" **color version** of the Five Elements model, please go to:

www.ManagePersonalStress.com

Here's to de-stressing and getting along better with everyone!

Dr. Vicki Matthews